GLOBAL CINEMA

Edited by Katarzyna Marciniak, Anikó Imre, and Áine O'Healy

The **Global Cinema** series publishes innovative scholarship on the transnational themes, industries, economies, and aesthetic elements that increasingly connect cinemas around the world. It promotes theoretically transformative and politically challenging projects that rethink film studies from cross-cultural, comparative perspectives, bringing into focus forms of cinematic production that resist nationalist or hegemonic frameworks. Rather than aiming at comprehensive geographical coverage, it foregrounds transnational interconnections in the production, distribution, exhibition, study, and teaching of film. Dedicated to global aspects of cinema, this pioneering series combines original perspectives and new methodological paths with accessibility and coverage. Both "global" and "cinema" remain open to a range of approaches and interpretations, new and traditional. Books published in the series sustain a specific concern with the medium of cinema but do not defensively protect the boundaries of film studies, recognizing that film exists in a converging media environment. The series emphasizes a historically expanded rather than an exclusively presentist notion of globalization; it is mindful of repositioning "the global" away from a US-centric/Eurocentric grid, and remains critical of celebratory notions of "globalizing film studies."

Katarzyna Marciniak is a professor of Transnational Studies in the English Department at Ohio University.

Anikó Imre is an associate professor of Critical Studies in the School of Cinematic Arts at the University of Southern California.

Áine O'Healy is a professor of Modern Languages and Literatures at Loyola Marymount University.

Published by Palgrave Macmillan:

Prismatic Media, Transnational Circuits: Feminism in a Globalized Present
By Krista Geneviève Lynes

Transnational Stardom: International Celebrity in Film and Popular Culture
Edited by Russell Meeuf and Raphael Raphael

Silencing Cinema: Film Censorship around the World
Edited by Daniel Biltereyst and Roel Vande Winkel

The Education of the Filmmaker in Europe, Australia, and Asia
Edited by Mette Hjort

The Education of the Filmmaker in Africa, the Middle East, and the Americas
Edited by Mette Hjort

Behind the Screen: Inside European Production Cultures
Edited By Petr Szczepanik and Patrick Vonderau

International Cinema and the Girl

Local Issues, Transnational Contexts

Edited by Fiona Handyside and
Kate Taylor-Jones

INTERNATIONAL CINEMA AND THE GIRL
Copyright © Fiona Handyside and Kate Taylor-Jones 2016

First published 2016 by
PALGRAVE MACMILLAN

The authors have asserted their rights to be identified as the authors of this work in accordance with the Copyright, Designs and Patents Act 1988.

Palgrave Macmillan in the UK is an imprint of Macmillan Publishers Limited, registered in England, company number 785998, of Houndmills, Basingstoke, Hampshire, RG21 6XS.

Palgrave Macmillan in the US is a division of Nature America, Inc., One New York Plaza, Suite 4500, New York, NY 10004-1562.

Palgrave Macmillan is the global academic imprint of the above companies and has companies and representatives throughout the world.

Hardback ISBN: 978-1-137-38891-9
E-PUB ISBN: 978-1-137-38893-3
E-PDF ISBN: 978-1-137-38892-6
DOI: 10.1057/9781137388926

Distribution in the UK, Europe and the rest of the world is by Palgrave Macmillan®, a division of Macmillan Publishers Limited, registered in England, company number 785998, of Houndmills, Basingstoke, Hampshire RG21 6XS.

Library of Congress Cataloging-in-Publication Data
International cinema and the girl : local issues, transnational
    contexts / edited by Fiona Handyside and Kate Taylor-Jones.
      pages   cm. — (Global cinema)
    Includes bibliographical references and index.
    Includes filmography.
    ISBN 978-1-137-38891-9 (alk. paper)
    1. Teenage girls in motion pictures.   I. Handyside, Fiona, 1974–
    editor.   II. Taylor-Jones, Kate E., editor.
    PN1995.9.G57I68 2015
    791.43'652352—dc23   2015020908

A catalogue record for the book is available from the British Library.

Contents

Part III Sonic Youth: Girlhood, Music, and Identity

Part IV Extraordinary Girlhoods

Figures and Tables

Figures

Tables

Acknowledgments

Fiona Handyside

I developed my research interest in the complex and flourishing area of the representation of girls in global cinema while developing a Final Year module with my friend and exemplary colleague Professor Danielle Hipkins. Conversations and film viewings with Danielle are always inspiring and I thank her very much for her invaluable input, and especially the particularly enjoyable trip to the Venice Film Festival. Dr Kate Taylor-Jones suggested we should collaborate on this book, and I am very grateful for her hard work and perseverance on this project and allied work on girlhood and cinema, especially the symposium held in Bangor in March 2014. Professor Aine O'Healy first suggested we approach Palgrave with the project and we are most grateful for her input and that of her co-editors in the Global Cinemas series, Professor Anikó Imre and Professor Katarzyna Marciniak, as well as the anonymous reviewers, all of whom strengthened and improved our ideas. Robyn Curtis and her assistant Erica Buchman provided quick and efficient editorial support, as has in latter stages Shaun Vigil. Of course, the volume would not exist at all without the good work, patience and enthusiasm of all the contributors, to whom many thanks. Dr Deborah Martin had the idea for, and was the driving force behind, a co-organised symposium on Global Girlhood and Cinema held at UCL in July 2013, generously supported by UCL's Faculty Institute of Graduate Studies and College of Humanities, University of Exeter. Many of the speakers are contributors to this book (Clara Bradbury-Rance, Kate Taylor-Jones, Danielle Hipkins) and I would also like to thank Dr Deborah Shaw, Professor Emma Wilson and Professor Catherine Driscoll for their papers. My very good friend Emma Goulart (née Hayes) has engaged in several fascinating and useful discussions about her experiences of raising a daughter, and Clara Goulart is a most engaging fellow film watcher and commentator (I especially enjoyed watching *Frozen* together). My niece Amelia Markham is very happy to discuss her experiences of girl film culture with me (and to sing to "Let it Go" together), and my nephew Henry Markham is just beginning to be able to participate too. It is to Amelia, Henry and Clara that Auntie Fi dedicates her portions of the book with lots of love.

Kate Taylor-Jones

I would like to reconfirm our thanks to Professor Anikó Imre, Professor Katarzyna Marciniak, Professor Aine O'Healy, Robyn Curtis and Erica Buchman. I would also like to thank Fiona Handyside for all her tireless hard work on the project and unfailing good humour. I am grateful to School of Creative Studies and Media, Bangor University for supporting the Girlhood Symposium held here in March 2014 and all the people who participated. I especially need to thank Louise Hoyle and Lyle Skains for their helpful comments and proofreading. This project has spanned two pregnancies and two daughters and both my girls have been at the forefront of all of my recent thoughts on girlhood. Having them has made me very aware of the complex issues of raising girls in this current age and I hope to do them credit in my attempts to balance cultural pressures, their own unique little personalities and my desires to raise feminists! I dedicate my portions of this book to all my family but specifically my mother-in-law Christine and my sister-in-law Vicky; two wonderful and inspiring women who both fought an extremely brave fight but ultimately could not beat cancer. We miss you everyday and I will use this space to encourage all "girls" whether old or young to please check your breasts regularly.

Introduction

Fiona Handyside and Kate Taylor-Jones

Girls and Girlhood in Media and Film

As Marnina Gonick, Emma Renold, Jessica Ringrose, and Lisa Weems note, there is a "current proliferation of images and narratives of girls and girlhood in popular culture."[1] In a similar vein, Sarah Projansky argues that "since approximately 1990, girls have appeared often and everywhere in U.S. media culture."[2] She supports this claim by tracking the number of girls to appear on the cover of mass market magazines such as *Newsweek* and *Time*, and analyzing the most discussed of the "literally hundreds of films featuring girls as central characters" released in US cinemas in the period 2000–2009. For John Hartley, commenting on the contemporary public sphere and its expression in the press, "a new figure has appeared in this already feminized, privatized, suburbanized and sexualized landscape; the figure of the young girl." He considers that girls are "up to their ankles, if not their necks, in public signification, becoming objects of public policy, public debate, the public gaze."[3]

This sense that girls have become hypervisible in the contemporary popular cultural formation, and that this is accompanied by a rise in debates about girls' identities, roles, and behaviors, has happened alongside a growth in the academic field of "girlhood studies." This interdisciplinary subject area draws from health, education, medicine, and psychology as well as the humanities, and even has its own journal, *Girlhood Studies*. One of its most notable subfields, and the broad context for our book on girls on film, is what Mary Celeste Kearney terms "girls' media studies." She defines this as "a unique area of academic research that has girls' media culture as its overarching area of study."[4] Given the historic interest feminist scholars have shown in the interaction between media representation and gender roles and the considerable debates concerning the impact of images on those who consume them, it is not surprising that girlhood studies pays considerable attention to questions of how girls are represented in the media, and how they consume it. From such pioneering monographs as Angela McRobbie's *Feminism and Youth Culture: From Jackie to Just Seventeen* (Macmillan, 1991), Susan Douglas' *Where the Girls Are: Growing Up Female with the Mass Media* (Times, 1995), and Dawn Currie's *Girl Talk: Adolescent Magazines and Their Readers* (University of Toronto Press, 1999) to the more recent Sharon Mazzarella and Norma Pecora's *Growing Up Girls: Popular Culture and the Construction of Identity* (Peter Lang, 2002), Kearney's *Mediated Girlhoods: New Explorations of Girls' Media Culture*, and Heather Warren-Crow's *Girlhood and the Plastic Image* (Dartmouth College Press, 2014), scholars have demonstrated the important role of the media in girls' lives and the construction of girl culture; explored the complex variety of girlhood representations; and debated the role of the media in either reinforcing or resisting gender stereotypes. Alongside this work on the sheer variety of media that characterizes girl culture— from traditional entertainment forms such as film, television, radio, music, comics, and magazines, to contemporary information technologies such as Web-based video-sharing sites, smart phones, and MP3 players—there is also scholarship that explores the specificity of representations of girlhood on film, such as Frances Gateward and Murray Pomerance's *Sugar, Spice and Everything Nice: Cinemas of Girlhood* (Wayne State University Press, 2002), Sarah Hentges' *Pictures of Girlhood: Modern Female Adolescence on Film* (McFarland, 2006), and Gaylyn Studlar's *Precocious Charms: Stars Performing Girlhood in Classical Hollywood Cinema* (University of California Press, 2013). Here, there is a concentration on film as one of the most highly significant cultural practices of the twentieth and twenty-first centuries, and thus as an important factor in the cultural imagination of girlhood, that stretches back to well before the contemporary period. Gateward and Pomerance's study of American cinema and girlhood further confirms the importance of girls to the narratives and images produced within films: adjusted for inflation, six of the ten top-grossing US movies of all time primarily concern teenage girls. These are *Snow White and the Seven Dwarves* (Cottrel, Jackson et al, 1937); *Gone With the Wind* (Fleming, 1939); *The Wizard of Oz* (Fleming, 1939); *The Sound of Music* (Wise, 1965); *Dr. Zhivago* (Lean, 1965); and *Titanic* (Cameron, 1997). The latter example also demonstrates the power of the teen girl audience, whose repeated visits to the cinema to see *Titanic* fueled a teen fan culture and prompted recognition of their significance as a market. Studlar's study of Hollywood female stars such as Mary Pickford, Deanna Durbin and Audrey Hepburn and their association with youthful femininity in the period 1914–1967 signals Hollywood's "remarkably long-lived attention to signifying girls and girlhood."[5] Furthermore, she traces this interest in children to the favorite Victorian pastime of "child-watching." Vicky Lebeau comments also on this Victorian compulsion to "represent the child" that early cinema rapidly mobilized into, inter alia, narratives of girlhood (e.g., there were no fewer than six silent versions of Lewis Carroll's *Alice in Wonderland* story).[6]

Clearly, the recurring theme in the contemporary media that girls are newly visible does not stand up to historic scrutiny, as the film scholarship discussed above reveals. This claim also masks earlier eruptions of public discourse about girls: for example, "the two decades between the wars [in the UK] were marked by great uncertainty about 'the modern girl'," as the figure of the "flapper" attracted debate about her conduct, morals, and suitability to participate in politics.[7] However, there is a sense that something is "different" in contemporary representations of girlhood, as the comments by Gonick et al, Projansky, and Hartley reveal. The late 1990s onwards saw an evolution of girl culture into what activists Marcelle Karp and Debbie Stoller deemed the "New Girl Order": a rebellious, fun, young, sexy notion of feminine power.[8] As Monica Swindle explains, it was in this period that "girl" began to be used as an adjective as well as a noun, as in "girl power," "girl culture," "girly girls," and "girl order," terms that attempted to articulate youthful femininity as a site of agency and enjoyment.[9] However, these terms also opened up girlhood to different forms of cultural surveillance and commodification, including in the world of films, which now frequently function as "lynchpin element[s] in a system of media synergies," and that continue to attempt to reach broad audiences.[10] Although the figure of the girl has frequently proven adept at working through any number of cultural anxieties from age-of-consent laws to consumer culture, the difference now is that, as Anita Harris explains, girlhood has come to function as a kind of container for narratives of both anxiety *and* progress: on the one hand, there is a continuous stream of popular anxiety texts, the most recent of which target princess culture, a continuation of a longstanding suspicion of the kind of media girls enjoy consuming; on the other, promotion of active and successful role models in the "girl power" mold.[11]

This book has at its core the idea that this linkage of contemporary girlhood to questions of risk and possibility means that the figure of the girl on screen both reflects and projects the shifting terrain of gender roles in a neoliberal postfeminist culture that emphasizes agency, choice, and empowerment for all, failing to take into account structural and institutional obstacles. The figure of the girl offers an accessible way to debate the legacies of feminism and the impact of globalization on gender roles and identities in the contemporary period. What possibilities might there be for alternative visions of girlhood, and thus potentially different modes of subjectivity, agency, and feeling, in the vast mediascape? It is important to acknowledge that girlhood has been spectacularized in film since the latter's inception, and to give back to the "girl on film" a visibility she may ironically have lost in feminist film theory. This has tended to be dominated by concern with the female body and the female look that, as Studlar explains, assumes "female" as "the middle-ground of an adult femininity amorphously defined at best."[12] This echoes perhaps a broader historical issue, whereby the relationship between feminism and girls has been uneasy, with women reluctant to be identified with/as girls.[13] Clearly, more notice is now being taken of girls, in feminist politics, in film studies, and in media studies. Yet in work on film, there remains an emphasis on studies of girls' film culture within the Hollywood system, whether in its classical studio era or in the contemporary era of mergers and conglomeration. This is hardly surprising, given the dominance of this cinema in terms of global coverage and the predominance of academic focus on this that has historically been seen in film studies. Nevertheless, the hegemonic cultural imaginary of its version of girlhood demands careful unpacking. In this book, we aim to build on the important insights into the specific ways in which films articulate girls and girlhood both for youth and adult audiences. We aim to broaden the scope of this previous work through a close attention to films produced from a variety of geographical contexts: as well as America, we explore films featuring girl characters living in Argentina, Democratic Republic of the Congo, Eritrea, France, Italy, Iran, Japan, Liberia, and the United Kingdom. Placing our study firmly into the period identified by Gonick et al. and Projansky as one of girl hypervisibility within a culture broadly defined as postfeminist, we aim to question the assumption that contemporary girlhood evinces the same themes, pleasures, values, and lifestyles regardless of national context. Our contributors examine films that reassert the singularity of individual experience even within the overdetermined context of the girl as a figure of either celebration or denigration (from Mia in *Fish Tank* (Arnold, 2009), challenging David Cameron's vision of a "broken" underclass in Britain to the inherent contradiction found in the presentation of girl-superheroes as seen in the Kick-Ass films (Vaughn, 2007, Wadlow, 2013)). While the dominant transnational reach of images of girlhood produced within Hollywood's globalized commodified structure means our sense of girl film culture is inevitably drawn from an eclectic array of textual encounters that cut across and blur national specificities, we aim to address how globalizing narratives are made sense of beyond a mainstream American social context; to offer a more complex account of girl film culture that compares the sonic and visual constructions of girlhood from different national cinemas; to challenge scholarship's tendency to look only at Anglo-American cultural production in its assessment of contemporary girlhood on screen. We argue that by attending to the individuality and particularity of film texts, produced from within a variety of national settings, we are able to dig down into both the local specificity of girl culture, and its participation within, and contribution to, transnational discourses concerning the figure of the girl. Throughout the book, we trace continuities and similarities, as well as marked differences and diversities, in how girlhood is embodied, understood, and mediated across various cultural and national formations, bringing films from different national spaces into dialogue across all four sections. Thus, this book is both national in scope, via the diverse range of national cinemas that our respective essays engage with and develop from, but also transnational in approach as we traverse national borders to examine the globalized nature of contemporary images of girlhood. In our first section, "Girlhood and Postfeminism: Global perspectives," we address three specific film cultures—those of France, Italy, and Japan—and interrogate how performance of girlhood is (re)presented in film. Our second section, "Philosophies of Girlhood on Film," compares and contrasts how films attend to the sensations, feelings, and desires of their girl protagonists, tracing feminist phenomenological and queer theoretical frameworks for analysis across films from Argentina, the United Kingdom, France, and America. The third section, "Sonic Youth: Girlhood, Music, and Identity" continues this attention to questions of film form, here arguing that soundtrack, and in particular music, is vital to communicating diverse experiences of girlhood that seem to escape conscious articulation, even as it may well repackage some of these experiences back as commodification. The ambivalences and possibilities of film music are traced across French and American cinemas. Our final section, "Extraordinary Girlhoods," considers extreme and unusual depictions of girls such as murderers, soldiers, prisoners, superheroes, and finds transnational constants here. The girl is potentially both more vulnerable and more wicked than her boy counterpart when placed at such extremes. Lisa Downing remarks on the difficulty culture has in coming to terms with the girl-killer, and discusses a puppet-animated short film, suggesting that this figure still remains problematic for mainstream feature films to depict. Overall, we aim to investigate how girlhood is simultaneously transnational and tied closely to particular national and/or cultural contexts. Thinking outside of the US dynamic helps address intercultural questions, partaking in what Ella Shohat calls polycentric, multicultural feminism, incorporating an intersectional perspective, regardless (or perhaps because) of the dominance of Anglophone, white, heterosexual, middle-class girls in the foreground.[14] Second, it provides a counter-weight to feminist media studies analysis that has a tendency to a tautological approach, in which texts are selected for analysis to the extent to which they conform to the promotion of what Rosalind Gill labels a "postfeminist sensibility."[15] This is not to deny the interest or validity of her findings, but rather to suggest that attention to the mediascape as a global force, carving out alternative perspectives as well as shoring up oppressive and narrow views, could potentially provide a way out of what Diane Negra calls the "echo-chamber of repetition and reinforcement" that characterizes dominant media representations of postfeminist girlhood.[16] As a form with considerable economic outlay and cultural capital, the feature film writes large contradictions, tensions, anxieties and ambivalences, providing the best opportunity for transgressive and complex reworkings of girls and their meanings (as well as constraint and conformity). While films may well reproduce stereotypes, close attention to the variety of narratives produced about girls and the attention to the embodied sensations and experiences of girlhood articulated here demonstrates possibilities of modification and critique, from Danielle Hipkins' assertion that the seemingly oppressive reproduction of beauty culture in film, especially in the Italian context of its association with the political corruption of the Berlusconi regime, may also speak to tenderness and care between mothers and daughters, to Deborah Martin's discussion of how "the established order is transgressed by the young girl's enhanced perceptual capacity, her ability both to see the realities to which others are blind, and to move beyond the visual into other sensory epistemologies."

Through attending to an international, diverse range of films, this book situates itself alongside scholarship by Catherine Driscoll and Timothy Shary and Alexandra Seibel, which has begun to complicate the elision of "teen movies" with Hollywood cinema. For Driscoll, writing from Australia, "the question of where teen film comes from, what it represents and for whom, is [...] complicated."[17] Driscoll discusses Shary and Seibel's edited collection *Youth Culture in Global Cinema* that focuses on a range of films from various nations.[18] As Driscoll comments, the replacement of the word "teen" with "youth" is telling, as if the authors were trying to avoid tackling head-on the issue of whether the teen film is fundamentally an American form. Driscoll traces the way key tropes of the teen film— coming-of-age; conflict with parents; youth as problem, institution, and party—navigate between the local and the global. While for Roz Kaveney, the US teen film has "colonized" the imaginations of the Western world, creating a US-centric "folk memory" of teen life,[19] Driscoll understands rather a convergence between the teen's own organization around boundaries and thresholds and films' complex hybrid blending of global tropes and specific local occurrences.

Teen film not only has narrative content centred on coming-of-age trajectories and the question of maturity but has produced, and continually refines, a historically significant audiovisual vocabulary that cannot be reduced to film style. This language crosses borders—a fresh-faced smile to camera, a shadowed pout [...], the structured tableau of a classroom, the energy of contemporary beats [...]—but they are not only national ones.[20]

Driscoll's identification of a shared set of iconographies and gestures that crosses a variety of borders (of nation, but also class and race, for example) is useful for thinking about how cinemas of girlhood too can speak to multiple sites. While teen film has a generically contained, if ambiguously delineated, canon, cinemas of girlhood are potentially even more amorphous, stretching across differences of genre, popularity, and audience address. Nevertheless, we can also identify an audiovisual vocabulary and narrative traits that we could tentatively suggest defines a cinematic girlhood, as we find time and again the motif of threatened/lost innocence against corrupting experience; girlhood as both performative and discursive; close attention to the bodily and the sensual, and to heightened, disrupted emotions; the multisensory awareness of the girl, often privileging sound and decentering the visual; attention paid to the rhythms, patterns, and different temporalities of girlhood; frequent comparisons and competition between different generations of "girls"; interest in girlishness as commodity. We should at this point note that, while attention to how actual girls consume and produce film media is obviously of great relevance and importance, it is beyond the scope of this collection. We are concentrating here on the already highly complex and involved questions of representation and identity: what narratives about girls are made available for cultural work; how film mediates girlhood experiences (probably, depending on the genre of the film, to an assumed adult audience); how this is framed in different ways in a variety of national and transnational contexts. We would refer readers to important work on girls' reception and production of media available elsewhere. Kearney's edited collection includes several chapters on girls as audiences, using both standard ethnographic/focus-group methodology and innovative auto-ethnography, and is excitingly international in its scope. [21] Projansky's account of girls in the mediascape includes a chapter on "girls as media critics."[22] As for girls as producers of media, Kathleen Sweeney advocates for education programs to include filmmaking, giving an impassioned account that argues that "given the proper Geek Girl tool belt, which includes the language of media literacy, anyone can become a Super Girl,"[23] while Leslie Regan Shade and

Sarah Banet-Weiser both strike more cautionary notes, arguing that girls' production is subject to various disciplinary logics that limit its progressive potential.[24]

Defining Girls and Girlhood

For all that girls are represented everywhere, it seems difficult to define what exactly constitutes girlhood and find the line where girlhood ends. We live in a culture where youth is revered, and girls and "girlish" characters on screen have had massive appeal over the last century, from the captivating "precocious charms" of Shirley Temple enumerated by Studlar to the 2013 record-breaking box-office behemoth *Frozen* (Buck and Lee, 2013) with its two young female leads Anna and Elsa. These films offer dynamic archetypes that have a special relevance in late capitalist culture, which creates the conditions for girlhood to flourish as identity, representation, and aspirational role.

The term "girl" has a discursive and performative volatility, with Swindle explaining that the "feeling" and "doing" of girl can attach to bodies of those other than young females (as in the expression "like a girl"). Anita Harris locates the paradigm shift in the denotation of girl in the late twentieth and early twenty-first century, as part of the girls' movement, commenting that,

> even the issue of how "old" a girl is—previously a fairly simplistic categorisation of females between the ages of approximately 12 and 20—has been complicated by both the "tweenies" phenomenon and the "Girlie" movement, which together girlify 7 year olds in midriff tops and 40 year olds with "Hello Kitty" barrettes.[25]

It is notable here that Harris quickly moves from the question of definitions of girlhood to material commodity objects that alter the appearance of the body—hair slides and midriff tops—speaking to the entanglement of contemporary expressions of girlhood with consumer culture and bodily surveillance. Contemporary consumer culture has an intense focus on beauty and youth, with cosmetics and fashions targeted at girls, and also promising that the experience of "girliness" can be bought by "adult" bodies. Women and girls are thus caught in an elastic construction that blurs the boundaries between the two. While, as Swindle comments, there is potentially a considerable affective pleasure to be had in this "girlish" presentation of the body (theoretically open to all bodies, to different degrees of subversion/conformity), historian Joan Jacobs Brumberg suggests that this leads to the girl body being constructed as a project in need of continual improvement and refinement.[26] Furthermore, this makes the construction of the girl contingent and indeterminate, always necessarily ongoing and incomplete, as Judith Butler describes: "to the extent that the naming of the 'girl' is transitive, that is, initiates the process by which a certain 'girling' is compelled, the term or, rather, its symbolic power, governs the formation of a corporeally enacted femininity that never fully approximates the norm."[27] In other words, if, from Simone de Beauvoir's famous dictum that "one is not born a woman, one becomes one," feminists have understood woman as a construct, the question remains what is one before one becomes a woman? Is one a girl? And how does this girl become a woman? And, pace Butler, isn't this girl in the process of becoming girl herself, as she is interpellated into discourse? Far from the dizzying and celebratory rhetoric of choice, girlhood is theorized as the forcible citation of an unachievable norm that disciplines and regulates even as it seems to offer up pleasure and freedom. The complex process of becoming a woman, and managing the transition from girlhood to womanhood, is thus still ambivalent, ambiguous, and fraught.

To be seen as "girly" has become a desirable position for many female-identified subjects, including chronologically adult women, for whom the subject position girl may well contain connotations of escape, evasion, and transcendence of the norms governing adult femininity. Michelle Lazer explains that women's entitlement to leisure and pleasure depends on a celebration of "girliness." [28] Furthermore, Yvonne Tasker and Diane Negra note, "the 'girling' of femininity more generally—the competent professional adult woman who is made safe by being represented as fundamentally still a girl—is itself a characteristic of postfeminist representations."[29] These technologies of gender together with the disciplining techniques that are employed to maintain the desire for youth have led to a continual need to achieve and then maintain a non-adult approach to looks and active participation in the world of "fun." This can be understood as part of a general cultural valuation of youth, in which media aims to appeal to audiences via a process that Hartley calls "juvenation": the over-representation of signs of youthfulness. He argues that this leads to ambivalent and contradictory effects, because as soon as this adult-dominated media juvenates its audiences, there is an opposing drive to enforce and entrench age boundaries between children and adults. He concludes that children are rarely celebrated, but either pathologized or victimized.[30] Studlar takes Hartley's concept, and argues that such juvenation practices were also the way in which Hollywood cinema constructed the appeal of many of its female stars. It would thus seem that the blurring between girls and women that Harris locates at the turn of the century has a longer pre-history than she acknowledges, with precedents set for this blurring of boundaries between girl and woman, child and adult.

In the current cultural moment of postfeminism, however, and concomitant girlhood hypervisibility, this blurring of boundaries suggests both the appeal of girlhood for all female-identified subjects—who after all would not want to indulge in an identity marketed as fun, empowering, and playful—and the problematic constraints that still mark "woman" as an identity position. Attention to girlhood on film thus follows two main directions in this book: we investigate the varied textures and experiences of female-identified children, but we also take into account the desirable qualities of "girliness" for adult women. The book does not privilege any one expression of girlhood over another, and our contributors draw our attention to the "girling" of womanhood in a variety of national contexts as well as discussing girl children and adolescents. Our book thus takes into account the slippery and precarious nature of the term girl, allowing a variety of accounts of how girlhood finds its sonic and visual shape within contemporary cinema cultures.

An Atlas of Girlhood onscreen

With such an expansive and amorphous topic, we could not possibly hope to cover everything, and such fascinating topics as the dominance of girls with supernatural powers in contemporary Korean cinema, the delightful girl teen punks of Lukas Moodysson's *Vi är bäst!/We Are the Best* (2013), and the use of girls in Bollywood cinema all offer intriguing avenues of enquiry, to name but a few. However, it is worth bearing in mind at this juncture Dudley Andrew's important intervention in discussion of what, exactly, it means to tackle teaching or researching the category of "international" cinema. Rather than offering a survey suggesting a distant gaze that "panoptically monitors the foreign for our use," we should be ready "to travel more than oversee."[31] Andrew thus uses the analogy of the atlas, whereby each map produced varies according to aspects that are significant to its user. When mapping international cinema through the focus of girlhood, various hotspots appear that this book draws attention to: the visibility and importance of girlhood in European as well as American cinema; her central role in articulating challenges to pre-existing gender regimes in Iranian, Japanese, and Argentine cinema; the attention to, and interest in, queer girlhood, or girlhood *as* queer, across national divides; the significance of music to the representation of girlhood; films that represent lives far removed from dominant media girls. Rather than aiming to offer an illusion of total coverage, this book seeks to "displace" the reader, offering a variety of perspectives from which to consider cinematic girlhood. It seeks to complicate the emerging topos of centers and margins. Whereas Projansky comments that, "girls [. . .] remain central to [and] in fact likely will become ever more important to celebrity and media culture," Sherrie Innes notes, "girls are ignored or overlooked in many societies around the world . . . . For many reasons, *all* the world's girls are placed in the margins of existence."[32] Partly the difference between Projansky's and Innes' comments is to do with the difference, touched on of necessity only briefly here, between mediated and actual girls' experiences. However, it also speaks to a tendency to see US media culture as a center (even as one challenges the ideologies of this center) and everywhere else as a margin (even existence within the hegemonic United States when one is outside of this media culture). By mixing together films that, for a contemporary Western audience, come from the hegemonic centers of the United States and critically acclaimed European art house, to those that come from a peripheral location (US queer culture, Latin America, Japan, Africa), the book aims to displace the reader from a comfortable position of knowing where the center and the margins are, to argue for a plurality of girlhoods, making possible as expansive and liberatory a view as possible of the girl in international cinema.

Organization

This book is divided into four main sections, each designed to facilitate a greater and in-depth understanding of the myriad of issues involved in filmic engagement with the girl. "Girlhood and Postfeminism: Global perspectives" examines the local, situated, embodied responses that girls make on demands to perform girlhood in a certain way. Danielle Hipkins, Mary Harrod, and Joel Gwynne draw on a variety of frameworks to shape their arguments, but in all three chapters in this section what emerges is a sense that postfeminism's imbrication with the globalizing forces of neoliberal governance and citizenship shapes the experiences and representations of girls outside of the dominant Anglo-American filmic sphere. These chapters show that while it would be a mistake to assert that postfeminism is a cultural sensibility that operates seamlessly across all societies, neoliberal attitudes toward the individual and society, often combined with the power and appeal of American popular culture, have had an impact across national borders in terms of attitudes concerning girlhood, agency, and empowerment.

This presentation of the interaction between nationally specific ideas of girlhood and frameworks constructed from broader transnational neoliberal economic regimes begins with the compelling example of contemporary Italy. While some theorists, such as Maristella Cantini, argue that postfeminist rhetoric can only be tangentially applied to the Italian context, Danielle Hipkins finds some contemporary Italian film sympathetically engaged with the appeal of transnational consumer culture for economically disadvantaged girls from the peninsula. Italy provides a particularly spectacular example of the way girlhood acts as a lightning rod to debate sexuality, empowerment, and control. Ex Prime Minister Silvio Berlusconi's political corruption has become entangled in debates about his sexual behavior, in particular his interactions with girls (young women under the age of 18). Furthermore, these girls have been interpreted as possibly victims of abuse, but also as empowered entrepreneurs well aware of potential financial and lifestyle rewards for their activities. In "The Show*girl* Effect: Adolescent girls and (precarious) "technologies of sexiness" in contemporary Italian cinema," Hipkins examines how the "velina" (television showgirl) in Italian popular culture has become a key figure in the postfeminist cultures of girlhood. Hipkins argues we see a figure that negotiates the taut boundaries of sexual liberation and the postfeminist desire for economic success within a workplace where desire and "sexiness" is a commodity to be bought and sold. Despite the bleakness of a situation where the choice is sexiness or unemployment, Hipkins sees the possibility of renewal and rescue within female friendship bonds.

Genre has played an important role in the filmic presentation of girlhood across national boundaries. The "chick-flick" has been a common marker in the narratives surrounding girls, women, and their viewing patterns and preferences. While the chick-flick is overwhelmingly associated with popular American cinema and its global dominance, Mary Harrod argues that this genre has begun to be appropriated within non-American contexts, in the light of shifting gender relations in Europe. "Girlfriends, Postfeminism, and the European chick-flick in France" examines how a series of films since 2006 have begun to inflect the chick-flick narrative from multiple and diverse perspectives, exploring the national specificity of inter-generational relations and attitudes toward girls and girliness within a genre that encourages cultural cross-fertilization (a fertilization occasionally visible within the film, as in the casting of British actor Andrew Lincoln as love interest in *Comme t'y es belle/Gorgeous* (Azuelos, 2006), a move Harrod interprets as a nod to the Anglo-American generic parentage of the film).

Joel Gwynne's chapter "Warrior of Love: Japanese Girlhood's Postfeminist Asian Body in *Cutie Honey* (Hideaki Anno, 2004)" engages with the way in which postfeminist discourse has been taken up in modern, neoliberal Japan. Rather as Hipkins finds the velina a fulcrum in which nationally focused stories of corruption and decline and broader postfeminist debates find expression, so Gwynne identifies the female action hero of *shōnen* manga as equally adept at expressing specifically Japanese fears of transformation and transnational accounts of women's empowerment within the workplace. Cutie Honey performs a contradictory and quintessentially postfeminist identity as both active (physically strong) but also passive (sexually objectified). However, Gwynne contends it is in attending to the incompetencies of her real-world female boss, Natsuko, that we find the most problematic expression of backlash culture. Meanwhile, Cutie Honey's comparative indifference toward heterosexual romance possibly spells a potentially more liberating, if far from radical, image of postfeminist girlhood and empowerment within the context of a film that still ultimately works to contain feminine progress within traditional models of subordination.

In "Philosophies of Girlhood in Film," we explore how the girl has been inflected across the contemporary field from several philosophical and critical angles. Moving the focus to Latin America in "Feminine Adolescence and Transgressive Materiality in the Films of Lucrecia Martel," Deborah Martin examines how the Argentinian filmmaker challenges hermeneutic and scopic drives via her focus on female adolescence. Martel's films, with their focus on the affective, visceral, and bodily experience of the girl, place adolescent femininity at the heart of a broader aesthetic and political project. The focus on the abject, the physical, and the materiality of the body allows new modes of thinking around the girl to be articulated via the New Argentina cinema's preoccupation with political, sexual, and economic upheaval. In a similar way, Lucy Bolton's chapter on the British film *Fish Tank* (Arnold, 2009) considers the way film can offer a highly situated, phenomenological experience of how it feels to be a particular girl. In "A Phenomenology of Girlhood: Being Mia in *Fish Tank* (Andrea Arnold, 2009)," we see a girlhood marked by disenfranchisement, rejection, and lack. In her examination of Mia's positioning inside the wider narratives of sex and class, Bolton argues that *Fish Tank* comments more widely on adolescence and the family in contemporary British culture, but never stops attending to the very particular experience of how it feels to be Mia, preventing her from simply being a stock figure of "Broken Britain." The section then moves onto thinking about the possibilities offered to girls through female bonds within the arena of queer sexuality. This experience of girlhood has remained highly marginalized from the mainstream discourses surrounding femininity and the postfeminist moment, as the recurrent anxiety about sexualization and girlhood remains firmly within a heterosexual and patriarchal worldview, in which passive/innocent girls are victims of active/predatory men. Taking the American film *Pariah* (Dee, 2011), Clara Bradbury-Rance's examination places queerness not only in the sexual orientation of the subject but in the spatial and temporal journey that she takes. In "Desire, Outcast: Locating queer adolescence," Bradbury-Rance shows how queerness potentially disrupts dominant modes of girlhood. Alternative modes of girlhood are a continued focus in the next chapter. In "Bye-Bye to Betty's Blues and "La Bonne Meuf": Temporal Drag and Queer Subversions of the Rom-Com in *Bye Bye Blondie* (Virginie Despentes, 2011)," Lara Cox examines how the controversial director Virgine Despentes utilizes a "return to girlishness" as a positive tool to disrupt and debate the omnipresent figure of "la bonne meuf" ("the good woman"). Cox argues that via the film's use of intertextuality, punk, and flashback, and the subsequent privileging of "queer time" over heteronormative experiences the film subverts and destabilizes the romantic comedy genre, producing a "spectral" girlhood that disrupts narratives of maturity and "coming-of-age."

In the third section, "Sonic Youth: Girlhood, music, and identity", we focus on alternative methods of breaking the silence surrounding how it feels to be a girl, paying a renewed attention to questions of film form, extending feminist film's commitment to searching for new form into the postfeminist era. For Chantal Akerman, creating a new subject position for women in film must go beyond content. Women filmmakers must "look for formal ways to express who they are and what they want, their own rhythms, their own way of looking at things," and we might add here, their own way of hearing things.[33] Angela McRobbie argues that the ideal girl subject of postfeminism is "called upon to be silent, to withhold critique in order to count as a modern sophisticated girl [...] indeed this withholding of critique is a condition of her freedom."[34] This section asks how postfeminist girlhood can find a voice within a cinema that remains sympathetic to her need to "withhold critique," and finds that dynamic and inventive use of music offers potential for an articulation of some of the paradoxes involved in navigating this slippery terrain.

As already discussed, youth films made in Hollywood typically focus on a white, middle-class, suburban coming-of-age experience. Inclusion of diversity tends to be a token gesture and rebellious girls often conform to traditional gender roles by the film's end. While a few mainstream youth films do have African-American protagonists and some attempt to tackle racism, very few explore the experiences of Latino youth in the United States. In " 'Chica Dificil': Music, identity, and agency in *Real Women Have Curves* (Patricia Cardoso, 2002)," Tim McNelis argues that the hybrid subjectivity of the Latina girl is expressed via the diverse and meaningful soundtrack even if the film's narrative seeks to define and ground a "real" Latina woman. Fiona Handyside's chapter "Emotion, Girlhood and Music in *Naissance des pieuvres* (Céline Sciamma, 2007) and *Un amour de jeunesse* (Mia Hansen-Løve, 2011)" takes this focus on sound further with an examination of French female directors Céline Sciamma and Mia Hansen-Løve. Via an affective engagement based on both stylistics and sound, this cinema allows for sound to channel and articulate the "illegible rage" that accompanies the experience of growing up in a postfeminist cultural landscape. Giving girls a voice is as much based around understanding and promoting a notion of fun and enjoyment over rigorous bodily discipline and to this end Samantha Colling's chapter "The Pleasures of Music Video Aesthetics in Girl Teen Film" explores the pleasurable spectacle of music and performance in the teen film. Girlhood and the music video has been a topic of much debate with the rise of stars such as Britney Spears, Christina Aguilera, Katy Perry, and Miley Cyrus. Colling's focus on the inter-media relationship between movement and sound presents a distinct moment of visibility in which "fun" supersedes all else. Whilst this moment of "girl fun" is fleeting and ultimately powerless in the face of established gender and narrative norms, nevertheless it presents a space where dominant cultural girlhood signals and embraces its own artificiality.

The final section "Extraordinary Girlhoods" allows us to explore girlhoods that are exceptional. The term extraordinary draws attention to the ways in which girlhood as a construct operates as a highly normative term, bound within strict understanding of gender and age and behaviors that are suitable for these categories: as Butler indicates, an interpellation that sows the seeds of its own failure. We have chosen extraordinary rather than transgressive for a specific reason. To "transgress" means in some small way to acknowledge conventional codes and normative behavior if only via one's own rejection of them. The girlhoods that we have in this final chapter in many ways undermine and destabilize the whole notion of girlhood itself. This chapter will look at how these extraordinary girlhoods are created and then presented for cinematic consumption.

Possibly the most extraordinary of all these girls is the child murderer Mary Bell, whose crimes, as Lisa Downing argues, were so culturally unintelligible as to be almost unrepresentable and unknowable, unlike those of adult serial killers such as Ian Brady and Myra Hindley. In "Where's Girlhood? The Female Child Killer in *Where's Mary?* (Tony Hickson, 2005)," Downing explores how the figure of the girl as murderer sheds light on the dominant articulation of girls as both other to and exemplars of childhood: other to it, as universal human norms are still posited as male (so that "the child" is usually by default "the boy"), and exemplary as girls embody the innocence and passivity associated generally with children. Downing argues that cultural norms that posit girlhood and childhood more broadly as a place of non-agency, "innocence" and purity deny the violence and rage that can also characterize this life stage. We then turn to a very different type of extraordinary girlhood in Margherita Sprio's "Performing

History: Girlhood and *The Apple* (Samira Makhmalbaf, 1998)." Spiro turns to the fraught issue of how girlhood is performed on camera, and what it means to ask girls to perform as girls. This chapter examines the extraordinary recreation of the true-life story of twin girls who were locked up by their parents. The film's reenactment begs questions about authenticity and performance, placing the role of the girls as symbols of Iranian oppression of women under the auspices of art rather than documentary—an art that aims to speak about local issues to a global audience via the recognizable "universal" humanism of the child.

The global audience is again returned to in "Girlhood in a Warzone: African Child Soldiers in Film." In this chapter Kate Taylor-Jones focuses on how female African child soldiers have been utilized in the global space to uphold gender and national stereotypes whilst denying the individual experiences and narratives of these most complex of female figures. Female child soldiers are doubly marginalized as figures that are imbued with the stigma of sexual assault together with the uncomfortable linkage to violence and aggression. Violence and aggression are of course seen as an antithesis to an idealized girlhood and we conclude with "Daddy's Little Sidekick: The Girl Superhero in Contemporary Cinema," where Marty Zeller-Jacques explores how the controversial child assassin Hit-Girl in the popular *Kick-Ass* (Vaughn, Wadlow: 2010, 2013) films presents a highly contradictory figure. Although dominated by an overbearing patriarch and rehabilitated into a quasi-normative role though the films, she simultaneously embodies a repudiation of traditional models of submissive girlhood in favor of her aggressive exercise of power.

Spanning a wide range of nations, directors, and genres, the chapters in this book are focused on extending, heightening, and developing the debate surrounding the girl in international cinema on both the local and the global stage. Moving between European, Asian, Arabic, and North and Latin American cinemas; analyzing successful female auteurs such as Céline Sciamma, Francesca Comencini, and Andrea Arnold; moving from popular genre cinema to niche shorts and art-house film; thinking about girls as friends, lovers, super-heroines, or murderers, this collection offers an accessible range of new ways to think about girls in the cinema, carving out a more nuanced understanding of the pleasures, potentials, and pains of girls in film.

Notes

1. Marnina Gonick, Emma Renold, Jessica Ringrose and Lisa Weems, "Rethinking Agency and Resistance: What Comes after Girl Power?," *Girlhood Studies* 2:2 (Winter 2009), 1–9 (1).

2. Sarah Projansky, *Spectacular Girls: Media Fascination and Celebrity Culture* (New York: New York University Press, 2014), p. 2.
3. John Hartley, " 'When Your Child Grows Up Too Fast': Juvenation and the Boundaries of the Social in the News Media," *Continuum* 12:1 (1998), 9–30 (15).
4. Mary Celeste Kearney, *Mediated Girlhoods: New Explorations of Girls' Media Culture* (New York: Peter Lang, 2011), p. 2.
5. Gaylyn Studlar, *Precocious Charms: Stars Performing Girlhood in Classical Hollywood Cinema* (Berkeley and Los Angeles: University of California Press, 2013), p. 2.
6. Vicky Lebeau, *Childhood and Cinema* (London: Reaktion, 2008), p. 4.
7. Carol Dyhouse, *Girl Trouble: Panic and Progress in the History of Young Women* (London: Zed Books, 2014), p. 70.
8. Marcelle Karp and Debbie Stoller, eds., *The "Bust" Guide to the New Girl Order* (London: Penguin, 1999).
9. Monica Swindle, "Feeling Girl, Girling Feeling: An Examination of "Girl" as Affect," *Rhizomes* 22 (2011), online. http://www.rhizomes.net/issue22/swindle.html
10. This definition of the role of film in culture comes from Hilary Radner, *Neo-Feminist Cinema: Girly Films, Chick Flicks and Consumer Culture* (London and New York: Routledge, 2011), p. 9.
11. Anita Harris, *Future Girl: Young Women in the Twenty-First Century* (New York: Routledge, 2004). The "Princess Panic" books referenced are Peggy Orenstein, *Cinderella Ate My Daughter: Dispatches from the Front Lines of the New Girlie-Girl Culture* (New York: Harper Collins, 2011); Jennifer Harstein, *Princess Recovery: A Guide to Raising Strong, Empowered Girls Who Can Create their Own Happily Ever Afters* (Avon, MA: Adams Media, 2011); and Rebecca C. Hains, *The Princess Problem: Guiding Our Girls through the Princess Obsessed Years* (Naperville, IL: Sourcebooks, 2014).
12. Gaylyn Studlar, *Precocious Charms*, p. 16.
13. Catherine Driscoll, *Girls: Feminine Adolescence in Popular Culture and Theory* (New York: Columbia University Press, 2002), p. 9. Kearney traces the desire to distance women from (girl) children to the problem their close identification posed for the advancement of women's suffrage and claims to equality before the law recognized from at least the time of the Victorian reformer John Stuart Mill. As Kearney explains, in a section of his *Principles of Political Economy* Mill specifically opposed women to immature and incapable youth in constructing his arguments for women's rights as citizen-subjects. "The larger women's movement developed an increasingly adult-centered perspective and thus uneasy relation to female youth as it narrowed its focus to gaining women the right to vote." See Kearney, "Coalescing: The Development of Girls' Studies," *NWSA Journal* 21:9 (2005), 1–28 (16).
14. Ella Shohat, *Taboo Memories, Diasporic Voices* (Durham, NC: Duke University Press, 2006).
15. Rosalind Gill, "Postfeminist Media Culture: Elements of a Sensibility," *European Journal of Cultural Studies* 10:2 (May 2007), 147–166.

16. Diane Negra, *What a Girl Wants: Fantasizing the Reclamation of Self in Postfeminism* (London: Routledge, 2009), p. 9.
17. Catherine Driscoll, *Teen Film: A Critical Introduction* (Oxford: Berg, 2011), p. 2.
18. Timothy Shary and Alexandra Seibel, *Youth Culture in Global Cinema* (Austin, TX: University of Texas Press, 2007).
19. Roz Kaveney, *Teen Dreams: Reading Teen Film from* Heathers *to* Veronica Mars (London: IB Tauris, 2006), p. 2
20. Catherine Driscoll, *Teen Film*, p. 162.
21. See in particular Shiri Reznik and Dafna Lamish, "Falling in Love with *High School Musical*: Girls' Talk about Romantic Perceptions' and Catherine Driscoll, 'Becoming a Country Girl'," in *Mediated Girlhoods*, pp. 151–170 and 135–150.
22. Projansky, *Spectacular Girls*, pp. 181–216.
23. Kathleen Sweeney, *Maiden USA: Girl Icons Come of Age* (New York: Peter Lang, 2008), p. xi.
24. See Leslie Regan Shade, "Surveilling the Girl via the Third and Networked Screen" and Sarah Banet-Weiser, "Branding the Post-Feminist Self: Girls' Video Production and You Tube," in *Mediated Girlhoods*, pp. 261–276 and pp. 277–294.
25. Anita Harris, *All about the Girl: Culture, Power and Identity* (London and New York: Routledge, 2004), p. xx.
26. Joan Jacobs Brumberg, *The Body Project: An Intimate History of American Girls* (New York: Vintage, 1997).
27. Judith Butler, *Bodies That Matter* (London and New York: Routledge, 1993), p. 576.
28. Michelle M. Lazar, "Entitled to Consume: Postfeminist Femininity and a Culture of Post-critique," *Discourse and Communication* 3:4 (2009), 340–371.
29. Diane Negra and Yvonne Tasker, "InFocus: Postfeminism and Contemporary Media Studies," *Cinema Journal* 44:2 (2005), 107–110 (109).
30. John Hartley, "When Your Child Grows Up Too Fast," 9–30.
31. Dudley Andrew, "An Atlas of World Cinema," in *Remapping World Cinema: Identity, Culture and Politics in Film* edited by Stephanie Dennison and Song Hwee Lim (London: Wallflower, 2006), pp. 19–29 (19).
32. Projansky, *Spectacular Girls*, p. 214 and Sherrie Innes, *Running For Their Lives: Girls, Cultural Identity and Stories of Survival* (Lanham, MD and Oxford: Rowman and Littlefield), p. xi.
33. Chantal Akerman, "Chantal Akerman on Jeanne Dielman," *Camera Obscura* 2 (1977), 118–119.
34. Angela Mc Robbie, *The Aftermath of Feminism: Gender, Culture and Social Change* (London: Sage, 2009), p. 18.

Part I

Girlhood and Postfeminism: Global Perspectives

I

The Show*girl* Effect: Adolescent Girls and (Precarious) "Technologies of Sexiness" in Contemporary Italian Cinema

Danielle Hipkins

Introduction

The eponymous working-class protagonist of bestselling Italian novel, *Marina Bellezza* (Silvia Avallone, Milan: Rizzoli, 2013), trades on her outstanding beauty by training hard to become a singer, and breaking into television talent contests. She is depicted as dedicated, but ruthlessly ambitious, dangerously promiscuous, and unreliable. In pathologizing Marina's desire for celebrity as the product of a broken home, the novel is the latest product of an Italian media discourse that "spectacularizes" girlhood in relation to the female television celebrity. Sarah Projansky has described how the "spectacularization" of girlhood works in the US media, making anxiety and ambivalence, and (usually) an exclusive whiteness, the conditions of the girls' appearance as "visual objects of display." Projansky suggests that the anxious dichotomies between "adoration and denigration," between the "can-do" girl of "Girlpower," and the "at risk" vulnerable girl, structure contemporary interpretations of girlhood, in which the girl can easily move between the polarities and transform from "fabulous" into "scandal."[1] In the text's "adoration" of Marina's blonde good looks, and the "denigration" of her disregard for others' feelings in order to get ahead, but also in the novel's emphatic context of poor job prospects, we can read a distillation of the peculiarly Italian take on contemporary girlhood and female futures. In this chapter I consider the ways in which a particular set of constrictions concerning "girlhood" and its representation rotate around the "velina" (television showgirl) in Italian cinema, revealing what Projansky labels "resistant potential" in contemporary postfeminist cultures of girlhood. There is a common notion that the Anglo-American framework of postfeminism is, in Maristella Cantini's words, a "cultural paradigm" that can only be tangentially applied to Italy," largely for reasons associated with Italy's economic situation, women's working conditions and their one-sided representation in the media.[2] With this chapter, in fact, I will argue that it is precisely in the depiction of how Italy's economically disadvantaged girl faces the broader trend of a female-focused transnational consumerism that Italian cinema interpellates postfeminist culture.

In previous work,[3] I suggested that the figure of the "velina" has become a fulcrum in Italy for "at risk" narratives of girlhood, particularly for recent popular, moralizing feminism.[4] Furthermore, I have suggested that this anxiety channels concern about youthful female sexuality and consumption. "Velina" is a term that stands in for a whole panoply of television showgirls, who have ranged in age from 15 to 30, but have always invoked a performative mode of "girliness." These performances have also traditionally targeted younger audiences as key consumers, many critics citing Mattel's controversial release of a Barbie velina in 2002 as an example of this.[5] More moralizing discourses came to the fore, when it recently transpired that young women aspiring to work in television were exchanging sex for money and/or placements in television with high-ranking men in politics and the television industry, including Italy's then PM, Silvio Berlusconi. As Valeria Ottonelli has also observed, media discourse about these scandals condemned the young women rather than the corrupt male politicians and managers "for having gone along with it [...] for 'futile reasons', that is, just for the love of luxury, money and an easy life."[6] As Catherine Driscoll has commented about the figure of the girl more broadly:

> The significance of late modern girls to consumption is not that they consume (everybody does), or that their sexuality is in fact bound up in commodification, but that they are perceived to derive an inordinate amount of pleasure from commodification and commodity fetishism.[7]

In the Italian context, there has been a particular focus on the entanglement of the desire for consumer goods with what is deemed sexually inappropriate female behavior in the figure of the girl. In this form of "slut-shaming," commentators are repeatedly drawn back to the figure of the girl, over whom there is an assumed right to comment, rather than the more intractable issue of corrupt (male) political power.

Responses to the "velina" and other high-profile girls in Italy as dangerous consumers are linked to the advent of what Hilary Radner calls "technologies of sexiness." For Radner, "the task of the Single Girl is to embody heterosexuality through the disciplined use of make-up, clothing, exercise and cosmetic surgery, linking femininity, consumer culture and heterosexuality."[8] In what I label here as "the showgirl effect," I argue that in contemporary Italian cinema the "velina" becomes herself a technology of sexiness that invokes the hypervaluation of the "girled body" in "today's relentlessly visual landscape."[9] A new emphasis on the performance of sexual knowledge makes the showgirl a particularly apposite focal point for anxieties about how girls employ various "technologies of sexiness," particularly when invoked in relation to traditional expectations of childlike innocence. Whether a girl herself, or the imaginary object of a girl's ambition, the "velina" invokes the "cause for panic" that Projansky associates with the female teen star: "who has entered puberty/adolescence but who is not yet adult" and "brings together child and sexuality."[10] Through the "velina," however, film narrative examines the way in which girls "negotiate and are being negotiated through the sexualisation of culture."[11]

These narratives also often challenge the pervasive "role modelling" approach to youthful female spectatorship, such as that evidenced by cultural commentator and academic, Michela Marzano, who suggests that "as a result of identifying with 'fashion dolls', [adolescent girls] end up internalizing the role that men want women to continue to play."[12] Recently, academic research in Italy has brought empirical understanding to this supposed proliferation of the desire to become a "velina," through focus groups with a cross-section of schoolchildren around the age of 16. Rossella Ghigi reports that this research demonstrated that in fact few young people seem to aspire to be "veline." Their responses to the figure articulate what Ghigi describes as a peculiarly Italian response to the backlash against feminism. On the one hand the schoolchildren interviewed have no problem with the neoliberal commodification of the body, and do not see the girls as victims so much as freely acting entrepreneurs. At the same time they criticize showgirls for potentially transgressing ideals of traditional femininity and are particularly wary of their apparent sexual availability and their lack of talent, blaming the women themselves for the mechanisms of televisual gender representation. Although admitting to a desire to look like the women, the children do not see themselves as negatively influenced by the images, but subscribe to what is known as the "third person effect," in which they claim that other viewers are negatively influenced. According to Ghigi, this allows them to express their own discomfort whilst conforming to the system.[13]

To what extent do recent film narratives provide "resistant potential" to the narrative "denigration" of girls, in particular to the association of beauty culture with stupidity and culpable promiscuity? How do they challenge the idea of girl spectators as "sponges," but also possibly complicate young people's claims that the "velina" does not have any impact upon them? I will discuss two films with an unusually explicit teen girl address (both are based on teen novels), *Un giorno speciale/A Special Day* (Comencini, 2012) and *Come tu mi vuoi/As You Desire Me* (De Biasi, 2007), which privilege the notion of female agency through their young protagonists. Both films draw upon the romantic comedy genre, if much more faithfully in the case of *Come tu mi vuoi*. Both films use the transformative demands of "velina" culture, from makeovers to make-unders, to interrogate the relationship between feminism, femininity, and consumption. They also work to problematize the female relations that are constructed through beauty culture, and foreground the precarity and political corruption that constrain the girls' behavior, particularly in relation to expressions of their sexuality.

Makeovers and Make-unders: The (Post)Feminist Gaze

Come tu mi vuoi reveals the female protagonist's alienation from mainstream gender practices in Italy through her response to the "velina" image. The film opens with images of a reality TV game show, in which attractive young women wearing hot pants and bikini tops are required to eat blancmange-type puddings without using their hands, and the overweight presenter, who brings the cakes onto the set, makes a joke about her own "lovely little figure." This reconstruction of an absurd Italian game show introduces what Rosalind Gill has described as the process of "subjectification,"[14] which will be the film's key theme: how neoliberal society encourages women to take pleasure in objectifying their own bodies through lifestyle and consumer choices. If, initially, this opening TV scene appears mediated only to one degree, suddenly the quality of the image changes and we realize that the diegetic spectator is watching the program on her computer, preparing for her exam on the mass media. As she prepares her notes, hard-working university student Giada (Cristiana Capotondi), whose exaggeratedly plain appearance contrasts with the made-over images of the young women on screen, angrily voices a classic feminist semiotic critique of the representation of woman as object, and asks the rhetorical question that has dogged the feminist mainstream:

"Why aren't women saying anything?." Even as we are introduced to our heroine, hard at work in this analysis, her argument is never labeled as feminist, rather merely "intellectual." The refusal of the feminist label parallels that of US teen makeover film *She's All That* (Iscove, 1999),[15] and reminds us of the haunting of postfeminist culture by second-wave feminism, in which

> Although the postfeminist text is often marked by amnesia, its historicizing manoeuvres leave traces of the very histories they seek to erase. The postfeminist text, then, might usefully be understood as a kind of palimpsest […] presenting the possibility of remembering and recovering a past which is supposed lost.[16]

The make-under/makeover pattern structures the relationship between feminism and postfeminism, as the protagonist learns to find a position of compromise between the two polemicized versions of female performance. When Giada falls in love with rich wide boy, Ricky (Nicolas Vaporidis), she reluctantly sacrifices her (feminist) beliefs on the altar of fashion and beauty in order to woo him. Sarah Gilligan identifies two types of cinematic "make-under":

> in the first, the subject starts out as "natural" or "made under" and is subsequently "improved" through the processes of the makeover; in the second conversely, the subject begins as "made up," before being "made under" to appear more "natural" (and thus more desirable).[17]

In *Come tu mi vuoi*, Giada's original made-under appearance is marked not as natural, so much as a stubborn mask, while the makeover scene itself echoes the industrial one in *Miss Congeniality* (Petrie, 2000), in which Yael Sherman has noted the "physical discomfort and labor of femininity."[18] In a highly parodic scene, Giada's transformation is presented as a form of initiation into a secret sect. The film thus renders all forms of feminine appearance problematic and explores the uncomfortable seams of what Angela McRobbie terms the "postfeminist masquerade."[19] Giada's ultimate sell-out lies in her acquisition, with money stolen from her waitressing job, of the uncomfortable "Cool-tura" G-string ("it rubs!," she declares naïvely). The exploitative advert for this product dominates the view from her flat window, and has previously generated her loathing. In embracing this culture, however, Giada is forced to become one of the girls she previously denigrated, and to understand them; indeed for all its parody, the film still engages with the familiar pleasures of the transformation scene typical of the genre, and therefore beauty culture itself.

If the voice of second-wave feminism "haunts" the text of *Come tu mi vuoi*, *Un giorno speciale* has an explicitly feminist message, exhorting young women, in the director's words, not to sell their beauty short.[20] *Un giorno speciale* tracks the day in the life of a 19-year-old aspiring actress, Gina (Giulia Valentini) from a socially disadvantaged background in the Roman periphery whose mother encourages her to "visit" an influential male politician in the hope of getting her onto television. Hence, once again, we see "the showgirl effect" driving the narrative. After her mother's solicitous makeover, Gina is collected by a young driver Marco (Filippo Scicchitano) on his first day on the job. The appointment at the center of Rome is repeatedly delayed, causing the young couple to become closer over the course of a day spent driving round Rome. It gradually becomes clear that Gina's appointment with the politician will be her first experience of sex work. The film ends, indeed, with Gina fulfilling her engagement, and returning home visibly shaken. In a romantic gesture Marco attempts to find her. The director, Francesca Comencini, was one of the leaders of the feminist movement *Se Non Ora Quando*, started in 2011 in response to images of women in the media, which posed precisely Giada's question: "Why aren't women saying anything?." This strategy, rather like *Come tu mi vuoi*, served to obliterate the ongoing existence of feminist resistance in Italy, and the movement was also accused of scapegoating women involved in the Berlusconi scandals.[21] In the context of Ghigi's work on the reception of the "veline" amongst young people in Italy as entirely in control of their own destinies, Comencini's desire to contextualize certain kinds of choices is understandable. However, in keeping with *Se non ora quando*, the film runs the familiar risk of employing a moralizing framework toward certain "technologies of sexiness," blame for which appears to be offloaded onto the girl's mother.

Comencini aligns Gina's reluctance to engage in sex work with her reluctance to wear the shoes that her mother gives her in the film's opening "makeover" scene. "Are you trying to kill me?," Gina jokes as her mother hands her the glittering 12-centimeter heels, which she later removes to don her Converse All-Stars. In fact the film effects the second form of "make-under" described by Gilligan as, over the course of the day, Gina subverts her mother's morning makeover, and becomes more desirable (in Marco's eyes). Through the makeover Comencini ostensibly engages with the paradigm of the melodramatic victim-girl, sacrificed to the ambition of her mother "as heartless or unthinking tool of patriarchy."[22] What Comencini's film offers to nuance the association between attachment to the "wrong" beauty practices and institutional sexual exploitation of young women is a more sympathetic texture to that mother–daughter narrative. The affective quality of the "makeover" scene demonstrates the rituals of female grooming as a language of communication between mother and daughter, in which the beautician-mother's preparation of her daughter for "sacrifice" is loaded with tenderness, longing and regret. Comencini has a reputation for particular sensitivity to screening moments of mother–daughter intimacy, and the ambiguities of their physical closeness.[23] Gina's mother tut-tuts over her daughter's poorly shaped eyebrows, and the camera lingers in extreme close-up over her grooming of Gina. The two are shot physically intertwined, as her mother paints her toenails, and fondly remembers giving birth to her, having seen her oddly long toe first of all. In the pleasure and laughter shared in this moment, despite the darkness and claustrophobia of the flat foreshadowing Gina's implicit destiny, Comencini pays a rare attention to the powerful affective bonds of female beauty rituals, which makes them much more difficult to dismiss as simply "poor taste." The unusual emphasis on maternal care as an aspect of the makeover serves to highlight that "an investment in bodily capital makes particular sense where other capitals and opportunities, such as educational qualifications, are limited (Skeggs, 1997)."[24] If it is, as usual, the mother who fails, this aspect is nonetheless a powerful attempt sympathetically to root the working-class girl's attachment to certain images of success in her intimate domestic context. In this respect, like Lauren Berlant, Comencini analyses "impasses in zones of intimacy that hold out the often cruel promise of reciprocity and belonging to the people who seek them," but this is not entirely a form of "cruel optimism." Through Gina's resistance, Comencini troubles Berlant's idea that "the creativity of the children keeps being rerouted to repeating some version of their parents' perverse approximations of the normative good life (Figure 1.1)."[25]

Figure 1.1 *Un giorno special/A Special Day* (Comencini, 2012). Disciplinary femininity: Surveillance and the "girlfriend gaze" in *Un giorno speciale*

"The Girlfriend Gaze" Unmasked

In reading the mother's care as deadly, but sympathetic, it is useful to draw upon Alison Winch's recent analysis of the "girlfriend gaze" in contemporary media culture. For Winch the affect of female intimacy is often hijacked by consumer capitalism in the popular media in order to encourage women to police one another with the aim of maintaining an emphasis on (lucrative) beauty culture. In demonstrating Gina's make-under resistance to her mother's "makeover" ritual, that gaze is unmasked. In this respect there is another symbolically important scene in the film. When her appointment with the politician is delayed, Gina asks Marco, without explanation, to take her to the swimming baths. Here she watches a performance of synchronized swimming, and suddenly falls ill. The scene cuts with an increasing pace between Gina's point of view on two perspectives. One is the audience in the gallery behind her, scrutinizing Gina, whose absurdly elaborate dress in the sports center context marks her out as one of Projansky's "scandal" girls. The other is the synchronized dancers whose performance, diving and rising from the water to a dramatic musical crescendo, and whose kohl-rimmed hostile gazes, seem to point with equal venom toward Gina. The scene echoes Céline Sciamma's use of the same sport in her film *Naissance des pieuvres/Water Lilies* (2007) to explore female bonds, and Comencini makes a similarly powerful use of the trope to question the disciplinary control of femininity in Italian culture, without further vilifying the image of the "velina" (for more on *Water Lilies* and synchronized swimming, see Handyside in this volume). Since we might assume that Gina has gone to the show to look for a female friend, of which there are no other instances in the film, and since the gaze of the girl swimmers intensifies the judgmental gaze of the local community, it is possible to read this scene in the light of Winch's critique of "girlfriend media": "that regulate the body and libido through surveillance networks that garner and maintain their power through provoking feelings of shame and guilt."[26] Winch refers here to the critical gaze upon female sexuality that dominates the popular media, and with this scene Comencini also reminds us that the aspiring showgirl is socially isolated in the face of such "surveillance networks," thereby distancing herself from the scapegoating of young women associated with her movement.

Come tu mi vuoi also speaks to the issue of female gazes. If Sara, Giada's flatmate, gently mocks her for her non-conformist, "make-under" fashion choices, as a plump girl herself she does not conform to an idealized postfeminist body type, and thus together initially the girls challenge the diktats of the beauty culture. However, the film shows Giada jettison her friendship with Sara in favor of elegant and cynical Fiamma, who becomes responsible for Giada's dramatic makeover. Giada and Fiamma lack the intimacy that usually legitimizes the girlfriend gaze, in which "the figure of the friend in girlfriend culture disguises the technologies of misogynist governance by offering advice and support through a friendly rhetoric."[27] Fiamma is far from friendly, and the help she offers Giada is portrayed as a form of diabolical (the clue is in her name: "Flame") experiment. Thus the film undercuts the affective bonding power that many makeover scenes generate, dwelling instead on a moment of erotic narcissism between the two women, and exposes precisely "the technologies of misogynist governance" behind certain forms of female friendship.

Precarity and Lines of Flight?

Alice Bardan has identified a number of films coming out of Italy as typical of a new European cinema of precarity. By precarity she understands:

> on the one hand, the *multiplication* of precarious and unstable forms of living, an insecurity of income and livelihood that nowadays affects a variety of social groups (from unskilled workers to academics), and, on the other hand, *new forms of political struggle and solidarity* that go beyond the traditional models of the political party or trade union.[28]

If, like other teen films,[29] *Come tu mi vuoi* employed the makeover to negotiate between contemporary practices of femininity and second-wave feminism, we also see it take the genre into the context of the workplace. Diane Negra and Yvonne Tasker suggest that "in general, the chick flick has maintained an imperviousness to the recession,"[30] but while the narrative patterns explored here are mainstream, primarily those of heterosexual love and desire, they do explicitly critique the inescapable nature of young women's need to adhere to the "beauty system" in order to obtain work. Not only does Giada have to steal to achieve her transformation, but she can then use that new look to achieve the university position her intellect alone would not get her; to discover that, in McRobbie's words: "the successful young woman must now get herself endlessly and repetitively done up [. . .] to conceal the competition she now poses."[31] By the end of the film Giada has been forced to learn that only a transformation in her appearance and a softening of her views will allow her access to mainstream Italian society in the shape of romance, *and* an academic job at the university (obtained here not by sleeping with, but at least by flirting with, an elderly academic male). Through its consistent emphasis on Giada's impoverished background, the film makes it clear that the serious constraints on female social mobility leave girls with no choice but to conform submissively to heterosexual models of female appearance. This is underlined by the final shot in which the camera zooms out from the embracing happy couple, to include in the background the advertising image that has haunted Giada throughout the film. A pair of young female buttocks, barely clothed in the infamous Cool-tura G-string, is the final word, the red of the advertising hoarding picked up in the image of the Italian national flag fluttering to its right, underlining Italy's cultural priorities of consumption of the female image. Has the camera itself adopted the critical gaze of the feminist specter-spectator, reminding us of the palimpsestic postfeminist text that Munford and Waters identify?

Comencini, whose work typically demonstrates awareness of changing labor conditions, also situates Gina within a context in which the search for ordinary domestic work, as she tells Marco, has also exposed her to attempts at sexual exploitation, further underlining the difficulty for women in Italy to work without the continued muddying of all work as a form of availability. The film is also at pains, however, to allude to the potential for rebellion. These moments of respite are brief; the film's ending is decidedly downbeat, showing Gina ignoring or not hearing Marco's calls to her as she watches television, retreating back into the world of dreams that led her to the encounter initially. Instead the climax of the film focuses on a moment when the girl and her driver engage in a form of rebellion more characteristic of the organized youth rebellions that have taken place through Europe as a protest against rising unemployment: shoplifting.[32] Gazing through the windows of Rome's most prestigious shopping street, the two protagonists appear to conform to all the clichés of the passive subject of Neoliberal consumerism. However, to Marco's amazement, Gina playfully enters into *Alberta Ferretti*, where she tricks the shop assistants and steals a dress. In a chase down Via Condotti, she throws it into the air, where it is shot falling in slow motion, as Gina shouts "fuck off" to the stupefied shop assistants and runs off hand in hand with Marco to a popular upbeat song on the soundtrack. What this scene shares with those "precarious" political movements described by Bardan, such as "Yomango," is that this is not shoplifting to acquire goods. This is shoplifting as something akin to the "lines of flight" discussed by Deleuze and Guattari, often referenced in girlhood studies as part of the representational appeal of the girl, a body in "becoming."[33] Jessica Ringrose and Emma Renold have used this idea in their empirical study of "girls' utopic but also violent or aggressive fantasies"; they "aim to reposition these away from a psycho-educational discourse that might seek to pathologise them towards an understanding of these fantasies as energetic lines of flight outside of normative, oppressive boundaries of (working class) femininity."[34] Their interpretation explains why we feel so much sympathy for Gina's actions in this scene, and why

this remains the emotional climax of the film. Indeed it is the potential generated by this scene that renders Gina's later submission to sexual
exploitation at the hands of the politician all the more shocking.

Conclusions

If "the ease with which women and young people have been marginalised
within, or erased from, the [US] cinematic discourse of recession, is striking,"[35] these Italian examples in which young women sit at the center of
the recession narrative are important. The films offer apparently bleak
prospects for Italian girls on the cusp of adult life, but through their
particular take on "the showgirl effect," they do invite a critique of the
happy endings of romantic comedy, thus gesturing toward the need for
alternatives. Nor do they completely eliminate possible pleasures in the
affect generated by beauty culture, although the films' concerns about the
consequences of pursuing beauty culture bring us to Projansky's com-
mentary on the outstanding heroines of films like *Juno* (Reitman, 2007).
She argues that their reception "gravitates toward and embraces smart
girls who eschew romance and beauty culture," but that "the cultural
celebration of these girl films [...] requires the belittling of girls more
generally."[36] This risk is particularly acute in the case of *Un giorno speciale*
because of its greater dependence on realist filmmaking codes. Nonetheless, by imagining more complex narrative contexts in which to situate
girls' experiences of work and consumption, and by not closing down all
forms of possible autonomous action, the films do even allude toward the
need for less romantic heterosexual rescue than new forms of peer connection to bridge what Berlant describes as "the loneliness of collective
singularity."[37]

Notes

I would particularly like to thank friends, colleagues, and students, who provided
useful feedback on earlier versions of this material at the Universities of Strathclyde,
Exeter, Reading, Columbus, Ohio, and Miami, Ohio. I would also like to thank
Catherine O'Rawe for helpful suggestions on previous versions of this work.

1. Sarah Projansky, *Spectacular Girls: Media Fascination and Celebrity Culture*
   (New York: New York University Press, 2014), p. 5, p. 35.
2. Maristella Cantini, ed., *Italian Women Filmmakers and the Gendered Screen*
   (New York: Palgrave, 2013), p. 212.
3. Danielle Hipkins, "Who Wants to Be a TV Show Girl? Auditions, Talent and
   Taste in Contemporary Italian Popular Cinema," *The Italianist*, 32 (2012),

154–190; Danielle Hipkins, " 'Whore-ocracy': Show Girls, the Beauty Trade-off, and Mainstream Oppositional Discourse in Contemporary Italy," *Italian Studies*, 66:3 (2011), 413–430.

4. Valeria Ottonelli, *La libertà delle donne: Contro il femminismo moralista* (Genoa: Il melangolo, 2011).

5. See my discussion of this in "Who Wants to be a TV Show Girl?," p. 157.

6. Valeria Ottonelli, *La libertà*, p. 13.

7. Catherine Driscoll, *Girls: Feminine Adolescence in Popular Culture and Cultural Theory* (New York: Columbia University Press, 2002), p. 110.

8. Hilary Radner, "Queering the Girl," in *Swinging Single: Representing Sexuality in the 1960s* edited by Hilary Radner (Minnesota: Minnesota University Press), p. 15.

9. Alison Winch, *Girlfriends and Postfeminist Sisterhood* (London: Palgrave Macmillan, 2013), p. 28.

10. Sarah Projansky, *Spectacular Girlhoods*, p. 105.

11. Adrienne Evans, Sarah Riley and Avi Shankar, "Technologies of Sexiness: The-orizing Women's Engagement in the Sexualization of Culture," *Feminism & Psychology*, 20:1 (2010), 114–131.

12. Michela Marzano, *Sii bella e stai zitta: perché l'Italia di oggi offende le donne* (Milan: Mondadori, 2010), p. 67.

13. Rossella Ghigi, "Nude ambizioni: Il velinismo secondo le adolescenti," *Studi culturali*, 3 (2013), 431–455.

14. Rosalind Gill, "Postfeminist Media Culture: Elements of a Sensibility," in *European Journal of Cultural Studies*, 10:2 (2007), 147–166.

15. Sarah Gilligan, "Performing Postfeminist Identities," in *Women on Screen* edited by Melanie Waters (London: Palgrave Macmillan, 2011), p. 170.

16. Rebecca Munford and Melanie Waters, *Feminism and Popular Culture: Investi-gating the Postfeminist Mystique* (London: IB Tauris, 2014), p. 30.

17. Sarah Gilligan, "Performing Postfeminist Identities," p. 169.

18. Yael Sherman, "Neoliberal Femininity in *Miss Congeniality* (2000)," in *Femi-nism at the Movies: Understanding Gender in Contemporary Popular Film* edited by Hilary Radner and Rebecca Stringer (London: Routledge, 2011), pp. 80–92 (80).

19. Angela McRobbie, *The Aftermath of Feminism: Gender, Culture and Social Change* (London: Sage, 2009).

20. http://cultura.panorama.it/cinema/Venezia-2012-cinema-Francesca-Comen cini-un-giorno-speciale, accessed June 18, 2013.

21. Valeria Ottonelli, *La libertà*, p. 14.

22. Kathleen Rowe Karlyn, *Unruly Girls, Unrepentant Mothers: Redefining Femi-nism on Screen* (Austin, TX: University of Texas Press, 2011), p. 46.

23. See *Mi piace lavorare (Mobbing)* [I Love to Work], 2003.

24. Paula Black, "Discipline and Pleasure," in *Feminism in Popular Culture* edited by Joanne Hollows and Rachel Moseley (Oxford: Berg, 2006), pp. 143–159 (157).

25. Lauren Berlant, *Cruel Optimism* (Durham, NC: Duke University Press, 2011), p. 22, p. 166.

26. Alison Winch, *Girlfriends*, p. 32.

27. Ibid., p. 14.

28. Alice Bardan, "The New European Cinema of Precarity," in *Work in Cinema: Labor and the Human Condition* (New York: Palgrave, 2013), pp. 70–85 (p. 71).

29. Joel Gwynne, "The Girls of Zeta," in *Postfeminism and Contemporary Hollywood Cinema* edited by Joel Gwynne and Nadine Muller (New York: Palgrave, 2013), pp. 60–77.

30. Diane Negra and Yvonne Tasker, "Neoliberal Frames and Genres of Inequality," *European Journal of Cultural Studies*, 16 (2013), 344 (351).

31. Angela McRobbie, *The Aftermath of Feminism*, p. 67.

32. Alice Bardan, *The New European Cinema*, p. 84.

33. Deleuze and Guattari cit. in Rebecca Munford and Melanie Waters, *Postfeminism*, pp. 158–9.

34. Jessica Ringrose and Emma Renold, "Teen Girls, Working-class Femininity and Resistance," *International Journal of Inclusive Education*, 16:4 (2012), 461–477 (465).

35. Diane Negra and Yvonne Tasker, "Neoliberal Frames and Genres of Inequality," 344.

36. Sarah Projansky, *Spectacular Girls*, p. 106.

37. Lauren Berlant, *Cruel Optimism*, p. 201.

2

Girlfriends, Postfeminism, and the European Chick-Flick in France

Mary Harrod

Anglo-American feminist film and television scholarship has of late been increasingly concerned with the negotiation by onscreen narratives of so-called postfeminist values, as well as their close cousin, "chick" culture. While postfeminism is often seen to succeed second-wave feminism in a neatly chronological way from the 1980s to today, the chick "cultural explosion" is located by Suzanne Ferriss and Mallory Young from the mid-1990s onwards, catalyzed for its most prominent theorists by the international success of the British novel *Bridget Jones's Diary* (Helen Fielding, London: Picador, 1996). For Ferriss and Young, "chick culture is vitally linked to postfeminism," through an aesthetic defined by: "a return to femininity, the primacy of romantic attachments, girlpower, a focus on female pleasure and pleasures, and the value of consumer culture and girlie goods." It can be seen as a collection of popular culture media forms principally concerned with middle-class women in their twenties and thirties, which are mostly American and British in origin.[1] The starting point of this essay is the deracination of what I am calling "chick texts" at the point of production. Specifically, it argues that elements of the Anglo-American chick-flick—a term used by the popular press connoting female-focused narratives with an emphasis on traditional feminine concerns such as heterosexual romance, designed to appeal to a largely female-identified audience—have begun to be appropriated by filmmakers in different European contexts.[2] Taking France as a case study, it compares local and global models of the genre as a means to shed light on some of the specificities of national (post)feminist culture, in particular the meanings of girlhood and the broader notion of girliness in French versus transnational popular cultural discourse.

While it is of course possible to define chick-flicks rather broadly, to define any film made with a female audience in mind, the current trend is toward a concentration on a very specific kind of femininity that is above all characterized by girlishness. This creates an intriguing connection between the figure of the girl as an aspirational role model, consumerism, and empowerment in popular film that warrants sustained analysis in a book concerned with how girls and girlhood are represented onscreen. While several of the films I discuss feature females of a range of chronological ages, "girlie" behaviors and desires are presented as desirable and rewarding. This emphasis within the chick-flick on empowered but girlie femininity is accompanied by an obsession with consumer culture—the *Sex and the City* TV series and films are clearly paradigmatic here. It is perhaps unsurprising that Hilary Radner's analysis of the rise of the chick-flick and girlie femininity in Hollywood cinema, *Neo-Feminist Cinema: Girly Films, Chick Flicks and Consumer Culture* features an image of Sarah Jessica Parker as Carrie Bradshaw on its cover, the outsize flower corsage on her dress signaling the entanglement of excessive consumption, fashion, and girlie pleasure and empowerment vehicled by the series. Scholars have questioned and critiqued this notion of empowerment via the performance of "girlie femininity."[3] Particularly useful to understand this enmeshment of consumerism, femininity, and girliness within a particular type of postfeminist film is Chris Holmlund's well-known 2005 description of "chick postfeminism," which she argues is a "white 'chick' backlash that denies class, avoids race, ignores (older) age, and "straight"-jackets sexuality."[4] (Older) age is at best ignored, at worst denigrated, in a dominant film culture where femininity is characterized by the desire to remain youthful in spirit and appearance, even through artificial means.

There is a recent and ongoing cycle of European filmmaking that speaks to this chick postfeminist culture, making films that promote values of girliness and youth as symbolic of female empowerment and agency. Nor is the choice of France as my focus accidental. While there exists today a popular European cinema that uses very similar generic structures to Hollywood, making films aimed largely at domestic audiences, as Europe's largest film-producing and -consuming nation, this country has succeeded in nurturing a more fully fledged genre cinema than its continental neighbors. French cinema is arguably the only national European cinema equipped to compete somewhat convincingly with Hollywood on the latter's own terms. By the same logic France is well placed to deploy "Hollywood" generic traits in a popular national cinema that can be marketed as such—as opposed to relying heavily on differentiation in terms of European prestige. It is thus paradigmatic—and will likely in future emerge as at the vanguard—of the new European chick-flick trend. Nevertheless, gestures toward the contemporary genre should be acknowledged in a number of other national cinemas. Young has argued that a "new European romance" she calls the "chic flick" has emerged in various national contexts (as well as France) through such female-centric narratives as German language films *Der Krieger und die Kaiserin/The Princess and the Warrior* (Tykwer, 2001) and *Bella Martha/Mostly Martha* (Nettelbeck, 2001). At the same time, Young notes the limitations of these romantic comedies as chick-flicks "proper," due to the absence of a close-knit group of female friends as a key trait, which some have seen as an essential element of the category.[5] Films that come a little closer to the chick aesthetic from this perspective include the Spanish *A mi madre le gustan las mujeres/My Mother Likes Women* (París and Féjerman, 2002), an intergenerational female gay comedy, and Italian *Scusa ma ti chiamo amore/Sorry if I Love You* (Moccia, 2008), which draws on the Hollywood model articulated in *Mean Girls* (Waters, 2004) and *Gossip Girl* (2007–2012), depicting a posse of manicured, bitchy high-school girlfriends as a backdrop to its heterosexual romance between a teenaged girl and an older man.

In France, meanwhile, not only has the rom-com become a key feature of national filmmaking since 2000, often thanks to the nation's relatively high proportion of female filmmakers and in ways that promote a focus on women and issues highly pertinent to them,[6] but the female friendship chick-flick (or girlfriend film) is also becoming familiar. As in previous examples, these categories often overlap; however, it is my contention that in a number of recent French films—major domestic box-office successes among them—relationships between women vie for importance with romantic ones, while other narrative and formal elements echo directly the contemporary global chick-flick. Consequently, the films contribute to a discourse about the nature and value of feminism and women's status today that has transnational resonance at the same time that it must be understood in its specific geo-cultural context. These films include, among others: *Tout pour plaire/Thirty-Five Something* (Telerman, 2005); *Comme t'y es belle!/Gorgeous!* (Azuelos, 2006); *LOL (Laughing Out Loud)* (Azuelos, 2008); *La Vie au ranch/Chicks* (Letourneur, 2009); *Tout ce qui brille/All That Glitters* (Mimran and Nakache, 2010); *Les Coquillettes* (Letourneur, 2012); and *Mince alors!* (De Turckheim, 2012). This chapter discusses these films' intervention in postfeminist chick discourse, exploring how "girlie" femininity is constructed in French film in ways that are both framed within localized concerns and politics but speak to global ideas of equality and agency within the paradoxical terms of postfeminist cultures.

Gorgeous!: Representable Femininity and Commodifying Girliness

Several of the traits of chick culture listed by Ferriss and Young could be summed up under the heading of the cult of looking good. This is to the fore in the many chick-flicks epitomized by the trope of the cathartic makeover discussed by such commentators as Charlotte Brunsdon and Alison Winch. Both these scholars underline the ambivalence of makeovers in films from *Pretty Woman* (Marshall, 1990) to *The Devil Wears Prada* (Frankel, 2006), where in fact it is apparent that the protagonist was "pretty" before the change. In this way the narratives both disavow and endorse the (capitalist) values of high fashion. Interestingly, Brunsdon also notes the recourse here to espousal of a fairly traditional "natural" code of femininity linked to her description of the emphasis placed by second-wave feminism on "sincerity, expression [and] truth-telling."[7] As Winch recognizes, however, the desire to look "good" must simultaneously be understood in terms of what Diane Negra has described as the (postfeminist) drive for female representability, that is acceptance according to constructed norms of legitimate femininity.[8]

In her analysis of the post-2005 "girlfriend flick," Winch is particularly interested in the makeover as part of the cult of slimness negotiated by films. She cites as a possible explanation for the trend both Susan Bordo's work on thinness as a response to unease about women's greater cultural presence and Susan Orbach's linkage of the slenderness ideal to (class) aspiration.[9] Thinness also bears an ambivalent relationship to issues of femininity, girliness, and female sexuality. The androgynous female form might be seen as more or less threatening for patriarchy, because it is more or less similar to men's bodies. Certainly it is closer to the contemporary youthful ideal of girliness than images of mature womanhood; however, that ideal too might be viewed from outside as either anodyne, because relatively sexually undifferentiated,[10] or, in the girlpower mold, a potent mobilization of hyper-feminine signifiers. In other words, just as girliness as a mobile, discursive concept takes on much of the weight of gender signification that is tentative in the actual girl, so a profusion of physical absence (i.e., lack of body) verges paradoxically on grotesque over-signification (the paradoxically potential meaning of the slim physique), especially when twinned with rampant materialism.

Given the cult of female beauty in France, it is unsurprising that French chick-flicks are centrally concerned with such questions.[11] However, they are not always worked through in quite the same way as in their US predecessors. The film that comes closest to the consumer ethos of Hollywood shopping films is perhaps *Gorgeous!*, whose title emphasizes the pleasures of performing attractiveness in the film—although these remain distinctly secondary to a focus on supportive relationships between women and there is no shopping at all in the narrative. Indeed, it is revealing that when this cycle of films does include a rare shopping sequence, at the start of *Thirty-Five Something*, it ends with the character rejecting the "outrageously expensive" clothes she has tried on. The animated opening credit sequence to *Gorgeous!*, however, depicts cosmetic accessories, heralding the film's setting around a beauty salon owned by one of the four lead characters, Isa, played by well-known comedian Michèle Laroque. The narrative is concerned with the emotional and domestic lives of, in addition to Isa, her sister Alice (Valérie Benguigui) and other members of her extended Jewish family Léa (Aure Atika) and Nina (Géraldine Nakache). Both Benguigui and Atika were fairly well-known in 2004, not least from roles in the chauvinistic male-centric Jewish comedy series *La Vérité si je mens!/Would I Lie to You?* (Gilou, France, 1997, with sequels in 2001 and 2012) to which this film is something of a feminized response, while Nakache would later co-direct and star in popular success *All That Glitters*. Also noteworthy is the age range of the main actresses, who were 46, 41, 36, and 26 respectively at the time of the film's release, broadening its appeal across various generations and doubtless helping it to pass the million ticket sales mark at the French box office. 26-year-old Nina's status as the apprentice at full womanhood is accentuated from the start of the film, by an opening scene in which she snacks on children's food, and later by her role as Léa's tutee in "hooking a man" through an extended makeover sequence. As befits her maiden status, Nina's principal storyline is one of romantic desire, directed at her distant cousin Simon, a handsome playboy for whom her frankness and casual attire spell friendship as opposed to sexual attraction. Léa, by contrast, is the queen of raunch. Separated from a husband with whom she is still in love, she seduces him at nightspots through a combination of revealing clothes, semi-drunken availability and calculated flirting with other men. In classic chick-flick fashion, seeing Nina's plight, the older woman helps the girl-like ingénue perform feminine desirability, not through a shopping spree but a combination of dieting, exercise, and painful beauty treatments.

Such an approach to "revealing" inner beauty is consonant with French uneasiness about unbridled capitalism, disavowing the consumerist aspect of exploiting France's immense beauty industry. As with the Hollywood films mentioned above, the work of this narrative is to gloss feminine perfection as natural, since Nina looks fundamentally unchanged—notwithstanding the adoption of more feminine attire—after her makeover. Even more than those films, however, emphasizing thinness, in this sequence and through recurrent—disingenuously light-hearted—discussion of diets throughout the film, occludes the role of money in image-creation. It thus legitimizes feminine self-sacrifice as an accessible route to happiness, theoretically for all. This is also the case in *Mince alors!*, whose title means both "Oh dear!" and, roughly, "Thin then!" and which is set in a residential spa geared toward weight loss. In this film, the main character, also called Nina, who is slightly overweight, is pointedly brought a spa holiday by her husband, who is having an affair. The film's discourse on weight goes further than recent US chick-flicks' fear of fat as, in Winch's words, "the unacceptable face of having it all," with weight here portrayed as a problem for the self-esteem of all the main characters, from obese Émilie to skinny Sophie. Although the ending sees Nina, flanked by her new girlfriends, confront and spectacularly ditch her husband at a work function to launch a swimwear line for curvier ladies, the triumph of liberation is undercut by her comment as she struts away: "It's amazing what losing six kilos can do for you." As Nina in *Gorgeous!* puts it, "Nutella is psychological!"—encoding weakness. It is worth noting that while for Winch men in the US chick-flick typically act as the voice of sanity about female characters' fears over their image, in both the French narratives the men actively prefer an ideal of "perfection," including extreme thinness.[12] Thus in Azuelos' film male family members cruelly gossip about the figure of an acquaintance who has recently given birth, while Simon's more appreciative registering of Nina following her "transformation" is expressed through a comment that she has lost weight. These details contribute to a more negative depiction of male characters, who frequently end up alone, in these female-authored films than in many (more often malescripted and directed) US chick-flicks. However, they also articulate an overall less conflicted cultural attitude toward slimness, which a recent survey has shown may be seen as more unquestionably desirable for women in France than anywhere else.[13]

As hinted, the (conflicted) ethic of female empowerment and entitlement that permeates chick-flicks is partly a question of their typically bourgeois, white settings, often mirroring their (in France in fact almost exclusively) female[14] directors' own backgrounds. In *Gorgeous!* Azuelos's own (on her father's side) moneyed Sephardic Jewish milieu is characterized by the construction of work as a choice for several characters, as well as such indulgences as beauty treatments and, for Isa, a $2,000 night out and a trip to New York—the latter following her divorce, with Nina in tow, to underscore an ideology of female entitlement as a refusal of victimhood. Yet stereotypes of affluent female empowerment are elsewhere combined with clichéd notions of female incompetence. This is striking in the protagonists' depiction as metropolitan drivers. As A. Rochelle Mabry has noted, an almost obligatory feature of the chick-flick is a trailer showing the heroine involved in a clumsy mishap; accordingly, the trailer for this film shows us Isa carelessly backing her massive four-by-four into the bicycle of handsome Englishman Paul (played by Andrew Lincoln, with whom her subsequent affair nods to the film's Anglo-American generic parentage).[15] Another prominent joke also featured in publicity materials comprises a sequence where Léa parks illegally—not, we sense, for the first time—and uses her feminine wiles to attempt to persuade the enforcement officer not to tow her Mini, on the pretext that: "I've got a manicure in an hour ... I'm completely overwhelmed." Léa's lack of self-awareness is played for laughs, while she and Isa are portrayed in such everyday scrapes as likeable and easy to identify with. As Maureen Turim has observed: "It is indeed hard for female-centred comedy to escape from under the misogyny that gives credence to the ditzy, the easily distracted, the hysterical female. Bad women (or teenage girl) driver jokes are a feature of a culture that historically only reluctantly allowed women to venture behind the wheel."[16] In Isa's case, the conjunction of "feminine" ditziness with "masculine" power, through the vehicle and her ability to take charge of the situation, immediately swapping numbers with Paul and promising stress-free financial reimbursement, resumes well the tension between increased female authority and the need to represent femininity as incapable.

In fact, the film is intermittently self-aware about the unnaturalness of representable codes of both femininity and class. In the first case, in one scene Léa is shown wearing a bandage over her recently cosmetically altered nose, while in a similar position on the opposite side of the frame Isa's nanny Fatima sports an almost identical dressing due to an injury inflicted on her by her brother (who disapproves of her same-sex "marriage"—or rather PACS—of convenience to Isa, on which more later). The equation of women's search for physical perfection with violence to their persons could scarcely be clearer (Figure 2.1).

More humorously, in a joke that points up the artificial and sometimes arbitrary nature of gender and class norms, when Léa asks if a T-shirt saying "I [heart symbol] caviar" looks slutty, one friend answers, "No, but your [heavily decorated, glittering] toe-nails really do"—only for another to assert the opposite! Léa's class aspirations specifically are even less subtly sent up by a scene in which she complains to her masseuse about her daughter's choice of circus school as a pastime. When the masseuse says she has had to endure weekly football matches in all weathers to support her son, Léa observes with ill humor that at least there's money in football, only for her interlocutor to chide her for short-sightedness, since "at circus school she might meet Princess Stephanie of Monaco's son"!

However, the narrative appears less ironic in its presentation of Isa's status relations with her live-in Arab nanny-cum-housekeeper, Fatima.

Figure 2.1 *Comme t'y es belle!/Gorgeous!* (Azuelos, 2006). Plastic Surgery is equated with abuse in *Gorgeous!*

Although Fatima is treated with superficial equality following the narrative development that sees Isa marry her in order to secure her a work visa, so highly does she value her domestic services, elsewhere it is quite clear who is in charge, as for example, at the playground Isa suddenly asks Fatima to supervise her sister's children as well as her own. In the end, postfeminist "empowerment" in this film, as typically in Hollywood, remains circumscribed to a highly elite stratum. The only film of this group to depart substantially from the paradigm is *All That Glitters*, whose title advertises a suspicion of wealth, and where *banlieue* girl Lila's pretense at cosmopolitan bourgeois status in order to court a man "above her station" ends in failure and almost in the loss of her more meaningful, life-enhancing relationship with her close girlfriend Ely (played by Nakache).

It should finally be noted that, despite its vituperative attitude toward unreconstructed masculinity, *Gorgeous!* shares with most other chick texts a romantic focus. Although Isa's PACS with Fatima superficially reimagines the lavish wedding rom-com finale along more muted and feminine lines, much of the film's emotional investment is in Isa's love-story with classic British new man Paul, alongside courtships for Nina and Alice. The fact that all these are happily resolved at the end reinforces the relative conservatism of this text in gender as well as class terms. However, divergences from this picture both here and in other films, where narrative and other elements afford relationships between women a status more comparable to those between the genders, are multiplied by considering female–female relationships across as well as within different generations.

Woman to Girl

The exception to the romantically resolved plotlines of *Gorgeous!* is Léa's trajectory, through which she learns to value her relationship with her young daughter over sexual exchange with her ex-husband. This parallels similar moves in the central story of both Azuelos' later smash-hit *LOL* and also a rom-com about divorce from the following year *Une semaine sur deux (et la moitié des vacances scolaires)/Alternate Weeks (And Half the Vacation)* (Calbérac, 2009). In all three films, the use of instant messaging allows access to the subjectivity of a preteen or teen girl character who is suffering due to uncertainty around parental relations and/or neglect by her mother. Such a charge is relatively implicit in *LOL* and *Alternate Weeks*, possibly informing the girl's overinvestment in a romantic relationship; in *Gorgeous!*, though, it is much clearer. Both Léa and Isa lie to their children about being unavailable due to work, when they are in fact pursuing romantic attachments. Léa goes further, taking out her own frustrations on her daughter by snapping: "How do you expect me to find a husband if I stay at home watching DVDs with you all day?." The effect of a close-up on her pre-teenaged daughter's hurt expression is not fully recuperated by Léa's immediate apology and smothering display of affection. In general, if the relative significance accorded to same-sex friendships versus romantic relationships for women in chick-flicks varies somewhat from film to film, but with friendship occasionally eclipsing romance (as in *All That Glitters*), mother–daughter relations are more likely to be accorded greater importance than female–male bonds. Moreover, unlike in some Hollywood films such as *The Women* (English, 2008),[17] the tentative prioritization of either career or romance over motherhood by women is a narrative still scarcely tolerated in France. This chimes with the cult of maternity in Gallic culture—a cult whose original architects were historically male. This truth underlies the fact that in *Gorgeous!* Léa's "education" is catalyzed by the attentions of a doctor, who she says has made her feel like she exists by taking an interest in her life—and indeed her role as mother—rather than her appearance. In other words representability, in the Kristevan sense of entry into a symbolic realm determined by patriarchy, remains the key mode for self-definition even in the notionally female-only space of maternity.

The price of a "proper" maternal role in both *Gorgeous!* and *LOL* appears at least a partial eschewing of girliness, in the sense of feminized display, for the adult woman. The difficulties of reconciling the girlie and woman positions is to the fore during a scene in the first film when roles are reversed and Léa's daughter sends her mother anxious text messages about her whereabouts after a night out, as the latter piles semi-intoxicated and scantily clad into a taxi. The boundaries of individual identities are made even more porous in *LOL* by the close structural parallelism between the sexual relationships of the central mother and daughter pair, Anne (Sophie Marceau) and Lola. This is further enhanced by the intertextual specter of Marceau's well-known performance as a teenager in the film series *La Boum/The Party* (Pinoteau, 1980, 1982) whose music is here reprised. Lola's habit of borrowing Anne's clothes, to which Anne reluctantly agrees, symbolizes the role confusion between mother and daughter, as the former fails to control her child, and the latter wears "seductive" clothing. Numerous reviews of the film in the popular press criticized Anne's immaturity here, and Marceau also distanced herself from Anne's acquiescence to her daughter's demands.[18]

According to Winch, the intergenerational conflict common in chick-flicks is also a question of competing versions of feminism. In Hollywood films, the youngest generation of girls—still resistant to full representability due to their inchoate femininity—may question their mothers' obsession with consumer goods (*The Women*); meanwhile, likeable young women like Andy of *The Devil Wears Prada* are pitted against the post-fifties woman's "unfriendly, powerful" and more traditionally feminist womanhood.[19] A contrast can be drawn here too with the French situation. There is no "masculinised," older professional woman—epitomized by Meryl Streep's iconic turn as Miranda Priestley—in the French films. This reflects the somewhat less extensive reach of second-wave discourses of equality in France: as recounted for example by Claire Duchen, the prominence of egalitarian currents in French feminism in the late 1970s (notably the work of the *Mouvement de Libération Feminine* or MLF) was counterbalanced to an extent by a strand that sought to reclaim femininity and maternity especially for its very specificity.[20] That is, femininity never lost as much cultural purchase there as it did for example, in the United States; consequently the post-ness of postfeminism has a different meaning in this context. The greatest conflict of ideas between women of disparate generations comes through the presence of openly pro-patriarchal grandmothers in both of Azuelos' films. Differences between Anne's 40-something generation and that of teenager Lola in *LOL* are of degree rather than category. The substance of the debate in France is in these films portrayed as hinging not on the desirability of girlie femininity, which is taken as read, but on the latter's precise parameters. Both Anne and Lola seek to be attractive; but Anne is troubled by the extreme sexual permissiveness implied by "liberation" today, as symbolized by the thongs sported by the girls in the changing room at school and banned by one of their mothers.

What Ariel Levy has described as "raunch culture" also underpins the world of the eponymous heroines of *Chicks*.[21] Heavily improvised using non-professional actors, this film about middle-class university students—still financially supported by their parents—depicts young French girls today, in the director's words, "as they really are"—as slobbish, narcissistic hedonists lacking goals.[22] The effect of realism is achieved through the film's documentary look, its juddering hand-held camerawork and indistinct location soundscape a far cry from the medium-shot sit-com aesthetic and clearly delivered, highly scripted lines that typify *Gorgeous!* especially. The girls' interest in partying for its own sake meanwhile colonizes the traditionally masculine territory of US "frat boy" films such as *Animal House* (Landis, 1978). Boys themselves are a background presence, albeit a friendlier one than in films about older generations; sex itself has no visual or narrative prominence. The French title, *La Vie au ranch* ("life at the ranch"), as well as the casting of gravel-voiced Sarah-Jane Sauvegrain in the lead role as Pam, further underscore the pseudo-masculinity of the girls, who come and go as they please and enjoy the metropolitan delights of Paris—including peeing in the street and tottering about drunkenly with their clothes falling off—to the full.

This combination suggests how on the one hand ideas about equality are making their mark in a film by a younger director (Letourneur was 31 in 2009), yet they are still paired with signifiers of feminine sexuality. Girliness is redefined in a more hybrid form in this micro-budget piece.

Chicks' exclusion from the mainstream, including any kind of theatrical release, suggests the extent to which the co-opting and transformation of Hollywood chick narratives is an aesthetic and ideological choice, not merely a commercial one. Here lies the importance of pinpointing the specificities of the French chick-flick, as a site for negotiating Gallic norms about girls and femininity in general. In this group of films these specificities in relation to Hollywood may be resumed as: a greater disingenuousness about the centrality of wealth to postfeminist ideals of girlhood and womanhood; a greater investment in maternity over personal fulfilment; and a less troubled relationship with previous versions of feminism and femininity. All of these arise from France's highly pronounced culture of gender differentiation historically. However, *Chicks*, like Letourneur's equally unconventional if more romance-focused follow-up *Les Coquillettes* (meaning literally "pasta shells," referring quirkily to the film's seaside setting as well as, ironically, to its [un-] "coquettish" female protagonists, this time aged around 30), shifts representations in a direction more obviously informed by global notions of equality—although these films' marginal, cultish status does complicate their relation to popular culture.[23] *Chicks* perhaps more than any other film analyzed here also crystallizes how chick-flicks' multivalency is further complicated by their transnational textual makeup in European contexts. To illustrate this point

I shall conclude by citing a scene from the film in which, while the girls dress up together for a smart event, Pam's friend Jude adopts a deep, manly voice to comment neutrally in American-accented English that, in her typically short and tight dress, "you look like a baby prostitute." The parade of girliness, revealed here in its grotesquely incongruous components, is thus marked as other, constructed through both the masculine and the foreign. Yet both the characters' and the film's precise relation to this, the culture that defines them, is left fluid and open to interpretation.

Notes

1. Suzanne Ferriss and Mallory Young, "Introduction: Chick Flicks and Chick Culture," in *Chick Flicks: Contemporary Women at the Movies* edited by S. Ferriss and M. Young (New York and London: Routledge, 2008), pp. 1–25 (1–4).

2. It might be noted that my conception of chick-flicks as a generic category, albeit one that intersects with others, owes a debt to the new genre criticism of Richard Maltby, Steve Neale, and especially Rick Altman, who have emphasized film genres' hybrid nature. Other scholarly publications that have found the designation "chick-flick" to be a productive organizing category in various ways include Roberta Garrett, *Postmodern Chick Flicks: The Return of the Woman's Film* (New York and Basingstoke: Palgrave Macmillan, 2007) and Hilary Radner, *Neo-Feminist Cinema: Girly Films, Chick Flicks, and Consumer Culture* (London and New York: Routledge, 2010).

3. Diane Negra, " 'Quality Postfeminism?': Sex and the Single Girl on HBO," *Genders Online* 39 (2004), http://www.genders.org/g39/g39_negra.html; Yvonne Tasker and Diane Negra "Introduction: Feminist Politics and Postfeminist Culture," in *Interrogating Postfeminism: Gender and the Politics of Popular Culture* edited by Y. Tasker and D. Negra (Durham, NC and London: Duke University Press, 2007), pp. 1–25; Deborah Jermyn, *Sex and the City* (Detroit: Wayne State University Press, 2009), p. 56.

4. Chris Holmlund, "Postfeminism from A to G," *Cinema Journal* 44:4 (2005), 116–121 (116).

5. Mallory Young, "Chic flicks: the new European romance," in *Chick Flicks: Contemporary Women at the Movies* edited by S. Ferriss and M. Young (New York and London: Routledge, 2008), pp. 175–190 (187).

6. See Mary Harrod, "The *réalisatrice* and the rom-com in the 2000s," *Studies in French Cinema* 12:3 (2012), 227–240.

7. Charlotte Brunsdon, "Post-feminism and Shopping Films," in *The Film Studies Reader* edited by J. Hollows, P. Hutchings and M. Jancovich (London: Bloomsbury, 2000), pp. 292–296.

8. Diane Negra "Structural Integrity, Historical Reversion, and the Post 9/11 Chick Flick," *Feminist Media Studies*, 8:1 (2008), 51–68; Alison Winch, " 'We Can Have It All": The Girlfriend Flick," *Feminist Media Studies* 12:1 (2012), 69–82 (71–5).

9. Winch, "We Can Have," 72.
10. cf. Negra, "Quality Postfeminism?," 12.
11. For more on the power of the beauty cult in France, see Mona Chollet, *Beauté fatale: les nouveaux visages d'une alienation feminine* (Paris: Zones, 2012) and Laure Mistral, *La fabrique des filles: comment se reproduisent les stéréotypes et les discriminations sexuelles* (Paris: Syros, 2010).
12. Winch, "We Can Have," 73, 76.
13. Marie Piquemal, "La Pression à la minceur est plus forte pour les françaises," *Libération,* October 29, 2013 http://next.liberation.fr/beaute/2013/10/29/la-pression-a-la-minceur-est-plus-forte-sur-les-francaises_943133?utm_source=dlvr.it&utm_medium=twitter.
14. For details of the relatively high numbers of women film directors across the board in France since 2000, see Carrie Tarr, "Introduction: Women's Film-making in France 2000–2010," *Studies in French Cinema* 12:3, (2012), 189–200 (191).
15. A. Rochelle Mabry, "About a Girl: Female Subjectivity and Sexuality in Contemporary Chick Culture," in *Chick Lit: the New Women's Fiction* edited by S. Ferriss and M. Young (New York and London: Routledge, 2007), pp. 191–207 (194).
16. Maureen Turim, "Popular Culture and the Comedy of Manners: *Clueless* and Fashion Clues," in *Jane Austen and Co.: Remaking the Past in Contemporary Culture* edited by S. R. Pucci and J. Thompson (Albany: State University of New York Press, 2003), pp. 33–52 (41).
17. See Winch, "We Can have," 79.
18. Emmanuel Frois, "Sophie Marceau: Avec 'LOL' son coeur fait 'Boum'," *Le Figaro,* February 4, 2009.
19. Winch, "We Can Have," 78.
20. Claire Duchen, *Feminism in France: From May '68 to Mitterrand* (London and New York: Routledge and Kegan Paul, 1986), p. 49.
21. Ariel Levy, *Female Chauvinist Pigs: Women and the Rise of Raunch Culture* (New York: Free Press, 2005).
22. Sophie Letourneur, interview in Shellac Sud edition of *Chicks* DVD (2009).
23. *Les Coquillettes'* very poster acknowledges global influence by pastiching that of the American indie satire on postfeminism *Spring Breakers* (Korine, 2012).

3

Warrior of Love: Japanese Girlhood's Postfeminist Asian Body in *Cutie Honey* (Hideaki Anno, 2004)

Joel Gwynne

It would be a mistake to assert that postfeminism as a cultural sensibility operates in all societies across the globe. It is, however, perhaps accurate to suggest that it more commonly operates in economically prosperous neoliberal nations, irrespective of their geographical location. Postfeminism is, after all, strongly implicated in neoliberal governance and citizenship and should be understood as imbricated with global neoliberal ideologies that serve to affirm not only the individualistic values of late-capitalist culture, but also to position feminism as redundant within democratic and ostensibly egalitarian societies. Neoliberalism has expanded its borders beyond the Western free-market, and thus the assumption that postfeminist discourse operates exclusively in Western contexts discounts not only the multinational trajectory of neoliberalism and its influence on economic, social, and policy reform on a global scale, but also the international impact of American popular culture and its multifarious manifestations of popular (post)feminism that are regularly consumed by a global media audience. Simply put, postfeminist discourse cannot be localized into convenient geographical and cultural spaces, for to do so would also entail a rejection of the visible effects of globalization and the cross-fertilization of global popular and consumer culture. With this in mind, and by drawing on the cultural significance of manga in modern, neoliberal

Japan, this chapter seeks to understand the culturally loaded figure of the Japanese schoolgirl within postfeminism.

Created by Go Nagai, *Cutie Honey* first appeared in volume 41 of the 1973 edition of the weekly magazine *Shōnen Champion*, and was significant in featuring the first female protagonist of a *shōnen* (boy) manga series. The franchise rapidly expanded beyond the pages of manga and into anime via a number of television and film adaptations. While the depiction of the protagonist, 15-year-old Honey Kisaragi, varies across these versions and mediums, some commonalities remain; she is almost always portrayed as an ordinary girl in outward appearance and thus representative of the texts' target audience—and, non-representatively, always loses her clothes during moments of magical transformation. The film adaptation on which this chapter focuses is unique in three ways: first, it combines both live action (i.e., real actors) and several very brief anime sequences; second, Honey is not ordinary in appearance but is rather played by Eriko Sato, one of Japan's leading swimsuit models; and third, while her age is unspecified it is clear that she is in her late teens or early twenties, and therefore much older than previous manifestations of her character. It is precisely because of these interesting variations that I have chosen to focus on the live-action representation of Cutie Honey as opposed to the original manga source material, since live action embodiment and film performance compli-cates our understanding of the relationship between girlhood, femininity and the place of contemporary women in Japanese society. The narrative premise of the live action film is simple: Honey Kisaragi is an office worker by day yet transforms, when called upon, into a superhero (Cutie Honey, Warrior of Love). Prior to his death, Honey's father (Professor Kisaragi) developed important research into the invention of the "AI System" which, while its function is not adequately explained in the narrative, appears to preserve the life of those who use it. This is now being continued by his his brother, Honey's Uncle Utsugi. A criminal organization named Pan-ther Claw hear of this research, and kidnap Utsugi in order to steal his invention with the aim of extending the life of their ageing leader, Sister Jill. Honey is thus required to employ her superhuman skills in order to save her uncle, protect the legacy of her father's research (while simulta-neously paying homage to his memory), and defeat the growing criminal presence of Panther Claw in Japanese society.

In Anno's adaptation, Honey is clearly not a teenage girl (thus departing from previous incarnations of the franchise); however, girlhood is central to both the narrative and the construction of her identity in a manner that parallels the dilution of the space between girlhood and womanhood in Japanese society. This dilution has caused a number of moral panics since the mid-1990s, often oriented around the sexualization of schoolgirls in

Japanese popular and porn culture.[1] While one can only speculate on the reasons that motivated Anno to hire the then 23-year-old Eriko Sato to play Honey, both her career as a swimsuit model and the filmic sexualization of her body imply that assigning an adult to a role usually occupied by a teenage girl serves to circumvent the negative reactions that may have occurred in response to the visual presentation of the character's eroticized body. Furthermore, it could also be asserted that since the original source material for the live adaptation is indeed manga—where teenage girls are routinely depicted as possessing developed bodies signified by large breasts and wide hips—then the recruitment of an adult actress serves to meet the demands of male consumers who expect to consume an eroticized female form.

Even so, while Sato's character is not a teenager in physical form, her mannerisms and behavior embody the "girling" of womanhood in Japanese society in much the same way that girlish behavior is extolled as the most acute form of femininity in postfeminist media culture.[2] Postfeminist culture has, after all, reconfigured our entire understanding of the relationship between age and femininity, as Sarah Projansky contends:

> If the postfeminist woman is always in process, always using the freedom and equality handed to her by feminism in pursuit of having it all (including discovering her sexuality) but never quite managing to reach full adulthood, to fully have it all, one could say that the postfeminist woman is quintessentially adolescent no matter what her age.[3]

Likewise, Eriko Sato's Honey is an inscription of what it means to be a young Japanese woman in a process of "becoming" in a neoliberal society that has embraced many of the advantages fostered by second-wave feminism—such as women's right to sexual and economic agency—but remains culturally obsessed with the notion of girlhood as ideal femininity. This obsession can in part be attributed to Japan's status as a highly patriarchal society in which the valorized traits of ideal femininity—sweetness, docility, and passivity—are synonymous with the location of children and childhood in the cultural imaginary. As such, to understand the implications of the film in terms of its depiction of young womanhood in modern Japan, it is necessary to briefly interrogate the origins of the term *shōjo*, a relatively modern phenomenon.

As Rika Sakuma Sato argues, the emergence of the word *shōjo* "coincides with the spread of the notion of 'adolescence' in Anglo-American societies,"[4] and specifically signifies girls in their adolescence. The word is "rarely used for a girl below the age of puberty or a woman beyond the age of twenty,"[5] thus clearly differentiating it from the notion of womanhood (*onna*). And as other critics have argued, the word *shōjo* is difficult to translate into English since the most accurate literal translation, "young woman," "implies a kind of sexual maturity clearly forbidden to *shōjo*."[6] *Shōjo* has therefore been understood as a signification of "the girl who never grows up,"[7] and the closely related identity of the *kawaii* girl has been described as attractive, but "lack[ing] libidinal agency of her own."[8] The cultural currency of *shōjo* as ideal femininity for unmarried adult women is evidenced by the dominance of *shōjo* behavior and mannerisms by women who are not *shōjo*, most explicitly in terms of women performing a *kawaii* (cute) aesthetic. While it is perhaps not surprising that many critics have positioned the childish, hyper-feminine performance of *kawaii* as disempowering, it can potentially be viewed as empowering in much the same way that femininity has been reclaimed in postfeminist and neoliberal culture. The construction of *kawaii* may represent a move from objectification to subjectification, and may be especially agentic for young women given the cultural constraints of Japanese womanhood. As Merry White argues, "childish cuteness soothes and provides a release from adult responsibilities," such as the pressure to conform to the valorized role of *ryōsai-kenbo* (good wife, wise mother).[9]

Honey's persona is *kawaii* in a number of ways. In combat with enemies, she is continually referred to as "little girl" despite her adult, sexualized body. In other scenes, the audience witnesses her skipping along the street and singing to herself, and visiting playgrounds to use the swings when she is feeling sad. After being informed that she needs to stay at work alone to complete her admin duties, she pouts and declares, "Gee, everyone's got it so nice. I want to go out and play too." Given the cultural ubiquity of *shōjo*, it is not surprising that Honey behaves in this manner, yet her *kawaii* persona is also validated by narrative events. Midway through the film, it transpires that she is, despite her adult form, in fact neither woman nor girl, but rather an android "based on human cells" with "a heart just like humans," created by her father after the human Honey died in a car accident. As Honey is a product of both her father's research and his emotional grief, the theme of paternal love is central to the narrative, actualized in a manner that corresponds with the construction of the action heroine in Hollywood cinema. As Yvonne Tasker notes, "the female hero may be represented as identified with the father, in search of authority, and sometimes reconciliation with authority."[10] Honey's agency as a superhero with incredible physical skills is thus tempered by her quest to protect the legacy of her father and, by doing so, achieve paternal (and possibly patriarchal) affirmation. Her positioning as a girl rather than a woman is further entrenched by key omissions in terms of cinematic tropes. Hollywood constructions of the action heroine are permeated by the notion of "heroine as mother," and it is this role that bestows primary agency. Films such as *Alien* (Scott, 1979) and *Terminator 2: Judgment Day* (Cameron, 1991) demonstrate the maternal motif recurring as a catalyst of women's agency, with female heroes acting to protect their children, whether biological or adoptive.[11] Yet, commensurate with Honey's construction as *shōjo*, we do not witness her adopting a maternal role for she is portrayed as unable to cope with the responsibilities that adult women confront in the real world. She is represented as incompetent in her administrative role as an OL (Office Lady) (described by a colleague as "useless"; another suggests "would someone fire her?"), and it is only through magical transformation that she achieves empowerment and respite from the complexities of women's role in society. Returning to Merry White's observation that *kawaii* may provide a release from adult responsibilities and constraints, Honey's ambivalent construction within the real-world location of the narrative—as either unable to succeed as an adult career-woman or, alternatively, empowered by her abdication of the responsibilities of womanhood—raises important issues. In the next section, I discuss how the processes of transformation summon questions regarding the status of contemporary Japanese womanhood, and the extent to which agency can be achieved in the real world and beyond the territories of both fantasy and *kawaii* ideal femininity. I will demonstrate how Honey's "empowerment" is evidently postfeminist in a way that corresponds to the emergence of the "action babe" in Hollywood cinema as a marker of (post)feminist backlash culture.

Transformation and Backlash Culture

Mary Celeste Kearney comments that, over the last 50 years, "traditional notions of female coming-of-age have been troubled greatly by transformations in American society and female anatomy," such as the earlier onset of menstruation and delayed marriage among women who pursue educational opportunities.[12] As entrance into adulthood is defined not merely by physical age but by both traditional and neoliberal cultural landmarks such as the beginning of career and marriage, the recent cultural and physical transformations experienced by young women have contributed to female adolescence being drawn out to its lengthiest state ever, providing girls with "a much longer period to experiment with a variety of identities, lifestyles, and interests," including those that take them beyond the realms of domesticity and heterosexual relationships.[13] Kearney's observation is no less true of contemporary Japan than of America, and Frances Gateward has likewise noted the manner in which Japanese sci-fi genres bring to the fore "cultural anxieties" concerning social transformations such as the advent of gender-based equality.[14] Furthermore, even on a semantic level, transformation is understood as problematic in Japan; a popular word for almost any kind of ghost or monster is *bakemono* (literally: a thing that changes). An alternative word for *yôkai* (hobgoblin) is *henge*, both the characters of which mean "change." The connotations surrounding transformation are clearly negative, yet the ubiquity of the transformation motif in Japanese sci-fi and girl manga suggests not merely abjection but also attraction, and hence acute cultural ambivalence surrounding the changing status of young women. As a narrative that focuses on a central character who obscures the line between girlhood and womanhood, transformation is a central element of *Cutie Honey*.

On a superficial level and in accordance with the genre of sci-fi, Honey's transformation from "ordinary" girl to Cutie Honey bestows a number of extraordinary powers and abilities. She is able to perform extreme acrobatics, including jumping hundreds of feet into the air and the ability to move at a high speed. Her physical abilities are complemented by high-tech paraphernalia such as sound-enhancing earrings, X-ray glasses, the "Honey Boomerang" (a blade that can slice through any material), and a sword that emits a laser beam: the "Silver Fleurette." Beyond her initial transformation, her superhero identity permits the performance of further identities. Upon her first transformation within the film, the audience is informed—through a montage of costumed multiple identities—that while her "true identity is Warrior of Love, Cutie Honey," she is also "at times a bike racer," at other times a female police officer, and even "a Panther Claw minion." What is perhaps significant, though not surprising given her real-world representation as a *shōjo* who cannot meet the demands of her career, is that Honey's "true identity" is not Honey Kisaragi—the woman whom the viewer watches living and working in the real world—but her warrior alter-ego. In a corporate world in which she is perpetually reminded of her inadequacy, Honey is only empowered when she transcends this environment by morphing into Cutie Honey. If she is passive in the real world, it is transformation, then, that elicits a more active form of feminine agency that is marked out as distinctly globalized and neoliberal.

Indeed, following the trajectory of Hollywood heroines in action films such as *Lara Croft: Tomb Raider* (West, 2001), *Charlie's Angels* (McG, 2000), and *Kill Bill* (Tarantino, 2003)—all commercially successful in Japan and released prior to *Cutie Honey*—Honey likewise combines readily apparent strength and skill with a more traditionally feminine, and often emphatically sexualized, physique. Yet, characteristic of postfeminist forms of empowerment, Honey's physical strength and ability can be understood as a form of invisible power divorced from both the wider social context and, even, corporeality itself. Her physical prowess is performed silently and effortlessly, her femininity as spectacle undisrupted by naturalistic signs of exertion or strength. Honey is a postfeminist heroine for our times; her agency enunciated by her ability to colonize the masculine territory of the action genre (by defeating scores of men in combat and by riding a motor-bike aggressively down the streets of Tokyo) while also reclaiming and reconfiguring the historical meaning of femininity. Indeed, by celebrat-ing feminine adornment and the presentation of the sexualized body, her neoliberal femininity is distinctly postfeminist as it contains "an implicit rejection of many tenets held by second wave feminists," such as the mutual exclusivity of female agency and the corporeal spectacle of femininity. [15] Honey enacts her transformation, for example, by pressing a magical neck-lace and shouting "Honey Flash," and thus jewelry becomes not a passive form of beautification but the means to enact a process of transformational empowerment.

Lisa Purse observes that the contemporary action heroine performs a sexualized femininity, and while she is certainly an "active, indepen-dent agent," she is also "eroticized with the terms of a conventionally objectified femininity."[16] Similarly, the sexualized aesthetic of *Cutie Honey* parallels the contradictory—both active and passive—neoliberal construc-tion of what has been termed "new femininity." New femininity can be recognized as a form of "empowerment" enacted by the financially emancipated neoliberal consumer-citizen through a self-regulation and self-presentation/objectification of the body, which ultimately serves to reconfigure traditional femininity. Its construction is linked to a relatively new phenomenon that critics have termed the "makeover paradigm," for in accordance with longstanding narratives that inculcate the importance of female desirability, the global media in recent years has employed the makeover narrative to further entrench the notion that female desirabil-ity is a goal to be relentlessly pursued. As Hilary Radner has argued, this process of "becoming" feminine is framed by postfeminist media culture as a form of liberation, inviting women to reject the notion of a "stable, untested and fixed" self and embrace female identity as "subject to a mul-tiple and on-going process of revision, reform and choices."[17] *Cutie Honey* emphasizes this sexualized neoliberal agenda in a number of ways. The film contains numerous scenes that centralize Honey's body, and the viewer witnesses her soaking in the bathtub and, later, performing extreme forms of acrobatic yoga in her underwear. These scenes have no relevance to the narrative; however, they underscore her sexual desirability and, more sig-nificantly, the fastidious management of a toned body through personal grooming and physical training. In a particularly noteworthy scene at the start of the film that signifies her new femininity, Honey receives a call from her distressed uncle while bathing. As she has no clothes to hand, the

Figure 3.1   *Kyūtī Hanī/Cutie Honey* (Anno, 2004). Cutie's neoliberal femininity contingent upon rigorous self-management

audience then witnesses her running down the street in only her under-wear, resulting in distracted elderly men falling off their bicycles. Eager to transform into her alter ago, Honey shouts "Honey Flash" and presses her necklace; however, her transformation fails as she does not have enough energy. Only after she stops to eat *onigiri* (white rice in seaweed) is she able to transform: magical transformation, then, does not entirely resolve all of the limitations of her physicality, but is in fact dependent on maintaining a healthy body through a nutritious diet. The film thus constructs her body as occupying a simultaneously active/passive space, as a visual spectacle yet one that yields a power carefully cultivated by its owner (Figure 3.1).

Cutie Honey's configuration of femininity as both active (physically strong) and passive (sexually objectified) raises an important question: Does this form of new feminine identity affirm women's progress and constitute the positive outcome of feminist activism, or merely embody (post)feminist backlash discourses through a carefully contrived facade of empowerment? To answer this question, it is important to look beyond the central character of Honey toward characters in the film that firmly inhabit the "real," social world, especially given the changing status of young womanhood in contemporary Japan. Indeed, in the 1970s rapid economic growth and the decline of the neo-leftist movement brought vast shifts to Japanese society, with industrial transformation, the diversi-fication of the employment sector, a declining birthrate, feminist activism, and the mechanization of housework all directly and indirectly contribut-ing to women's entry into employment. Reflecting on the effects of these changes on women in the late twentieth century, Susan Napier declares that "nowhere is the dizzying rate of change in post-war Japan more apparent than in the shifting and varied identities of the modern Japanese woman."[18] Shifting and varied identities are indeed necessary, for the postfeminist female subject is required to perpetually negotiate and reconstruct the terms of her empowerment in the context of a backlash culture that aims to inhibit and deride women's progress. Commenting on postfeminist backlash in the Western cultural imaginary, Imelda Whelehan notes that television produced for a young female audience in the 1990s transmitted "coded threats to women on the verge of self-definition with suggestions that feminism made you unattractive, unmarriageable and miserable," and a similar misrepresentation pertaining to feminism is apparent in contemporary Japanese media culture.[19] Hilaria Gossmann has observed that since the 1980s the majority of married Japanese women do work outside of the home, and yet the majority of TV dramas still depict wives as predominantly contained within the domestic space.[20]

Likewise, a pernicious misrepresentation of the lived experiences of career women is central to *Cutie Honey*. This misrepresentation is made most explicit through the character of Detective Aki Natsuko—the Squad Chief of the Public Safety Division. When the viewer is introduced to Natsuko, it is clear that her status as a woman in a man's world is significant: she is presented at the center of the screen, the only woman in the frame standing in front of hundreds of male police officers. In accordance with her role as an ostensibly powerful leader of men, she is desexualized through the masculine attire of a smart trouser suit and glasses that accentuate her intellect rather than her sexuality, and she speaks in a dull, monotonous tone in counterpoint to Honey's sweet, high-pitched, and childlike voice. Yet, while Honey and Natsuko are presented as antithetical in terms of appearance and demeanor, they share an absence of real-world autonomy. Natsuko appears to encapsulate the empowered modern woman through her high-status career position, yet she is nevertheless constructed to be as incompetent in her vocation as Honey is in hers. Lacking the independence that she purports to possess, Natsuko's catchphrase— "I can take care of this situation myself"—becomes a running joke, for she consistently fails to control the dilemmas in which she is embroiled and always calls upon Honey to save her. Despite her dependency on others, she is represented as alienated from her femininity, declaring "I hate women who cry," and yet—in what could be seen as another marker of backlash culture—receives an internal "makeover" at the close of the film by ultimately acquiescing to femininity. After sacrificing herself to the leader of Panther Claw in order to save Natsuko (after another failed attempt at independence and assertion) Honey almost dies and Natsuko finally

learns to cry, facilitating her connection to a more emotional (and implicitly maternal) feminine identity. The career woman is thus contained, and
Honey's subordinate femininity is further extolled through her willingness
to sacrifice herself in service of others.

Conclusion

Any conclusion concerning the sensibilities of empowerment and backlash within *Cutie Honey* needs to place the film within its genre, for
doing so may demonstrate the increasingly progressive trajectory of the
girl superhero in ways that may not be apparent when analyzing the film in
isolation. Indeed, in her study of Japanese female superheroes in the 1980s
and 1990s, Susan Napier notes that while fantasies of exceptional abilities
are a staple of *shōjo* manga, protagonists often have "ambivalent or simply
negative feelings about these powers" that "capture[s] the young Japanese
girl at a time of great change or uncertainty."[21] By recognizing that girl
superheroes do not emphatically embrace their power, Napier taps into
a cultural hesitancy concerning young women's movement toward new
formations in subject positions and identities. Likewise, in her study of
the popular manga series *Sailor Moon*, Anne Allison argues that a central character, Serena, "longs to be pretty and attractive; primps over her
hair and makeup; diets; and mentally imagines herself in a wedding gown,"
and therefore aspires to achieve a conventionally idealized form of feminine identity despite her extraordinary abilities.[22] In counterpoint, Honey
entirely embraces her power and shows no sign of caring for her status
as a sexually desirable object. Indeed, for while she maintains her body
and manages her health—and while this body is presented as spectacle for
the consumption of the viewer—she does so for the purpose of enacting a
magical transformation, rather than for the purpose of securing a romantic relationship as in earlier forms of *shōjo* manga. In this manner, the film
could be seen as projecting a more independent vision of young womanhood, even if Honey's status as a sexual object when in battle commodifies
her independence and agency and thus drains her filmic representation of
any radical thrust.

Given the conceptual contradictions within *Cutie Honey*—namely the
positive affirmation of the sexually visible and physically active female form
juxtaposed with a more reactionary representation of the "ordinary" career
woman—what conclusions can we arrive at when attempting to position
the text as an inscription of non-Western postfeminist discourse? Following on from Gina Marchetti's suggestion that "particular genres tend to
be popular at certain points in time because they somehow embody and
work through those social contradictions the culture needs to come to

grips with," the immense popularity of both *Cutie Honey* and the magical girl genre could be read signifying the double bind that entraps young woman in modern Japan as they attempt to fulfill their potential in the aftermath of feminism, yet under men's terms in what remains a highly patriarchal society.[23] Indeed, the film registers both recognition and fear of the social progression of women in the late twentieth century by affirming their sexual and physical power while also devaluing their contribution to the world of work. The film's promotion of empowerment through magical transformation is, therefore, highly problematic, as it implies that empowerment is unattainable to "ordinary" young women. It also suggests, perhaps more insidiously, that the only way for young women to attain a desirable femininity is to disavow an assertive identity in favor of a childlike persona. In short, to adopt the appearance and demeanor of Honey Kisaragi the office lady (OL), but not the skill and physical ability of Cutie Honey, Warrior of Love.

Notes

1. See S. Sato, "What Are Girls Made Of?: Exploring the Symbolic Boundaries of Femininity in Two Cultures," in *Millennium Girls: Today's Girls around the World* edited by Sherrie Innes (Lanham, MD: Rowman and Little field), pp. 15–44.
2. See McRobbie, *The Aftermath of Feminism: Gender, Culture and Social Change* (London: Sage, 2009).
3. Sarah Projansky, "Mass Magazine Cover Girls: Some Reflections on Postfeminist Girls and Postfeminist Daughters," in *Interrogating Postfeminism: Gender and the Politics of Popular Culture* edited by Diane Negra and Yvonne Tasker (Durham, NC: Duke University Press), p. 45.
4. Sato, "What Are Girls Made of?," p. 17.
5. Ibid., p. 16.
6. J. W. Treat, "Yoshimoto Banana Writes Home: Shōjo Culture and the Nostalgic Subject," *Journal of Japanese Studies*, 19:2 (1993), 364.
7. Susan Napier, "Vampires, Psychic Girls, Flying Women and Sailor Scouts: Four Faces of the Young Female in Japanese Popular Culture," in *The World of Japanese Popular Culture: Gender, Shifting Boundaries and Global Cultures* edited by Dolores Martinez (Cambridge: Cambridge University Press, 1998), p. 94.
8. J. W. Treat, "Yoshimoto Banana Writes Home," 360.
9. Merry White, *The Material Child: Coming of Age in Japan and America* (Berkeley, CA: University of California Press, 1994), p. 126.
10. Yvonne Tasker, *Working Girls: Gender and Sexuality in Popular Cinema* (London: Routledge, 1998), p. 69.
11. Ibid., p. 69.

12. Mary Celeste Kearney, "Girlfriends and Girl Power: Female Adolescence in Contemporary US Cinema," in *Sugar, Spice and Everything Nice: Cinemas of Girlhood* edited by Frances Gateward and Murray Pomerance (Detroit: Wayne State University Press, 2002), p. 128.
13. Ibid., p. 29.
14. Frances Gateward, "Bubblegum and Heavy Metal," in *Sugar, Spice and Everything Nice: Cinemas of Girlhood* edited by Frances Gateward and Murray Pomerance (Detroit: Wayne State University Press, 2002), p. 278.
15. Stephanie Genz and Benjamin Brabon, *Postfeminism: Cultural Texts and Theories* (Edinburgh: Edinburgh University Press, 2009), p. 76.
16. Lisa Purse, *Contemporary Action Cinema* (Edinburgh: Edinburgh University Press, 2011), p. 188.
17. Hilary Radner, *Neo-Feminist Cinema: Girly Films, Chick Flicks and Consumer Culture* (London and New York: Routledge, 2011), p. 16.
18. Susan Napier, "Vampires, Psychic Girls," p. 91.
19. Imelda Whelehan, *Overloaded: Popular Culture and the Future of Feminism* (London: The Women's Press, 2000), p. 16.
20. Hilaria Gossman, "New Role Models for Men and Women?: Gender in Japanese TV Dramas," in *Japan Pop!: Inside the World of Japanese Popular Culture* edited by Timothy Craig (New York: East Gate, 2000), p. 213.
21. Susan Napier, "Vampires, Psychic Girls," p. 93.
22. Anne Allison, "Sailor Moon: Japanese Superheroes for Global Girls," in *Japan Pop!*, p. 273.
23. Gina Marchetti, "Action Adventure as Ideology," in *Cultural Politics in Contemporary America* edited by Ian Angus and Sut Jhally (New York: Routledge, 1988), p. 187.

Part II

Philosophies of Girlhood in Film

4

Feminine Adolescence and Transgressive Materiality in the Films of Lucrecia Martel

Deborah Martin

This chapter considers girlhood in the films of acclaimed Argentine director Lucrecia Martel, arguing for its central importance to their political and aesthetic project. It explores the local proliferation of girl-images which followed in the wake of Martel's influential début *La Ciénaga/The Swamp* (2001), and indicates some of their global resonances. Whilst Martel has come to be seen as a crucial player in the experimental-ism and aesthetic break with previous Argentine filmmaking that, in the late 1990s and early 2000s came to be known by the label "New Argentine Cinema," it is also vital to delineate the correspondences that exist between her work and that of other recent Argentine women filmmakers frequently excluded from this canon. As Jens Andermann suggests: "[I]t makes sense today to look beyond the uncertain boundaries of an 'independent' genera-tional project, which has been in many ways a critical fiction [. . .]. [W]hat this critical narrative missed was the wider, more contradictory and multi-layered landscape of film-making in Argentina."[1] I argue that Martel's work has also played a crucial role in the development of a new feminist and queer cinema in Argentina, made by women filmmakers and focused in particular around young characters and girl-figures.

If the New Argentine Cinema has been characterized as arising from and responding aesthetically and thematically to profound political and eco-nomic upheaval, the increased liberalization of the law in relation to gender and sexuality since the "progressive turn" in Argentine politics has, in turn, been accompanied by a striking set of cinematic challenges to gender and sexual ideologies.[2] The girl has been central to the ways in which Argentine cinema has formulated these challenges.

Lucrecia Martel's first three features, which are *The Swamp*, *La niña santa/The Holy Girl* (2004), and *La mujer sin cabeza/The Headless Woman* (2008), depict the private, intimate worlds of the middle classes in Salta, northeast Argentina. Within their feminine, domestic settings, the films explore complex micropolitical and discursive structures of desire, belief, and prejudice, through ambiguous narratives and an immersive, tactile film language that privileges sound and decenters the visual. Desire in these films is multiplicitous, exploding riotously in directions incestuous, inter-generational, lesbian, heterosexual, inter-species, and autoerotic, crossing boundaries of class and ethnicity; yet the films are also concerned with attempts to govern desire, to channel, contain, and regulate it. Desire is associated with the possibility for radical change that is the thematic under-current of all the films as well as with stasis and the deadening repetitions that in each film threaten to trap characters, and to perpetuate the neo-colonial and patriarchal power structures upheld by the institution of the bourgeois family.

In this filmic universe, children are everywhere; Martel describes her camera as "younger than an adolescent."[3] Whilst avoiding overarching narratives or central characters—the films prefer multiple allusions and potential storylines—each of Martel's features does privilege an adolescent girl figure. In *The Swamp* and *The Holy Girl*, these are, respectively, Momi and Amalia, who in each case assume quasi-protagonist status despite the proliferation of other characters. In *The Headless Woman*, which does feature a more conventional protagonist (the middle-aged Vero), the ado-lescent girl (her niece Candita) is nevertheless significant. And these three girls are always in some way transgressive in their desires and attitudes, caught up in unrequited or impossible crushes. Their lesbian desires, sexualities, or activities are often "backgrounded," pushed—sometimes literally—to the edges of the frame. As B. Ruby Rich has it: "Martel's films are concerned with lesbian desire in both vague and offhand ways."[4] It is not the principal focus, but it is always present as part of a multifarious landscape of desire. The girl's desire is transgressive and revolutionary: in *The Swamp* and *The Headless Woman*, Momi's passion for the Indian housemaid Isabel, and Candita's implied romance with the working class, *mestiza* Cuca, transgress the rigid boundaries of race and class govern-ing their bourgeois worlds; in *The Holy Girl*, Amalia's sexual awakening becomes entangled with her Catholic instruction, causing her to confuse the sexual attentions of the middle-aged Dr. Jano (he presses against her in the street) with a divine calling. This darkly humorous, subversive interpre-tation of events signifies a transgression of Amalia's religious education, as well as of the traditionally passive role in which Jano (and cinema) would cast her (as female and as child).

Each of Martel's films constitutes a meditation on perception and its social conditioning. Perceptual impediment and deprivation is associated with adult characters, dominant subjectivities, and oppressive attitudes. In this symbolic landscape, the established order is transgressed by the young girl's enhanced perceptual capacity, her ability both to see the realities to which others are blind, and to move beyond the visual into other sensory epistemologies. *The Swamp*'s Momi is the only character to confront her mother with the truth of the latter's alcoholism and mental deterioration, and the only character to penetrate the dirty waters of the family's swimming pool, around which the action revolves;[5] the holy girl, Amalia, is in a constant state of perceptual flux and experimentation, pressing on her eyes to alter her visual perception, pursuing Jano through touch and smell, and thus evading the logic of the gaze and transgressing classical cinema's ocularcentrism and coding of the feminine.[6] Amalia *perceives differently*; and it is against this backdrop of perceptual dexterity and flexibility that the film's major moral or ideological point is made, as Amalia is open to perceiving differently the gendered and sexual relations into which Jano initiates her. *The Headless Woman*'s Candita is outspoken: the plot revolves around the possibility that her aunt, Vero, has killed a boy from the slums in a hit-and-run, and whilst other characters ignore or cover-up this possibility, Candita is the only character (aside from Vero herself) to state, in a matter-of-fact way, that a murder has taken place. This straightforward understanding of this denied reality is mirrored by Candita's belief in the supernatural, which in Martel signifies an openness to realms of experience foreclosed to dominant subjectivities.

Martel's transgressive girls resonate with other figurings of young femininity in recent Argentine cinema. The work of Albertina Carri and Lucía Puenzo also contains a critique of the (bourgeois) family, a focus on childhood, youth, and desire, and privileges marginal sexualities. Both directors take up what are, in Martel, merely allusions, and develop their narrative potential, Carri in *Geminis* (2005) through the incest theme, and Puenzo in *El Niño pez/The Fish Child* (2009) through the cross-class lesbian romance. Puenzo's earlier film *XXY* (2007) has been acclaimed for the place it affords desire in a narrative about an intersex protagonist.[7] Its protagonist, Alex, has been brought up as a girl, a gender stability now secured by hormone tablets, and which is rejected by the character, who by the end of the film asserts her right to exist without medical intervention or the necessity of choosing a sex or gender. More conventional than Martel's work in terms of aesthetics and narrative, both *XXY* and *The Fish Child* are variations on the coming-out story, declarative where Martel's are assumptive on the topic of sexual dissidence or difference.[8] What they share with Martel is the queer girl character through whom a challenge to societal codes of gender and sexuality is effected.

We might think this moment in Argentine social, sexual, and cinematic history through the actress Inés Efrón (b. 1985), who plays the outspoken, intersex Alex in *XXY*, the outspoken, sickly Candita (who has hepatitis C, represented through yellow make-up) in *The Headless Woman* and Lala (a rich white girl in a relationship with her family's indigenous Paraguayan maid, with strong echoes of *The Swamp* and *The Headless Woman*) in *The Fish Child*.[9] Efrón (who was in her early twenties at the time) repeatedly embodies the adolescent girl protagonist whose defiant gaze and challenge to regimes of gender and sexuality has become a striking feature of the Latin American cinematic landscape in an era of transnational funding. For Deborah Shaw, this type of protagonist is a feature of a Latin American cinema now heavily defined by the decisions of European funding bodies (often social bodies and/or linked to film festivals) and their progressive gender and sexual politics. Shaw likens the rebellious gaze of *XXY*'s Alex to those of *The Holy Girl*'s Amalia, and the indigenous girls in Peruvian director Claudia Llosa's films, suggesting a way in which European imaginaries of young women as "a metaphor for social change,"[10] resurface in Latin American film.

In these films of the late 2000s, in roles that emphasize a transgressive corporeality or sexuality, Efrón's body is coded as liminal in relation to age, health, and gender. Through them, Efrón emerges as angry and outspoken, sexually and socially transgressive, figured visually through her fragile, feminine androgyny, and a sickly, or wan look. In *XXY*, Alex's skin appears to have a blue tinge; a visual code reinforced in the film by her associations with water and marine life. Martel has commented that it was this sickly look that led her to cast Efrón as the jaundiced Candita.[11] As either supportive or subversive of the dominant ideology, film stars have been understood as particularly associated with issues and negotiations of gender and sexuality. For Dyer, to think about them is to consider changing notions of identity, or "how we are human now."[12] In the late 2000s, through her characters and through her paratextual characterization as breaking with traditional acting styles, Efrón came to signify a challenge to existing categories and structures.[13] The youthful transgression of her characters reflects changes in process in public discourse on sexuality in Argentina; her visual positioning as liminal—blue, sickly, otherworldly, or even abject—underscores her disruption of normative categories of the human.

Carri's more recent *La rabia/Anger* (2008), and Julia Solomonoff's *El ultimo verano de la Boyita/The Last Summer of La Boyita* (2009) both privilege a girl-child's gaze and endow it with the ability to see beyond the world of rationality and the *status quo*; in *The Last Summer of La Boyita* this is explicitly an ability to see beyond restrictive social norms of gender and sex.[14] In interview, Solomonoff cites Martel as an important influence on *The Last Summer*, and suggests her impact on a generation of filmmakers:

> Lucrecia has had a very liberating effect on a lot of people, who have realized that one's own story, told well, is enough; there's no need to go searching elsewhere. In the intimate, in observation, in that "dead" moment of the afternoon, the siesta, there's so much. And in this way, she has established a kind of "Swamp World," opening the way for many filmmakers.[15]

Both *Anger* and *The Last Summer* are part of this world, of its experimentation with the creation of embodied and corporeal cinematic languages, and the evocation of the perceptual experience of childhood.[16] *The Last Summer* emphasizes a tactile or haptic gaze, and privileges time-images that suggest a child's temporal experience; *Anger* uses heightened, hyperreal sound reminiscent of *The Swamp*, emphasizing in particular bodily sounds such as breathing, to explore the inner world of its mute, autistic child protagonist.

In *The Swamp*, a film replete with bodily fluids, decay and sticky residues, which suggests a tactile and embodied relationship to these, Momi is taunted with the nickname "Dirty Momi" by her brother while her mother, Mecha, calls her "filthy girl," and "disgusting." After her dip in her family's putrid swimming pool, Momi, who always seems to be wearing the same gingham swimsuit, is scolded by Isabel for not washing for days. In other words, Momi is aligned with the transgressive materiality the film privileges, and thus with the disruption to the symbolic order posed by the abject. In Julia Kristeva's theory, the abject, ultimately the maternal experience repressed by every psyche, can be re-evoked by that which "disturbs identity, system, order. What does not respect borders, positions, rules. The in-between, the ambiguous, the composite."[17] *The Swamp* explores the abject nature of feminine adolescent experience, as well as the processes by which dominant culture "abjects" (the girl's) transgressive desires.

"In its abject, in-between state, adolescence troubles all identity categories."[18] In *The Swamp,* the abject gives expression to the combination of desire and disgust accompanying the "horrifying transgression of bodily and self-other boundaries" that, for Driscoll, is "especially relevant to feminine puberty."[19] The sticky, messy, smelly world in which the film immerses us is an evocation of the uncomfortable materiality of a changing body. In this way, the film subverts conventional horror's (misogynist) uses of abjection, instead, like Momi, embracing the "abject" as part of the everyday.[20] In *The Swamp*, then, the abject is not jettisoned, but rather recuperated. Through its tactile and olfactory visuality—especially images of the rubbing, sniffing, and touching of the body—the film dissolves boundaries between spectator and film, self and other, rather than (as conventional horror does) redrawing them. The film's materiality gets the spectator dirty and gives expression to the culturally and psychically repressed.[21]

If Momi is "abjected" by her family, it is because of the threat posed by her desire for Isabel to the social boundaries that maintain race and class segregation, and compulsory heterosexuality. Whilst her homosexual desire is never mentioned by her family, their words consign her to the same realm of abject bodies inhabited by the film's indigenous and poor, who are subject to constant racist abuse—especially from Mecha—which labels them as perverted, thieves, and dirty. Judith Butler suggests that abjection can be used "to understand sexism, homophobia, and racism, the repudiation of bodies for their sex/sexuality, and/or color," which consolidates identities based on exclusion and domination of others. "In effect," she posits "this is the mode by which others become shit."[22] *The Swamp*'s, and Momi's embracing of "shit"—of dirt, bodily fluids and decay—thus also constitutes a queer resistance, a subversive re-citation of the dominant ideology that also produces the *jouissance* associated with the transgression of taboo. It is this kind of subversive appropriation of the discourses of repudiation that Butler argues can function as a basis for queer opposition.[23]

The Headless Woman's Candita is similarly positioned, but she is older, and her challenge to dominant culture more potent than that of Momi, who for all this seems ultimately doomed to repeat the words and actions of her elders. Hepatitis C generates a physical resemblance between white, bourgeois Candita and darker-skinned, working-class girlfriend Cuca (and recalls Efrón's blue-tinged Alex of *XXY*). As a disease caused by contact with contamination, it represents Candita's sexual and social contamination by "undesirable" elements (Cuca, the "ladies"),[24] her abject status in the eyes of bourgeois society. As a virus that transforms her body into a rhizome, a connection with another organism, or organisms, hepatitis suggests Candita's as a body that is literally "becoming other," one that is hybrid and in a process of perpetual transformation.[25] Cuca, for her part is a go-between, moving easily between Candita's house and the slums. Subverting the spatial dynamics of the dominant order through this boundary-crossing, she is literally "matter out of place."[26] Together these girls offer a radical escape from the mutually reinforcing matrices of class, gender, and sexuality within which the adult female characters are enmeshed; of all Martel's girls, it is they who most clearly offer a metaphor for social change, justice, and integration, they who seem most likely

Figure 4.1 *La mujer sin cabeza/The Headless Woman* (Martel, 2008). A tactile, queer moment: *The Headless Woman*'s Candita massages her aunt Vero's hair

to reject and escape the oppressive codes upheld by adult society. Their positioning echoes the familiar figuring of the girl within poststructuralist theory as a site of escape from the oedipal matrix, especially through metaphors of movement and flight.[27] These metaphors are in particular suggested in the film by the peripatetic Cuca, whose motorbike riding both draws upon lesbian iconography and positions her beyond and able to move away from the social stratification symbolized in this film by the car (Figure 4.1).

Thirty minutes into *The Headless Woman*, Candita, who also sends love letters to, and makes passes at, her aunt, rubs jojoba oil into Vero's hair, shot in close-up from behind, whilst Candita is visible on her far side, smiling. Her hands extend around her aunt's head, such that what is closest to the camera is Vero's abundant blonde hair as it is massaged by Candita's hands, suggesting a de-organization of the erotic body through the touching of hair, a body element connoting both desire and disgust. As the camera lingers on this highly tactile, vaguely erotic image, the sound of background conversations momentarily fades to be replaced by the barely audible sound of breathing, adding to the erotic charge and to the invitation to shared embodiment briefly conjured here.[28] This queer, tactile moment is interrupted by the sound of motorbikes pulling up, and of Candita's mother Josefina's words: "The 'ladies' are here. Don't let them in the house. Not in the house." Candita gets up and goes outside to greet her (lesbian?) friends, exchanging tender embraces and words with Cuca. The pair are visible in the background through a partially open door, whilst in the foreground, inside the house, Vero sits, and listens to Josefina: "I don't know where she finds these people . . . messing about with that bike all day like a bunch of dykes." Candita's body—site of queer abjection, of becoming, of transgressive materiality—is pushed outside, to the boundaries of what is livable and thinkable, to the edge of the frame, to join the realm of abject bodies—servants, the poor, the "ladies"—always hovering at the film's visual periphery.

The transgressive materiality that is associated in Martel's films with adolescent girlhood and queer desire arises in *The Holy Girl* in relation to water. This element features prominently in all Martel's work: intense humidity, heavy rainstorms, water fights, showering and washing, droplets on windowpanes are all recurrent, as is the swimming pool. Water is of course connected to the feminine, the maternal, and the abject, but Martel's frequent allusion to John Cassavetes's *Love Streams* as an influence, and particular reference to the title image (Guest),[29] is important here. Like desire, water flows, transgressing boundaries, and this interest in the swimming pool stems from the preoccupation with the domestication, channeling, and containment of desire. In *The Holy Girl*, Amalia's frequent immersion in water, and emergence from it, also images moments of ideological rupture associated with the adolescent girl's enhanced perceptual capacities. These points help us to understand its representational significance, but beyond this, it gives the film an erotic and tactile charge, as water's action on skin is continually evoked. Such images and erotics give form to girls' queer desire in recent films including not only *XXY* and *The Last Summer*, but also in European productions such as *Naissance des pieuvres/Water Lilies* (Sciamma, 2007) and *La Vie d'Adèle—Chapitres 1 & 2 /Blue Is the Warmest Colour* (Kechiche, 2013).[30] The extended swimming, playing, and being in water of the young protagonists evokes a fluidity and freedom of desire, and invites a closer relation between film and spectator through tactility and embodiment. The notion of fluidity, the challenging of boundaries both symbolic and cinematic, is present in all these films, through their use of watery images as a means of communicating girlhood desire, desire that is dispersed, diffuse, and escapes inevitably from the attempts to channel and contain it constituted by social, symbolic, and cinematic systems. This is one sense in which Martel's depictions of adolescent girlhood, depictions that are corporeal, tactile, transgressive, and queer, resonate with recent such depictions in global queer cinema. Indeed, these resonances between the aesthetics of girlhood desire in contemporary global cinematic contexts suggest a rich avenue for future inquiry.

Notes

1. Jens Andermann, *New Argentine Cinema* (London: I. B. Tauris, 2012), pp. xii–xiii.
2. In 2010, Argentina became the first Latin American country to legalize same-sex marriage, and in 2012 passed a comprehensive transgender rights bill,

allowing transgender people to change their gender on public documents without undergoing surgery and without medical or legal permission.

3. D. Oubiña, *Estudio Crítico sobre* La ciénaga: *Entrevista a Lucrecia Martel* (Buenos Aires: Picnic editorial, 2009), p. 65, my translation.

4. B. Ruby Rich, *New Queer Cinema: The Director's Cut* (Durham, NC: Duke University Press, 2013), p. 180.

5. Laura Podalsky reads this as "an effective metaphor for Momi's compulsion, unique among all the characters, to penetrate the dirty realities ignored by others" (p. 109) in *The Politics of Affect and Emotion in Contemporary Latin American Cinema: Argentina, Brazil, Cuba and Mexico* (Basingstoke: Palgrave Macmillan, 2009).

6. For a fuller discussion of this argument, see Deborah Martin, "Wholly Ambivalent Demon-girl: Horror, the Uncanny and the representation of Feminine Adolescence in Lucrecia Martel's *La niña santa*," *Journal of Iberian and Latin American Studies* 17:1 (2011), 59–76.

7. Sophie Mayer, "Family Business," *Sight and Sound* 18:6 (2008), 14–15, (15).

8. B. Ruby Rich makes a useful distinction between the "assumptive" queerness of Martel's films and the "declarative" mode of more conventional gay/lesbian narratives (181) in *New Queer Cinema*.

9. Before these more high-profile films, Efrón starred as Andrea in Alexis Dos Santos' *Glue* (2006), which foregrounds adolescent male bisexuality, whilst Efrón's character experiments with giving herself a moustache and imagines being a man.

10. Angela McRobbie argues that "young women in Britain today have replaced youth as a metaphor for social change" in her book *Feminism and Youth Culture* (London: Palgrave, 2000), (201).

11. On the casting of Efrón, Martel said "What most interested me in Inés was that sickly look she has," Deborah Martin "Interview with Lucrecia Martel," October 23, 2011 Unpublished.

12. Richard Dyer, *Heavenly Bodies: Film Stars and Society* (Basingstoke: Macmillan, 1986), p. 17.

13. A publicity interview for *XXY*, which suggests differences between the acting techniques of Efrón and Ricardo Darín (who plays her father in the film), sums up Efrón's career as follows: "All the girls she plays as well as her own initiation into acting point to the same idea, which goes for a whole generation: it's the adults who are always trying to define and label. 'Because we are young' concludes Efrón 'we are destined to break existing models'." Available at: http://www.pagina12.com.ar/diario/suplementos/espectaculos/5-4750-2006-12-10.html online, my translation.

14. Deborah Martin, "Growing Sideways in Argentine Cinema: Lucía Puenzo's *XXY* and Julia Solomonoff's *El último verano de la boyita*," *Journal of Romance Studies* 13:1 (2013), 34–48 (41–42).

15. Deborah Martin, "Interview with Julia Solomonoff," April 16, 2012 Unpublished.

16. For discussions of Martel's aesthetic evocations of childhood experience, see Ana Amado, "Velocidades, generaciones y utopías: a propósito de *La ciénaga*,

de Lucrecia Martel," *ALCEU*, 6:12, (2006) 48–56 (54) and Deborah Martin, "Wholly Ambivalent Demon-girl: Horror, the Uncanny and the Representation of Feminine Adolescence in Lucrecia Martel's *La niña santa*," *Journal of Iberian and Latin American Studies* 17:1 (2011), 59–76 (71).

17. Julia Kristeva, *Powers of Horror: An Essay on Abjection*, trans. by L. S. Roudiez (New York: Columbia University Press, 1982), p. 4.

18. Rachael McLennan, *Adolescence, America and Postwar Fiction: Developing Figures* (Basingstoke: Palgrave Macmillan, 2009), p. 27.

19. Catherine Driscoll, *Girls: Feminine Adolescence in Popular Culture and Cultural Theory* (New York: Columbia University Press, 2002), p. 231.

20. Barbara Creed proposes that conventional horror, structured according to male anxiety, "stages and re-stages a constant repudiation of […] 'the abject' " (70), and that this operation is part of the process by which the abject is culturally repressed in order to uphold the symbolic order. Barbara Creed, *The Monstrous-Feminine: Film, Feminism, Psychoanalysis* (London: Routledge, 1990).

21. I draw here on the work of Laura Marks whose conception of haptic visuality is informed by the work of Aloïs Riegl, Deleuze and Guattari, and Maurice Merleau-Ponty. Marks proposes that haptic or tactile images may blur borders between film and viewer, inviting embodied spectatorship. Laura Marks, *Touch: Sensuous Theory and Multisensory Media* (Minnesota: University of Minneapolis Press, 2002). On embodiment and tactility in films and moving image culture, see also Vivian Sobchack, *Carnal Thoughts: Embodiment and Public Image Culture* (Berkeley: University of California, 2004) and. Jennifer Barker, *The Tactile Eye: Touch and the Cinematic Experience* (Berkeley: University of California Press, 2009).

22. Judith Butler, *Gender Trouble: Feminism and the Subversion of Identity* (New York: Routledge, 1990), p. 182.

23. See Judith Butler, *Bodies That Matter: On the Discursive Limits of "Sex"* (New York: Routledge, 1993), pp. 223–242.

24. "Leidiz" (from the English "ladies") is used in an ironic sense by Candita's mother Josefina when referring to Cuca and her working-class friends who seem not to fit bourgeois conceptions of femininity/heterosexuality.

25. Deleuze and Guattari propose that "We form a rhizome with our viruses, or rather our viruses cause us to form a rhizome with other animals" (11). Gilles Deleuze and Félix Guattari, *A Thousand Plateaus: Capitalism and Schizophrenia*, trans. by Brian Massumi (London: The Athlone Press, 1987).

26. Mary Douglas, *Purity and Danger: An Analysis of the Concept of Pollution and Taboo* (London: Routledge, 2000), p. 50. Cuca is also one of the working-class, *mestizo* characters who return the bourgeois gaze, and who in doing so seem to indicate an unspoken understanding of Vero's potential involvement in the hit-and-run.

27. Gilles Deleuze and Félix Guattari, *A Thousand Plateaus* and Catherine Driscoll, "The Woman in Process: Deleuze, Kristeva and Feminism," in *Deleuze and Feminist Theory*, edited by C. Colebrook and I. Buchanan (Edinburgh: Edinburgh University Press, 2000), pp. 64–85 (81).

28. For Davina Quinlivan, the use of audible breathing in film gives "a particular impression of embodiment" that can function as a means of suture (5). Davina Quinlivan, *The Place of Breath in Cinema* (Edinburgh: Edinburgh University Press, 2012).
29. Lucrecia Martel, "Artist in conversation with Haden Guest," BOMB Magazine, Available at http://bombmagazine.org/article/3220/lucrecia-martel
30. In a recent talk, "The sea nymphs tested this miracle: traces of a liquid world in *Naissance des pieuvres*" at "The Girl in Global Cinema" Symposium, July 12, 2013, Emma Wilson spoke of the use of intersensory cinema and water images for exploring girls' sexuality in *Water Lilies*. See also Handyside, chapter 9 in this volume.

5

A Phenomenology of Girlhood: Being Mia in *Fish Tank* (Andrea Arnold, 2009)

Lucy Bolton

In October 2009, David Cameron, then leader of the Opposition, attempted to persuade voters to entrust him to help mend Britain's broken society.[1] The elements of his Conservative party's discourse of "broken Britain" consist of single mothers, poor education, anti-social behavior, alcohol abuse, teenage sex, and lack of employment. This is the world of *Fish Tank*: a depiction of contemporary Essex housing-estate culture, in which 15-year-old Mia "swims frustrated circles, like a shark in a tank."[2] Mia is played by amateur actor Katie Jarvis, and her sullenness and rage are the beating heart of the film. *Fish Tank* may appear to suggest that Mia is a prime example of contemporary broken British culture, but it is a shot across the bows of such misperceptions, announcing that girls like Mia should not be dismissed or underestimated. The film achieves this by creating Mia's very particular experiences at this pivotal point in her young life, and evoking the rhythms and relationships of this 15-year-old girl in her place in contemporary British society.

There are clear ways in which the milieu of *Fish Tank* reflects the British social-realist tradition, and director Andrea Arnold has frequently been hailed as a successor to Ken Loach.[3] British social-realist cinema has traditionally been one of the places where girls' stories have been given prominence, even if usually as symptomatic of society's fears, such as teenage pregnancy in *A Taste of Honey* (Richardson, 1961) and *The L-Shaped Room* (Forbes, 1962), or sexual liberation in *Beat Girl* (Greville, 1960), *Girl with Green Eyes* (Davis, 1964), and *The Girl on a Motorcycle*

(Cardiff, 1968). Christine Geraghty describes how, in the 1960s, "the social and moral issues which clustered round young women were reworked in the cinema."[4] Dysfunctional families, where there were no fathers and only pleasure-seeking mothers, led to daughters seeking support, "often by members of the same generation, in a less restrictive but more careful way than that given by the family."[5] In this way, argues Geraghty, "cinema worked within the broader social context in its attempt to reflect contemporary attitudes to what was seen as a 60s phenomenon," namely "an unpredictable, spontaneous, emotionally honest, sexually active young woman."[6]

Incarnations of girlhood in more contemporary British cinema tend to fall broadly into one of three types: schoolgirls in uniform (saucy as in *St Trinian's* (Parker and Thompson, 2007), St Trianian's 2: The Legend of Fritton's Gold (Parker and Thompson, 2009) or "jolly hockey sticks" as in *Cracks* (Scott, 2009)); young ladies of heritage films (such as Jane Austen adaptations *Sense and Sensibility* (Lee, 1995) and *Pride and Prejudice* (Wright, 2005)) and the upper classes (*Room with a View* (Ivory, 1985), *Atonement* (Wright, 2007)); and sexual provocateurs (*My Summer of Love* (Pawlikowski, 2004), *Wish You Were Here* (Leland, 1987)). In recent years, there have been examples of British films concerned with a young woman as a character in a story revolving around her, as differentiated from a girl as emblematic of social ills or who "challenged conventional morality."[7] Films such as *Morvern Callar* (Ramsay, 2002) and *The Disappearance of Alice Creed* (Blakeson, 2009) are boundary-pushing genre movies, reworking gender stereotypes and reimagining conventional tropes.[8]

Fish Tank might look like social-realism but is also phenomenological experimentation.[9] This is a film about Mia, but it is not just a gritty exposition of her environment and the limits of her choices; nor is it a straightforward vision of teenage girlhood in broken Britain. It is an evocation of her individual personality and experiences, through an immersive cinematic phenomenology of her space, time, and movement. The phenomenological concept of the lived body, as Iris Marion Young argues, "can offer a way of articulating how persons live out their positioning in social structures along with the opportunities and constraints they produce."[10] The lived body, in Young's words, is "a unified idea of a physical body acting and experiencing in a specific sociocultural context; it is body-in-situation."[11] This existentialist phenomenological approach enables us to understand how *Fish Tank* evokes the experience of what is *to be* a modern girl in modern Britain, rather than presenting a more conventional story of what happens to her within her social and cultural context.

The first five minutes of *Fish Tank* assert that the film is all about Mia's lived body. The film's opening shots tell us very little in terms of plot: we meet a girl. In terms of Mia, however, they establish a great deal: she is a loner; she appears to not care what her peers or her elders think of her; she is opinionated, violent, surly, and funny. A close-up tracking shot follows her feet and her determined, aggressive footsteps, and there are close-ups of her worldly wise but young and hungry face. The camera picks up on her energy through its urgently unsteady hand-held motion and the accompanying sound of her exercised breathing. We know where we are: we are *with* Mia in her time and her space. If it takes Mia a few minutes to get from one side of the estate to the other then it will take us a few minutes too.

Through this phenomenological filmmaking, we know Mia's perspective even if we do not adopt it. That is, we might think her head butt of one of the other girls is inexcusably violent and that she is unruly and offensive, but we still view the world in Mia's time and from the position of her lived body. There does not need to be an adoption of perspective from a moral or psychological point of view, but the film creates alignment with Mia's perspective in terms of what she sees, hears, and does. As she sits on the fence watching the girls dance in an aggressively humorless and formal music-video style, Mia snorts derisively and mimics their poses. Point-of-view shots enable us to follow Mia's glance over to some boys watching the girls dance, as we overhear their lustful appraisals: "I'd 'ave that one." The dancing girls are framed as if they are performing for Mia and for the spectator, so we share her line of sight on their self-important car-park stage. We are therefore amused by Mia's ridicule, and affiliated with her mocking stance, albeit we would most likely stop short of the ensuing head butt when challenged by one of the girls.

Mia's world is very female. She lives with her hostile, resentful, and abusive mother Joanne (Kierston Wareing) and her younger sister, Tyler (Rebecca Griffiths). They insult and curse each other, and Joanne shows no interest in either of her daughters other than to ensure Mia is sent away to a school for problem children and to make sure neither girl is around when she has her friends over to party. Into this realm comes the sinewy phallus that is Connor (Michael Fassbender), having sex with her mother and asserting masculinity and fatherliness over the two daughters. The film's tension resides in the uncertainty over whether Connor is a benign potential ally or a predatory pedophile. This would be a tense enough narrative dynamic (like Teresa's quandary in *Shadow of a Doubt* (Hitchcock, 1943), or India's in *Stoker* (Park, 2012)—is he a good uncle or a murderous one?) but in *Fish Tank* the dilemma becomes palpably excruciating at the phenomenological level of Mia's lived body.

Christina Schües explains that one of the tasks of feminist phenomenology is to explicate the temporal constitution of the experience of sexual difference. This is founded on a belief in the intertwining between the temporality of experience and gender, and the idea that our experiences are bound to our body and to the world. The embodied self, Schües argues, articulates itself within a context for which it cannot account nor articulate entirely: "for feminist purposes it is especially the limits of what is narratable that are worth considering, for these limits mark out the futural possibilities for us and for generations to come."[12] This is an apt approach to bring to bear on Mia's liminal and experimental lived body in *Fish Tank*, as it allows for precise evocation of the specificity of Mia's experience, rather than an emblematic "noughties" British teenager.

A further idea discussed by Schües is that time has rhythm, and that this rhythm or pace is tied to the appropriateness of the time structure of our activities: "understanding the forces and the different structures of time lays the ground for understanding the relations between human beings, between men and women, between different groups and styles of living."[13] This clearly has particular resonance for film. Temporality and rhythm are constitutive in shot length, camera movement, scene duration, pace of performance, delivery of dialogue, and rapidity of soundtrack. It is in the rhythm and relations of *Fish Tank* that Mia's embodied character is developed and the cinematic style in which time is created, protracted, and interfered with, can be understood as a feminist phenomenological statement of *this* girl's experience.

The multilayered temporality of the film, focused on Mia, works to create a viewing experience of acute intensity and tension. These layers are, simply, the world as experienced by the striding Mia, the dancing Mia, the running Mia, and the stationary Mia, and how those elements relate to the other people and lives in the film. Present and partaking to various degrees are elements of nature, music, and nonhuman lives (a nocturnal hamster trying to sleep, an observational dog, a dying fish, a lonely horse). All these bring different types of physicality and different rhythms of life are present in the film's temporal landscape, thereby enabling the specific elements of Mia's experience to emerge.

The opening scenes set up various relations, and Mia's life then develops along distinct but intertwined strands of timescales and relationships. Mia is practicing street dance moves in an empty flat on her estate. The moves are contorted and demanding, and she practices them with seriousness and application. She surveys the estate from the flat's balcony: this is a place of exertion and stillness, retreat and promise, escape and creation. There is immediacy and intention here as she's in her dancing zone but she's also laying plans and trying to improve as she practices for an audition that might offer her a way out of her situation. Mia's little sister, Tyler, is shown as not only part of Mia's past through the presence of a baby photo in her bedroom, and her present through their foul-mouthed sibling banter, but

Figure 5.1 *Fish Tank* (Arnold, 2009). Mia makes a meaningful connection

the film also conveys a fear for her future. Tyler and her friend are shown smoking, drinking, and made-up with bright shiny cosmetics in a bedroom where little kittens are drawn on pink plastic paraphernalia. This contrast between the idea of the sugar and spice of little girls' lives and what Tyler's life is actually made of is pulled sharply into focus when we meet Keira later in the film as we will see in due course (Figure 5.1).

One of Mia's formative relationships is with the horse that she sees tied up at a travelers' site. Mia seems set on releasing the horse, trying unsuccessfully to smash the chains with rocks and returning to the site with more appropriate tools. Mia clearly feels the need to free her. She strokes the horse all over, caressing her skin, mane, and ears, tracing the lines of her bony haunches and whispering "sssshh" in her ears. This is tender and caring Mia, revealing a softness and connectedness that she does not seem to have any other outlets for in her life. She has an ongoing feud with the other girls on the estate. She has been rejected by her best friend Keeley and her peer group, and is in trouble with police for having broken one of their noses with that introductory head-butt. We see a photograph in Mia's bedroom of her with Keeley in better times when they were close, and we see Mia try to make contact with her by leaving mobile telephone messages that go unanswered. Mia's mother is violent and abusive, concerned with her own love life above her daughters' well-being. Talking to the social worker, she says of Mia that "she came out looking for trouble";

and when things go badly wrong with Connor, she tells Mia that when she knew she was pregnant with her, she made an appointment to have her aborted. Here, the film looks back to the time in Mia's life when she was created and born, shedding light on the relationship with her mother and the type of childhood she may have experienced. This adds to our understanding of Mia's exclamation that it is her mother that is "the matter" with her, but does so in a way that immerses us in the timespan of Mia's life, conveying the loveless circumstances of Mia's conception and birth.

Mia's age is central here, but so is her gender. The fact that she is female is constantly foregrounded. When trying to release the horse from its chains, the boys come back to the site and she has to fight off an assault that looks like turning sexual. She is rescued by one of the boys, Billy, and this slowly grows into a friendship, as they engage in playful and adolescent behavior. The girls insult her in terms of ugliness and dirtiness, and the most frequent term of abuse between Mia and others, including her little sister, is "cunt." The pivotal relationship, however, is with her mother's new lover, Connor. The development of their exploratory bond creates a tension between hope and fear as Mia, and we, assess the potential he might have as a friend and support, alongside the unease at his familiarity and intimacy with Mia and Tyler.

Mia's mother has a party, and makes it abundantly clear through verbal abuse and physical violence that Mia and Tyler are not allowed to come downstairs. During the party, Mia sees a couple having sex in the kitchen and she steals their vodka. She then forages in her mother's dressing table, like a little girl, playing with the perfume and make-up. This scene captures her precise in-between state: swilling vodka and playing with her mother's cosmetics. At the end of the evening, Mia pretends to be asleep as Connor lifts her tenderly and carries her from her mother's bed to her own. He takes off her trainers, pulls off her trousers, folds them neatly, and places them on a chair, covering her with a sheet. We observe Connor through the crook in Mia's arm. As the camera shows her glimpsed view of him, accompanied by her breathing, we are placed alongside Mia's head, not knowing how to interpret his gentleness and care with the undressing.

The tension around Connor's meaning is drawn exquisitely in the time of a 15-year-old girl. He drives the family to a lake where he wades into the water, lures a carp by tickling it, and skewers it brutally with a branch. His seduction of the carp echoes his coaxing of Mia into the water to help him, and prefigures the brutality of the future of their relationship. Mia cuts her foot as she wades out of the water. Connor tells her to jump on his back, and she holds onto him as he carries her back to the car. We hear his labored breathing, and the image is slightly slowed down: Mia's experience is on the cusp of both child and lover as she rests her head against his shoulder blades and closes her eyes. These are dual relations between Mia and Connor existing in the same time.

Mia goes to find him at the store where he works, creating a time that is just theirs. Connor offers her care as he tends to her injured foot, and encouragement as he tells her she dances well and should go for the audition. Connor says she looks nice when she smiles, and the impact of this praise is evident in Mia's subtly bashful downward cast of her eyes and shuffling feet. On another occasion, however, he dresses in front of her and offers her his neck to sniff his scent. Despite the erotic proximity between his neck and her mouth, she replies, like a cheeky teenager, that it smells of "fox piss." He puts her over his knee and spanks her bottom. There has been a clear shift, to more sexualized, flirtatious behavior; less fatherly, less friendly, sexier, so that the spanking is almost a parody of fatherliness.

Mia demonstrates her audition piece for Connor, to a piece of music he introduced her too on the day of the journey to the lake, and that he says is his favorite song. He invites her to join him on the sofa, patting the cushion as if beckoning a child or a pet. Having stroked her hair, they then begin to kiss and have sex. Connor's feelings are shown to be, or have become, sexual. Mia's desire to please him, the recognition that their trip together was meaningful to her, and the ambiguity about the response she expects, serve to create a situation of immense vulnerability and significance. The thought of Mia having had sex with Billy appears to be a catalyst for Connor's sexual advances, as he moves on top of Mia, enters her, and challenges, "I bet his cock isn't this big."

He then utters the predictable line of the abuser, "we have to keep this between you and me." In the morning he has left, and Mia's mother is in tears. Mia responds by finding out where he lives and breaking in to his house. She discovers that throughout the time they have spent together an alternative family life has been running in parallel. He has a wife and daughter, a semi-detached house, and a garden. Mia falls to a crouch and urinates on the carpet, conveying the overwhelming shock and bodily impact of the discovery. She watches while Connor and his family arrive home in the car, and his little girl scoots to and fro in front of her, presenting an irresistible opportunity to strike at the heart of Connor's duplicitous, nonchalant complacency. On the spur of the moment, Mia entices the little girl, Keira, away. Dressed like a Disney princess, riding a pink scooter, these images suggest that this Keira's childhood is very different from Mia's and Tyler's. Mia makes her run away, shouts at her, and treats her badly, dragging and chasing her through fields of wheat and corn. There are slow-motion shots of the sparkles on Keira's dress twinkling in the sunshine, with the breeze whistling around her, parodically, as the situation is far from idyllic. Soon the girls are standing by water. Keira kicks Mia, and she throws the girl into the water seemingly instinctively. Mia then rescues her too, and as she manages to pull her out of water she hugs the shivering but compliant child. Their shared near-death experience has put an end to their hostilities and Mia takes her home.

During this experience, which takes about ten minutes of screen time, and is probably intended to represent a few hours of real time, we stay with Mia and Keira. We can only imagine the horror and panic happening at Connor's home; but I am not sure that we do, so immersed are we in the ominous encounter between Connor's real daughter and his sometime daughter/lover. We see Keira run off toward home, and then Connor explodes out of the house and pursues Mia by car, then chases her on foot, catches her and slaps her, but they exchange no words. Both know why Mia took his daughter, and the extent of the betrayals involved in his deception and her abduction have ruptured their ability to converse.

The ending of *Fish Tank* is upbeat in that Mia survives Connor and her mother and leaves the estate to go to Wales with Billy. Before she leaves, she looks at her mother dancing to NaS's rap "Life's a bitch." Mia joins in, mirroring her steps, with Tyler behind her, as their dog watches them. This is an overdetermined but striking evocation of the rhythms they share as women in the same family, and the difficult dynamics from generation to generation.

When Billy explains to the desolate Mia that the old horse has died, he says "she was sixteen, it was her time." This sentence also aptly sums up Mia's situation, but rather than it being her time to die it is her time to break away from the people and structures that seek to limit her. There is hope in the fact that Mia is able to forge a friendship with Billy, a boy her own age. We have seen them playing together, getting drunk, and horsing around on a shopping trolley. Although Mia says they have had sex, we do not know if this is true. As they drive away from the estate, a heart-shaped helium balloon floats away over the rooftops. This is another overdetermined image, here of the disappearance of Mia's romantic delusions as a more realistic and age-appropriate relationship sets off on its way.

Arnold talks about this final scene in an interview with Lisa Mullen and describes how "Everything was one take and quick and grabbed and snatched." Arnold confides, "I'd like to find a way of being more like that if I could (...) What if I did a whole film where I just did one-takes. Something very real and raw would have to happen ...."[14] "Something very real and raw" is a good description of the viewing experience of *Fish Tank*. The medium of film enables a multi-layered concoction of relationships and, to borrow Schües's words, the limited articulation of this embodied self: there are lots of things we do not know about Mia. As Schües predicts, the limits of this narration are interesting, for they create the ambiguities that cause the tension. The film enables the positioning of Mia in relation to her gender, class, age, and whiteness, to be played out in timelines that cross-cut and intersect, without her verbal self-articulation.

Spending time with Mia in *Fish Tank* is to experience the uncertainties, ambiguities, and disappointments of a particular 15-year-old girl in modern Britain. We experience those ambiguities through our not knowing the extent of her relationship with Billy, the intentions and deceptions of Connor, or what her future holds. The film does not take a judgmental or proselytizing stance on the estate or the people that live there, but portrays fun, humor, anger, ugliness, and beauty in places that might, in another filmmaker's hands, have been bleak, gray, and driven by narrative earnestness. There is a danger and unpredictability to *Fish Tank* that resists simple stereotyping, such as the one we find in the more middle-class milieu of *Broken* (Norris, 2012) (a title that directly references the "broken Britain" discourse), which offers caricatures of broken Britain's young girls. The vulnerable tomboy Skunk is contrasted to the motherless Oswald sisters who can be seen as the source of malevolence and destruction in the film. In some ways, Mia is the Oswald girls' cinematic forerunner, having drawn to our attention the different ways a girl can be brought up in Britain today. Where *Broken* and *Fish Tank* differ, is that the former tells a conventional coming-of-age story in an exaggerated hothouse of today's Britain, whereas the latter is less concerned with narrative and morality than it is with the slipperiness and ambiguity of relationships and experiences for a girl at this time of her life.

It is interesting to consider Mia's experiences as a British girl on the cusp of "sweet sixteen" with the more traditional coming of age in *Twenty One* (Boyd, 1991). Here, the middle-class London milieu of Katie's (Patsy Kensit) dissatisfaction with 1980s girlhood, and Kensit's star persona, created a sense of zeitgeist about the film. Katie is a jaded and cynical protagonist, who addresses the camera with confessional monologues that evoke the spirit of a female Alfie as she echoes his desire for "a straightforward fuck." In *Fish Tank*, there is no star persona, moralizing message, overt political agenda, or pop-culture burden. *Fish Tank* articulates what it is to be Mia: not a cliché of "broken Britain," or a cinematic device for conveying the supposed concerns of a generation, but of one 15-year-old girl facing both constraints and possibilities within the confines of her class, age, and gender. In this way, the film articulates a voice of modern cinematic girlhood in Britain, asserting the existence of individual experience and social constraint against tired narratives of alienated youth and broken families.

Notes

1. Deborah Summers, "David Cameron: We'll Put Britain Back on Her Feet," *The Guardian* (October 8, 2009).
2. Lisa Mullen, "Estate of Mind," *Sight & Sound* 19:10 (October 2009), 16–19 (17).
3. Peter Bradshaw considers Arnold to be "Loach's natural successor": Peter Bradshaw, "Fish Tank," *The Guardian* (September 10, 2009).
4. Christine Geraghty, "Women and Sixties British Cinema: The Development of the 'Darling' Girl," in *The British Cinema Book* edited by Rob Murphy (London: British Film Institute, 2009), pp. 154–163 (314).
5. Ibid., p. 315.
6. Ibid., p. 319. Julie Burchill considers British cinema's "Chelsea girls" in the context of mods, The Beatles, Keeler and fashion also in Julie Burchill, *Girls on Film* (New York: Pantheon Books, 1986).
7. Carol Dyhouse, *Girl Trouble: Panic and Progress in the History of Young Women* (London and New York: Zed Books, 2013), p. 136.
8. See Richard Beck, "Tears in the Neighborhood," *Film Quarterly* 64:1 (Fall 2010) online http://www.filmquarterly.org/2010/09/tears-in-the-neighborhood/ on *The Disappearance of Alice Creed* and Lucy Bolton on *Morvern Callar* in *Film and Female Consciousness: Irigaray, Cinema and Thinking Women* (Basingstoke: Palgrave, 2011), pp. 128–166.
9. Graham Fuller, "Social Realism with a Poetic Lens," *The New York Times* (January 14, 2010); Nick Roddick sets Arnold's work in the social realist context and examines the film's "almost adversarial relationship with the real," "Estate of Mind," *Sight and Sound* 19:10 (October 2009), p. 19.
10. Iris Marion Young, *On Female Body Experience: "Throwing like a Girl" and Other Essays* (Oxford and New York: Oxford University Press, 2005), p. 25.
11. Ibid., p. 16.
12. Christina Schües, Dorothea E. Olkowski and Helen A. Fielding, eds., *Time in Feminist Phenomenology* (Bloomington, IN: Indiana University Press, 2009), p. 9.
13. Ibid., p. 11.
14. Lisa Mullen, "Estate of Mind," p. 19.

6

Desire, Outcast: Locating Queer Adolescence

Clara Bradbury-Rance

Picture the doubled image of a teenage girl in a baseball cap: she looks outwards but the darkened window of the bus on which she is travelling directs her gaze back in our direction. Her image resides in a movie poster next to a definition of the film's titular subject: "PARIAH [puh-rahy-uh] *noun* 1. A person without status. 2. A rejected member of society. 3. An outcast."[1] *Pariah* (Dee Rees, 2011) is a film of escape (about looking out) but also of self-recognition (about looking back inwards). This kind of mirror image is highly suggestive of the adolescent state itself: constructed through prepositions, the teen finds herself *after* childhood (if biology does its job); *before* adulthood (if society does *its* job); if not, then *alongside* both ... or neither. The word "pariah" and its definition riff on this prepositioning, sitting neatly in a poster in justified font between the girl's original image and her reflection.

A second citation, from Sara Ahmed's *Queer Phenomenology,* establishes a theoretical approach to the positioning of *Pariah*'s definition. "The differences between how we are oriented sexually are not only a matter of "which" objects we are oriented toward," Ahmed writes, "but also how we extend through our bodies into the world."[2] How do we consider queerly that passage of extension "through" the world? If the pariah is "without" (as in not with*in;* on the outside) how is she oriented? If she is rejected (from the Latin: thrown back), what is she thrown back *to*? If she is outcast, then from what? Alike (Adepero Oduye) is this film's pariah: queer in a Christian family, clever in a school of underachievers, the girl who just doesn't quite fit in. The spatial construction of Alike's queerness resonates all the more clearly when we read the pariah as a sign of adolescence:

without recognizable temporality; thrown back from childhood to a state as disorienting as infancy; cast out from childhood but not yet cast into adulthood.

This chapter reads Alike as pariah through her overlapping sexual, spatial, and temporal locations: in queerness, in the city, in adolescence. The chapter considers the location of adolescence in existing theory and, discovering its under-theorization, conceptualizes adolescence as *dis*located, theoretically and elsewhere. Concurrently, "queer" becomes a term that is undefinable as part of its very definition and therefore one that approximates this same dislocation in sexual terms. I propose "queer" and "adolescent" as metaphors for each other's dislocatedness, adjectivally qualifying each other's nounal forms. "Time is out of joint," declares Prince Hamlet in Shakespeare's play; in Elizabeth Freeman's adoption of that expression in *Time Binds*, queers are "denizens of time out of joint."[3] Returning to Freeman's concept throughout, I argue that the same could be said of adolescents. And so we come to perceive the archetypal adolescent narrative—the "coming of age" story—as an anachronism in the context of the individual lifecycle: if that genre depends on a journey toward location, position, orientation, then queer adolescence, such as is explored here in *Pariah*, dislocates, displaces, disorients spatially, temporally, and also generically. *Pariah* is a film that, on the surface, asks to be read as a typical coming-of-age drama that brings the queer adolescent into visibility through a familiar formula. But this ostensible paradigm teases us, exposing the anachronism it is perceived to endorse, leaving us instead with queer cinematic spaces that fragment the trajectory of the genre.

The chapter takes up the poster's emphasis on positioning but makes of it something queerer than the mere statement uttered toward the film's close: "I'm a dyke." *Pariah* is, yes, a story of adolescent desire, of self-narration, of an attempt for self-definition: the closing lines of the poem that ends the film, written and read aloud by Alike, tell us that "breaking is freeing, broken is freedom/I'm not broken, I am free." The poem itself, which accompanies the image of Alike on another bus out of Brooklyn toward a new life at college, wavers back and forth between different positions (within and without, inside and outside) and the different sentences of the pariah (broken, open, and free). Queerness in *Pariah* resides not in any literal or metaphorical destination (college, identity) but in those places in between. As Glen Elder, Lawrence Knopp, and Heidi Nast define it, queerness "does not universalize the experience of those who do not practice heterosex, but highlights the *contextual* nature of that oppositional [...] desire." For them, "queer" is primarily "a term of political engagement and not necessarily an identity."[4] In my terms "queer" is, moreover, *necessarily not* an identity. And it is through these temporal and spatial negotiations that we discover not only adolescence as a medium through which to explore queerness, but queerness as an expression of adolescence.

The first decade of the twenty-first century has seen the representation of lesbian desire in mainstream cinema bracketed by two psychosexual thrillers: *Mulholland Drive* (Lynch, 2001) and *Black Swan* (Aronofsky, 2010). These are the antitheses of the decade's other unignorable exhibits of lesbian depiction: Lisa Cholodenko's romantic tragi-comedy *The Kids Are All Right* (2010), critically praised but divisive in its postfeminist treatment of lesbian family life; and television's six-season account of middle-class West Hollywood, *The L Word* (2004–2009).[5] Pushing against these heterogeneous banners of either pathologization or homonormativity, *Pariah* and its female-directed international peers, the Iranian-American *Circumstance/Sharayet* (Keshavarz, 2011), the French *Water Lilies/Naissance des pieuvres* (Sciamma, 2007), and Swedish *She Monkeys/Apflickorna* (Aschan, 2011), to name but a few, resist these labels, and in so doing resist the easy categorizations sustained and demanded by an industry whose arthouse as well as blockbuster constituents often remain devoted to genre conventions. From *Pariah* and *Circumstance*, which exhibit the queerness of urban ephemeralities, to *Water Lilies* and *She Monkeys*, which convey the homoeroticism of the tension between discipline and risk that categorizes their sporting cultures, these films elicit an interrogation of their characters' sexualities by way of considering the in-between spaces they occupy as adolescents with desires that are queer because they are not yet named. The films allow their protagonists to linger in their sexual ambiguity and ambivalence. Alike's attempts to be representably queer—stuffing her jeans with a dildo so that she can act the part, for instance—come to parody the genre that *Pariah* knowingly diverts from: the LGBT branded "coming out" branch of the "coming of age" tale.

What makes adolescence an intriguing site of same-sex desire for so many filmmakers is to do with what makes the child strange and the adolescent even stranger: positioned in a time and space of in-between-ness, exploring desire but unable to name it, the scene of adolescence allows for desire between young women to be staged but not constrained by the coherence of a pre-constructed identity. Moreover, as the always failing production of selfhood, adolescence is located somewhat ephemerally in existing theory. "Whilst childhood is seen as a kind of alter-ego for the adult," Alison Waller writes, "there is no theoretical place for the adolescent."[6] The adolescent is placeless, dislocated. Despite the proliferation of images of teenage girls in popular culture, female adolescence in particular has, as Catherine Driscoll writes, "been excluded from theories of modern subjectivity despite being widely employed as both metaphor for modern life and crucial data source for developmental models of identity."[7] It is on screen that so many of these images of teenage girls prevail, and where the homosocial-homosexual lines that are so commonly blurred in adolescence become aesthetically charged.[8] While adolescence is understood as a time of imbalance and potential trauma in the journey toward a projected selfhood, it nonetheless functions to construct, as Driscoll writes, "both childhood and adulthood as relative stabilities" without being properly theorized in its own right.[9]

The introduction to Jerome Hamilton Buckley's 1974 book *Season of Youth*, a much cited work on the *Bildungsroman* (novel of formation or coming of age narrative), is entitled "The Space Between."[10] The third part of Driscoll's account of teen film is entitled "liminal teen film," a title that suggests a mode at the very heart of the genre that is undefinable, between childhood and adolescence.[11] For Alison Waller, it is "a liminal space onto which a distinct dichotomy of desires or fears cannot easily be projected."[12] Adolescence in these theorizations is in-between, placeless, liminal. In all of them its joints—to childhood, to adulthood—are perceived to be dislocated, just as ambiguous queer desires can be dislocated from sexual identity and, in their rendition on the cinema screen, from genre identity.

Adolescents are the exemplars of Elizabeth Freeman's "denizens of time out of joint," dislocated from what is before and after until a time as and when they are deemed to have "come of age," if that coming is ever allowed to happen. Judith Jack Halberstam sees a traditional chart of growth as anathema to girls' experience. "If adolescence for boys represents a rite of passage (much celebrated in Western literature in the form of the *Bildungsroman*) and an ascension to some version (however attenuated) of social power," Halberstam writes, "for girls adolescence is a lesson in restraint, punishment, and repression."[13] For Alike, queer adolescence means just this: for the pariah, a series of lessons in how to relocate, how to be cast back in. Torn between the different modes of girlhood that haunt her—her mother's fear of her lack of girly femininity and her best friend's rejection of it, her father's expectations that no matter what her orientation she will remain his "baby girl"—Alike wrestles with the imprint of her "dyke" identity against her desire to be free from an identity prescribed for her.

Alike is a teenage girl growing up in Brooklyn with her father, mother, and sister. *Pariah* narrates Alike's story through three places that vie for proprietorial rights to her identity. There is the club that opens the narrative, where Alike and her best friend Laura dance, seduce, and compare the numbers they have collected on their phones at the end of the night. There is the home that is presented as alienating; Alike's return to it means a return to chastisement and the imperative to be the girl that her mother wants her to be. The film's third key place is the school in which Alike takes extra classes with her favorite teacher, who listens to her poems and tells her honestly what she thinks of them. Do these places—each one an institution in its own way—come to define Alike? Nearly, if not for the spaces in-between. Foremost of these is the bus ride whose image began this chapter, that transitory space in which Alike passes from the multicolor-filtered utopia of the dance floor to a darkly shot home. The transition is made literal in her changing from cap and baggy shirt to girlish vest and let-down hair. This is an act she completes alone: even Laura is stubbornly ushered from the bus so that the change of clothes, and its necessity, is private (and yet simultaneously necessarily public). It is these spaces—the bus where she changes her clothes, the back room of the bar where she is given a dildo by Laura—that chart Alike's queerness, rather than spaces that self-identify (club: queer; home: straight). Alike negotiates the threshold—a liminal space like the window that provides her mirrored image—between the oppressiveness of domestic space and the lure of urban space, the boundary between self and other, and the erotic fascinations that lie therein. Doreen Massey suggests that, contrary to traditional opinion, the conceptualization of a place—which she defines as a particular articulation, or moment, formed out of the abstraction of space—is not dependent on the construction of boundaries; a place need not be defined "through simple counterposition to the outside" (where the outside is always positioned against, as in *counter* to) but can be formed "precisely through the particularity of linkage *to* that "outside" which is therefore itself part of what constitutes the place."[14] It is this very notion of "linkage" that is at the core of my theorization of queer female adolescence, denoting the threshold between inside and outside that makes possible the queering of space (Figure 6.1).

London Lesbian and Gay Film Festival (now BFI Flare, whose very name voices the provocation inherent in designation) programmer Brian Robinson writes that the success of directors like Lisa Cholodenko is still the exception in an industry in which "lesbian directors remain marginalised."[15] But *Pariah* belongs to a cycle of films that slip past the radar of "lesbian film" because they resist the categorizations that allow them to be reprimanded for being not authentically what their viewers want them to be (representative of all lesbians, of all women of color, of all teenage girls).[16] Recently, the Palme d'Or winning *Blue Is the Warmest Colour/La Vie d'Adèle Chapitres 1 et 2* (Kechiche, 2013) has centered this debate, the question it provokes resounding across the spectrum of media discourse: "is this a lesbian film?"[17] In *Black Swan* and *Mulholland Drive*, we witness journeys of self-discovery occurring via sensationalized episodes of lesbian sex. The sex scene provides a climactic transition point from innocence to experience or from disorientation to identity. This quintessential

Figure 6.1 *Pariah* (Rees, 2011). Alike (Adepero Oduye) rides the bus through Brooklyn in *Pariah*

lesbian narrative (coming out, coming to terms, coming of age), is ironically charted through a verb that signifies *arrival* even though its etymology emphasizes *motion*; the verb has come to signify the *accomplishment* of the movement, just as the "coming of age" genre points to the expectation of an end point at which the protagonist *has come of age*.[18] But despite its prevalent coupling with "coming out" and "coming of age," queer adolescence, as opposed to what we might think of as LGBT adolescence, refuses to arrive. *Pariah*'s sex scene between Alike and Bina (Aasha Davis), the daughter of a friend of her mother's, is intimate, moving, softly lit, and potentially erotic for its red tones, but it does not leave its protagonist in a developed state of awareness: it leaves her disoriented. Bina's rejection is cruel and arguably homophobic—"I'm not *gay* gay," she says, explaining her morning-after cold shoulder—but it also yields a vibrancy of anger and confusion for Alike as she spins in the street outside, a bright yellow scarf around her neck. As she kicks bins over the music on the soundtrack expresses her rage and the cinematography breaks up, through jump cut after jump cut, any notion of a path of growth.

The urban sidewalks of *Pariah* suggest the city as a space that queers adolescence because its rebellions and desires leak, merge, flow *across* sidewalks, *outside* of buildings, *between* people rather than *along* the familiarly constructed path of development.[19] The eponymous act of Michel de Certeau's "Walking in the City," its multiplication and concentration, "makes the city itself an immense social experience of lacking a place."[20] De Certeau's article implies a certain queerness—in placelessness—about the city itself. To return to Massey's theorization of place as a particular articulation, or moment, formed out of the abstraction of space, we might metaphorize "lesbian" as place, identity as a moment in space, and "queer" as that which is placeless, unarticulated, that which remains abstract. This, along with Larry Knopp's adoption of placelessness as "an embodied and material practice" of pleasure rather than of lack, seems to speak in particular to adolescence, where no place is quite one's own, not least of all the bedroom that has the illusion of privacy but remains open to penetration.[21] And so Alike and her friends must share their highs and lows outside of four walls. Although Alike and Bina's desire for one another is consummated in the familiar space of the teenage girl's bedroom, it is learnt on the streets, as they walk together to school at their mothers' insistence. Walking through the city is thus an act of linkage not only between home and school but between repression and resistance, between identities named for us by others and desires unnamable. The linkage encompasses all of these things and adheres to none of them. Ahmed writes that bodies become oriented through "responsiveness to the world around them."[22] The inhabitants of the various homes of *Pariah*—Alike's, Laura's, Bina's—offer these responses pre-made. For these teenage girls the streets of New York become the spaces where romance becomes confused, where heartbreak is manifest in anger, where desire is infused with a responsiveness to the surroundings rather than the walls of an already constructed home.

B. Ruby Rich writes in her review that "when Alike finds love, sex, and rejection all at once, *Pariah* turns explosive."[23] The film does indeed build up to a climactic fight between Alike, her zealous Christian mother Audrey (Kim Wayans), and her protective but blinkered cop father Arthur (Chris Parnell), in which Audrey accuses Arthur of letting their daughter "turn into a man" before them. When Alike enters the scene, the fight becomes physically and emotionally violent. This scene is a narrative manifestation of explosiveness that is elsewhere rendered visual through the film's vibrant use of color. But its sparks linger and it doesn't find its resolution: even as she leaves New York at the end of the film, Alike's relationship with her mother remains tempestuous—"I'll pray for you," Audrey says coldly to her daughter in response to a plea for reconciliation, as they continue to be separated by the framing, which maintains a two-shot that refuses to reunite them visually. Dislocated from her parents as she is, any settling picture of Alike's success in the next stage of her life is withheld from us; that joint is not yet stabilized. The bus ride marks not only the *before* and *after* of Alike's "growth"—bringing her home from the film's opening club scene, taking her away from an oppressive domestic situation—but the *during* of her queerness, a queerness that refuses a singular space in which to belong.

The distributor's website for *Pariah* tells us that the film is "a coming-out story that is also a coming-of-age tale, a much-honored narrative about how men and women learn to be themselves as adults."[24] And indeed the film's director, first-timer Dee Rees, adheres to this model: when describing the motives behind the film's aesthetic style, Rees says in interview that "as we get toward the end of the film it opens up [...] Alike is a butterfly she's in a cocoon."[25] Rees describes moments like the one in which Alike pulls the curtains away from her window as symbolic of her breaking away from the confines of her familial background, and simultaneously of opening up from inside her cocoon. As Alike moves toward self-definition "the shots open up," Rees says.[26] For all the beauty of Rees' spatial metaphor, however, it buys into a narrative of growth that I think the film itself manages to avoid. It is precisely a resistance to growth that marks *Pariah* and its contemporaries as different, in their eschewing of the coming out and coming of age cycles that marks so many narratives of teenage "development."

Halberstam's *In a Queer Time and Place* takes a stance in opposition to growth that operates the strategy of positioning that resonates through this chapter: "queers participate in subcultures far longer than their heterosexual counterparts," Halberstam writes, in a bold delineation of distinct queer and heterosexual "parts" (one which is "countered" to the other).[27] But *Pariah* is queer not simply because it sees its protagonist rejecting the oppressiveness of her heteronormative family upbringing. As this chapter has demonstrated, I am more interested in Freeman's terminology, that which describes, in another spatial metaphor, queers as "denizens of times out of joint" and, as such, as "a subjugated class [...] even as many of us occupy other positions of power including the economic."[28] Here is the adolescent as queer—not only because homosexual, but because a denizen of "time out of joint." *Pariah*'s characters' inabilities to name their desires allow for imaginative aesthetic and diegetic framings of the incoherence of desire at an age of broader incoherence and instability.

In this film neither the process of "coming out" nor the state of "having come out" can resolve. In a late scene, Alike stands on the roof of Laura's building, where she is staying following the fight with her parents. In the background the wide yellowed sky is overexposed and yields a sense of openness and potential. In the foreground Alike, and the figure of her father, stand looking away from each other. They discuss Alike's childhood, the house she grew up in. Her father's nostalgia for the space of origin is cut short by Alike's admission that she will not be coming back home. In Massey's theorization, home is not the imagined space of "security of a (false, as we have seen) stability and an apparently reassuring boundedness."[29] Indeed in *Pariah* and other films of the period the home is a space of high drama in which relationships are compromised because of the prior conviction of domestic stability.[30] *Pariah* avoids making home safe again; it avoids allowing its protagonist to come full circle into the arms of a loving family that accepts her for who she really is. In this penultimate scene the daughter and father never share the frame. The openness of the rooftop sky at sunset, which could serve to sentimentalize, instead suggests something too broad to be pinned down in reconciliation or recognition.

Rich's Sundance review of *Pariah* continues: "[t]he tone is tragicomic, the genre is coming-of-age, and the execution is impeccable."[31] Notably, in a version of the same paragraph on *Pariah* that made it into her anthology *New Queer Cinema: The Director's Cut*, Rich writes that *Pariah*'s "tone is tragicomic, the exaction impeccable."[32] In this subtle re-writing *Pariah* is still about "agency not abjection," still about "New York's mean streets"; Dee Rees still has "Scorsese in her blood."[33] But the film as a coming-of-age tale? Rich is no longer so sure. Time itself evidently reconfigures our ease with the assumption of identities (ours, the film's, its protagonist's). "The concept of identity as a process of 'becoming'", writes Hilary Radner, "has been understood as offering emancipatory possibilities to the individual who is invited, not to take up a stable, untested and fixed position, but, rather, to see her 'self', or even 'selves', as subject to a multiple and on-going process of revision, reform and choices."[34] The notion of becoming still positions its (ever revising) subject in a process of coming (to a place). The city in *Pariah* forestalls this process, allowing Alike to move about with a sense of placelessness, finalized in a closing scene that does not close but opens up (first a wide sky, then a bus journey). The contradictions of Alike's concluding poem—"open to the possibilities within/ pushing out […] I am broken/I am open"—attest to the contradictions of this search for subjectivity and locatedness. "How [do] we extend through our bodies into the world," Ahmed asks in the passage quoted at the beginning of this chapter. The queer adolescent as pariah complicates this extension (where is the join from outcast to in-cast?); our bodies (if still in formation and not yet "ours"); the world (as perceived by whom, if always in a state of representation, figuration, discovery?) The coming-of-age genre is charted through a verb that signifies arrival. But queer adolescence—or, as a metaphorical palindrome, "adolescent queerness," continually running back (and forth) again—is dislocated from the temporal and spatial joins of the genre's motive verb. Queer adolescence refuses to arrive.

Notes

1. "Pariah," *Focus Features*, (2011) http://www.focusfeatures.com/pariah [accessed December 9, 2013].

2. Sara Ahmed, *Queer Phenomenology: Orientations, Objects, Others* (Durham, NC: Duke University Press, 2006), pp. 67–68.

3. Elizabeth Freeman, *Time Binds: Queer Temporalities, Queer Histories* (Durham, NC: Duke University Press, 2010), p. 19.

4. Glen Elder, Lawrence Knopp and Heidi Nast, "Sexuality and Space," in *Geography in America at the Dawn of the 21st Century* edited by Gary L. Gaile and Cort J. Willmott (Oxford: Oxford University Press, 2006), pp. 200–208 (203).

5. See Clara Bradbury-Rance, "Querying Postfeminism in Lisa Cholodenko's *The Kids Are All Right*," in *Postfeminism and Contemporary Hollywood Cinema* edited by Joel Gwynne and Nadine Muller (Basingstoke: Palgrave Macmillan, 2013), pp. 27–43.

6. Alison Waller, *Constructing Adolescence in Fantastic Realism* (New York: Routledge, 2009), p. 5.

7. Catherine Driscoll, *Girls: Feminine Adolescence in Popular Culture & Cultural Theory* (New York: Columbia University Press, 2002), p. 9.

8. Alongside LGBT favorites like *All Over Me* (Sichel, 1997) and *The Incredibly True Adventure of Two Girls in Love* (Maggenti, 1995), other films that explore girls' friendship and desire include *Foxfire* (Haywood-Carter, 1996) and its 2012 remake *Foxfire* (Cantet, 2012) and *Thirteen* (Hardwicke, 2003) to name but a few.

9. Driscoll, *Girls*, p. 6.

10. Jerome Hamilton Buckley, *Season of Youth: The Bildungsroman from Dickens to Golding* (Cambridge, MA: Harvard University Press, 1974).

11. Catherine Driscoll, *Teen Film: A Critical Introduction* (Oxford: Berg, 2011).

12. Waller, *Constructing Adolescence in Fantastic Realism*, p. 6.

13. Judith Halberstam, "Oh Bondage up Yours! Female Masculinity and the Tomboy," in *Curiouser: On the Queerness of Children* edited by Steven Bruhm and Natasha Hurley (Minneapolis: University of Minnesota Press, 2004), pp. 191–214 (194).

14. Doreen B. Massey, *Space, Place and Gender* (Cambridge: Polity Press, 1994), p. 155.

15. Brian Robinson, "The Pride and the Passion: 25 Years of the London Lesbian and Gay Film Festival," *Sight and Sound* (April 2011) http://www.bfi.org.uk/sightandsound/feature/49705 [accessed August 21, 2011].

16. Jessie Daniels expresses concern that films like *Pariah* paint "a picture of a claustrophobic, hostile, and homophobic family that the lead character, Alike, must navigate away from in order to survive" and as such become stand-ins for generalizations of black lesbian life tout court.
    Jessie Daniels, "Black Lesbians: Visible, Not Pariahs," *GLQ* 19:2 (2013), 261–263.

17. For a cross-section of reviews, see for example: Joanna Benecke, "Why Don't Cinemas and Directors Show Proper Lesbian Sex Scenes?," *The Guardian* (November 14, 2013) http://www.theguardian.com/film/2013/nov/14/lesbian-film-blue-is-the-warmest-colour [accessed November 19, 2013]; Marcie Bianco, "Review: Is 'Blue Is the Warmest Color'" a 'Lesbian Film'?," *After*

Ellen (October 25, 2013) http://www.afterellen.com/blue-is-the-warmest-color-comes-stateside/10/2013/ [accessed December 5, 2013]; Manohla Dargis, "Seeing You Seeing Me: The Trouble with 'Blue Is the Warmest Color,'" *The New York Times* (October 25, 2013) http://www.nytimes.com/2013/10/27/movies/the-trouble-with-blue-is-the-warmest-color.html?_r=1& [accessed November 19, 2013].

18. OED Online.
19. There is an even more acute sense of this in a film released in the same year as *Pariah*, Maryam Keshavarz's *Circumstance*, set in Iran.
20. Michel de Certeau, *The Practice of Everyday Life*, trans. by Steven Rendell (Berkeley: University of California Press, 1984), p. 103.
21. Larry Knopp, "From Lesbian and Gay to Queer Geographies: Pasts, Prospects and Possibilities," in *Geographies of Sexualities: Theory, Practices, and Politics* edited by Kath Browne, Jason Lim, and Gavin Brown (Aldershot; Burlington, VT: Ashgate, 2007), pp. 21–28 (23).
22. Ahmed, *Queer Phenomenology*, pp. 8–9.
23. B. Ruby Rich, "Park City Remix," *Film Quarterly* 64 (2011), 62–65 (62).
24. "*Pariah*'s Team Remembers Their Coming of Age Stories," *Focus Features*, (January 9, 2012) http://www.focusfeatures.com/slideshow/pariahs_team_remembers_their_coming_of_age_stories?film=pariah [accessed December 9, 2013].
25. "*Pariah* + Q&A—Video," *BFI Live*, (2011) http://www.bfi.org.uk/live/video/751 [accessed December 9, 2013].
26. Ibid.
27. Judith Halberstam, *In a Queer Time and Place: Transgender Bodies, Subcultural Lives* (New York: New York University Press, 2005), p. 174.
28. Freeman, *Time Binds*, p. 19.
29. Massey, *Space, Place and Gender*, p. 169.
30. See *The Kids Are All Right* and the rest of Cholodenko's oeuvre.
31. Rich, 62–65.
32. B. Ruby Rich, *New Queer Cinema: The Director's Cut* (Durham, NC: Duke University Press, 2013), p. 278.
33. Ibid., p. 278.
34. Hilary Radner, *Neo-Feminist Cinema: Girly Films, Chick Flicks and Consumer Culture* (New York: Routledge, 2011), p. 6.

7

Bye-Bye to Betty's Blues and "La Bonne Meuf": Temporal Drag and Queer Subversions of the Rom-Com in *Bye Bye Blondie* (Virginie Despentes, 2011)

Lara Cox

When *Bye Bye Blondie* (Despentes, 2011) debuted in cinemas in 2011, critics were surprised by the uncharacteristically sentimental turn that the film's director appeared to have taken. As reviewer Jordan Mintzer summarized, this was a "more accessible sophomore effort" than the ultra-violent, rape revenge movie *Baise-moi* (Despentes, 2000) that made Despentes a feminist *enfant terrible* among fans of contemporary French pop culture.[1] As a novelist, director, and essayist, Despentes has become known as part of a third-wave anarcho-feminism in France. From her critical essay/manifesto *King Kong Théorie* (2006) to *Baise-moi* and her documentary on queer pornography *Mutantes* (2009), Despentes is not known to shy away from controversy, focusing on tropes of sex positivity and women's capacity for violence as a source of empowerment. Her films have been associated with the rise of an ultra-violent genre of "new extremism" in Europe while her explicit representations of women's sexuality have earned her a place alongside other sex positive feminists in France such as Wendy Delorme and Emilie Jouvet.[2] By contrast, *Bye Bye Blondie* unexpectedly seemed to curry favor with a generic mainstay of commercialized cinema (albeit with a lesbian twist): the romantic comedy. Diane Negra observes a common "enchantment effect" in films such as *Bridget Jones's Diary* (Mcguire, 2001), *13 Going on 30* (Winick, 2004), and TV series *Sex and the City* (1998–2004), which connects the rom-com genre to the ideals of the postfeminist *Zeitgeist*: "Over and over again the postfeminist subject is represented as having lost herself but then (re)achieving stability through romance, de-aging, a makeover, by giving up paid work, or coming home".[3] In accordance with this description, *Bye Bye Blondie*'s heroine Frances (Emanuelle Béart) renounces a faltering television career to reunite with someone whom she terms the "big one," her teenage sweetheart Gloria (Béatrice Dalle). In the film's closing shots, Frances's sham husband (a closeted gay novelist) encapsulates the film's principal theme of willful abandonment for the sake of love: "[Frances] was losing everything and she didn't care."

In this chapter, I propose three main ways in which *Bye Bye Blondie*, depicting the rekindling of an adolescent romance, makes a return to a past "girlishness" for its two heroines Frances and Gloria: via the film's use of intertextuality, punk, and flashback. I place "girlishness" in quotation marks to signal the way the film itself constructs the attributes of girlhood as discursive and mobile, able to be appropriated for transgressive purposes. The film mobilizes female adolescence for a reflection on the norms of female adulthood and the two heroines' chance for escape from these norms. I argue that Despentes, not one to renege on a radical counterpatriarchal position, mobilizes the three motifs of intertextuality, punk, and flashback in a way that diverges from what Sadie Wearing describes as the "simultaneously necessary and impossible" form of rejuvenation that determines postfeminist representation and makes girlishness desirable for adult women within a consumer culture that promises youth can be acquired. As Wearing elucidates, Hollywood rom-coms such as *Something's Gotta Give* (Meyers, 2003) and makeover programs such as *10 Years Younger* (UK, 2004–present) exhibit a "deference to quite rigid demarcations of the appropriate, the decorous, and the 'natural'";[4] maturing women are expected to act out assigned roles of mother, wife, grandmother, et cetera while still striving toward a cult of youth. Though there is a double-pull between young and aging femininities in *Bye Bye Blondie*, the film's intertextual reference to the past girlishness of *37° 2 le matin/Betty Blue* (Beineix, 1986) allows both heroines to *reject* an "age-appropriate" motherhood, and punk and flashback serve to jettison Frances's obsessive preoccupation with a broader notion of "the future" in its normative guise. I argue that *Bye Bye Blondie* thus conjures the past in a way that appeals to what Elizabeth Freeman dubs queer "temporal drag," which she defines as "the tug backward as a potentially transformative part of movement itself."[5] In temporal drag, a past time frame is recuperated in the present not for the purposes of shoring up an ideal of youthful feminine beauty. Rather, it serves the purpose of creating an open-ended version of futurity, disrupting "the appropriate, the decorous, and the 'natural' " for aging women (Wearing) or what Freeman similarly terms "chrononormativity," "the use of time to organize individual human bodies toward maximum productivity"—the nexus where ideologies of capitalism, the family, and linear (normative, generational) temporality meet.[6] Prioritizing queer time via intertextuality, punk, and flashback, Despentes's latest film thus subverts the codes of the romantic comedy, the very generic mold in which it sets itself.

Bye Bye *Betty Blue*

While Despentes's *Baise-moi* deployed a "designer violence" that parodied Quentin Tarantino's *Pulp Fiction* (1994) the violence of *Bye Bye Blondie* similarly remembers a cult classic, this time of Gallic descent: *37°2 Le Matin/Betty Blue* (Beineix, 1986).[7] The alliterative common ground of *Betty Blue* and *Bye Bye Blondie* hints at this intertextuality, and the casting of Béatrice Dalle in both films, two and a half decades apart, makes the overlap explicit. "Temporal drag" therefore occurs first on an inter-diegetic level: we are prompted to reflect on the slippage between a gamine Dalle in her characterization as Betty and her older adult counterpart as Gloria in *Bye Bye Blondie*. This reflection is encouraged, additionally, when turning to Despentes's novel *Bye Bye Blondie* (Paris: Grasset, 2004) on which the 2011 film is based, since the heroine Gloria in the book resembles Betty of Beneix's film to a striking degree. Gloria, in Despentes's novel, is given to uncontrollable outbursts of fury, which begin in her teens. She is not the lover of Frances but Eric, and the reunion of the heterosexual couple in adulthood, in sharp contrast to the film, only serves to worsen the heroine's all-consuming vitriolic attacks, as she is eventually swept away by her own anger and violently assaults her partner (e.g., "[s]eized [...] by a kind of giant hand [...] that obscures everyone else's point of view").[8] This act only stresses the heroine's position of social and economic vulnerability, as she decides to leave her partner but is forced to return to him out of pecuniary concerns. Similarly, the eponymous character of *Betty Blue* is prone to outbursts of rage and destruction, at one point setting her partner Zorg's house ablaze. As with Despentes's novelistic Gloria, the violence acted out by Betty is ultimately self-harming and self-defeating: the character, distraught after a miscarriage, drives out her own eye.

While the casting of Dalle in Despentes's film recalls for viewers Gloria's links to the hapless Betty, *Bye Bye Blondie* depicts a form of women's violence that stands apart from the self-punishing, miscarrying "failed mother" of Beneix's cult classic. Dalle's Gloria is only once driven to aggression in adult life, as she sublimates her impulses via the creation of metal sculptures, a material that complements her mental resilience. Indeed, no longer "the over-heated tantrum artist riffing off a cheesecake writer-drifter" Zorg of *Betty Blue*, Dalle-as-Gloria harnesses her tendency toward violence to defend the rights of those less fortunate during her one outburst in the film.[9] She overhears a conversation at a party peopled by Frances's self-important, television-industry entourage and is enraged by one of the guests' disdain for a notion of communitarianism, instructing the nameless partygoer to "shut your mouth" prior to slapping the man who steps in to defend his apolitical partner and storming out of the scene. Gloria thus uses violence only when she deems it necessary (to avenge social iniquity) in a way that transgresses patriarchal norms of femininity as passive and nonviolent, and she resists rebounding upon an implication of "feminine hysteria" that both the eponymous character of *Betty Blue* and Gloria in Despentes's original novel risk in the uncontrollable nature of their outbursts. The intertextual reference to *Betty Blue* in Despentes's film may thus be seen as a spectral "girlish" violence that Gloria—a "grown-up Betty" of sorts—successfully manages to reconfigure in adulthood to a queer temporal alternative to her predecessor Betty, whose failure to conform to the chrononormative role of mother (following her miscarriage) was the root cause of her turn of violence inward. Dalle's Gloria flouts all concerns for her circumscription within a temporally "decorous" motherhood: her aggression enables her to protect the under-privileged in society in the party scene, and elsewhere, in the sublimation of this same tendency, to create a makeshift metal haven for her and Frances in the latter's capacious condominium. These two caretaking roles make no particular allusion to motherhood.

The rejection of an "age-appropriate" maternity is further underscored in *Bye Bye Blondie* when considering the intertextual reference to *Betty Blue* in conjunction with the character of Frances. At first reticent to draw attention to her lesbian relationship and angered by her partner's violent act of retribution in the aforementioned party scene, Frances chastises Gloria: "Violence is the language of idiots, Gloria." Gloria rejoins: "But the violence is all on your side, Frances." While this retort at first appears surprising given the latter's ostensible absence of violence, the film's intertextual reference to the miscarrying, self-annihilating character of *Betty Blue* gestures toward another more diffuse, systemic form of violence visited upon women that Frances, similar to Betty, is at first willing to tolerate. Kathy O'Dell coins the phrase "everyday masochisms," the "acts of self-deprecation, denial of hunger in the name of beauty, suppression of anger for the sake of peace, and so on," to describe this type of violence.[10] Frances accepts the progressive bid by her television bosses to move her to a twee farmer's program, where she will enact the role of docile, motherly presenter complete with tractor and token toddler atop her knee, having been judged to be of an age where it is no longer expedient for her to be in the role of high-flying chat show host. Spurred on by the risk of losing Gloria at the end of the film, however, Frances emulates her lover's actions of the earlier party scene, as she punches her manager who promises disingenuously to meet to discuss the star's future. While Frances may choose to forsake her career for love—a typical motif of the romantic comedy (recalling Negra's description of the "enchantment effect")—it is therefore important to contextualize this decision in the postfeminist ideology that she actively rejects at the same time: the maternal future planned for her by her bosses. Frances thus joins Gloria in referencing the violence of the girlish Betty; crucially, both characters leverage such aggression to evade the chrononormative dictates that led to their predecessor's demise, enlisting temporal drag to reject motherhood.

Farewell to "the Future": Punk and Flashback

As the foregoing description indicates, the most significant intra-diegetic transformation in *Bye Bye Blondie* is undergone by Frances. This second part of the chapter discusses the ways in which the character's concern for a chrononormative "future"—that is, one tied to ideologies of heteronormativity and capitalism—are gradually derailed by way of punk and flashback. Frances, whose prospects in television are rapidly deteriorating as she reaches middle age, resembles the postfeminist subject who is "time-starved," "rushed, harassed, subject to her 'biological clock' in a permanent 'state of chronic temporal crisis.'"[11] She hectically splits her time between social engagements, private yoga lessons, and her television job. Although discontented and suffering the effects of this pressured lifestyle, the character does not outwardly object to her aging fate in television, as it is only at the end of the film, as we saw, that she seeks violent retribution for being forced out of her job. Frances is also deeply preoccupied with adhering to a standard of heteronormative femininity. When Gloria re-enters her life, she is reticent to draw attention to the relationship, preferring instead to uphold a public façade of being happily married to her novelist- husband.

The first way in which *Bye Bye Blondie* destabilizes Frances's chrononormative priorities is by way of punk music, which is coded triply in this film as queer, adolescent, and temporally chaotic (the soundtrack blends tunes from the 1970s and 1980s, such as The Ruts's *Babylon is Burning*, with contemporary artists such as Déborah Dégouts).[12] We are first introduced to the punk motif by way of a teenage Gloria, played by actress and musician Soko. Gloria expresses her love of the anti-establishmentarian music genre as a means of separating herself from her family and society, embodying a broader disaffection of the young adult generation of the 1980s living with the consequences of François Mitterrand's flagging socialist government.[13] Judged as needing to be "fixed" for her punkish tastes, the teenager is interned in a psychiatric institution where she meets Frances. Indexed from this point on in the film as adolescent, punk nonetheless remains a lifelong pursuit for Gloria and it instills a sense of temporal circularity at several points in the film. For instance, after her violent outburst during the party scene (described earlier), Gloria hastens to a punk club with Véro, the only member of Frances's entourage to appreciate the former's unabashed demeanor. As the pair dance among a crowd of mixed- and same-gendered pairings, they recall an earlier scene in which Gloria's teenage punk entourage festively dance around a car, drinking and smoking, while heteronormative codes fail to figure.

Punk progressively injects queer temporal circularity into Frances's life too. While a teenage Frances (Clara Ponsot) endeavors to impress Gloria with her love of punk-rock giants The Stooges and David Bowie, her taste for the genre remains secondary to other priorities. Unlike Gloria, a teenage Frances prefers not to assume punkish attire—towering hairstyles, heavy eye makeup, and tattoos and piercings—and instead wears clothing (jeans and T-shirts) that afford her gender-normative invisibility in society. A teenage Frances eventually renounces all ties to the punk genre and her relationship with Gloria. Chrononormativity—a wish to have a successful "future," career, and, as we later learn, a marriage—is at the heart of her decision. After the arrest of both teenagers following an incident of punkish antics in their hometown of Nancy, she writes to Gloria: "I cannot jeopardize *my future*, especially not for a summer fling" (my emphasis). Yet, decades on and entrapped in a stuffy lifestyle that ultimately has left her unhappy, Frances gains a new appreciation for punk rebellion when Gloria re-enters her adult life and comes to live with the chat show host and her husband. During one scene, Gloria unapologetically turns up her music to maximum volume while creating her metal sculptures. When the husband tries to complain about Gloria's disruptive demeanor, Frances tersely answers: "She is punk rock. [...] that's what I like." These words recall Gloria's similarly expressed dismissal of a therapist's suggestion decades before of her failure to conform to the codes of (passive) femininity with exhibitionist clothing and makeup: "I am punk." An insouciant punk discourse, transferred from an adolescent Gloria to an adult Frances, enables the television presenter to impugn the "future" that she had wished for before and which is now an unhappy reality: married, heteronormative life. Harkening back to (Gloria's) queer adolescence in adulthood, she refuses to bow to the demands of her husband.

But the resurrection of a punk past in the present is not only hinted at in *Bye Bye Blondie* via discursive repetition; it is also explicitly brought into existence via the film's extensive use of flashback, the final motif in our analysis. Past and present intersect in this film constantly and unceasingly. Both time frames occupy approximately half of the film's 90-minute duration, with eight flashback sequences in total. Emulating what Freeman describes as the "linear, serial, and end-directed time" of chrononormativity, flashback initially functions to elucidate the present-day plot.[14] Our first encounter with the past occurs when Gloria and Frances meet for the first time in decades in a scene in Gloria's local watering hole in Nancy. Cutting to a flashback sequence, a teenage Gloria (Soko) writhes on the floor, screaming in protest after a dispute with her father that turns violent. Her seizure occasions her tranquillization and institutionalization. Gloria's teenage all-black gothic-punk outfit is sharply contrasted with Frances's in adulthood as, in a flash-forward, the camera shifts focus to the latter in an all-white ensemble on the television screen in the Nancy bar. As the locals watch Gloria's ex on the television screen, Frances coincidentally walks into the bar, again clad in white. This reinforces the opposition between her and Gloria who, in this present-day setting, wears dark clothing, recalling her punk past. Frances's outfit is reminiscent of the lab-coat clad clinicians shown in flashback sequence who had tried (and failed) to make Gloria acquiesce in her teenage years. The calibration of Frances with Gloria's psychiatric oppressors in this first intersection between flashback and the present day preempts the television presenter's decision to ditch Gloria for conformism, a career, and her "future" later in the film.

Toward the end of the film, however, flashback begins to *derail* the current-day plot, diverging from a conventional use of the device as a means to make sense of the present.[15] In the club scene following the party (described earlier), Gloria reveals her utter contempt for Frances's preoccupation with (capitalist) chrononormativity: "When are we going to have fun? *I'm sick and tired of your office hours*" (my emphasis). The couple separate, furious with one another, against a musical backdrop in which two singers repeat the line "With time, everything, everything disappears," both in French and English. The lyric stresses the value of the past, as an evanescent phenomenon, functioning as a powerful counterweight to Frances's obsession with "the future." Further privileging a recuperation of the past, the camera cuts briefly to a teenage Gloria resting her head on Frances's shoulder in blissful repose, followed by a flash-forward to a lone and despondent Frances sitting in the metal shelter that her lover had constructed for them. It is this fleeting glimpse of adolescent felicity that spurs on the film's *dénouement*, causing Frances to reject her manager's empty promise to talk about her maternally inflected future in television in a way that closely resembles Freeman's exegesis on moments of temporal drag "when an established temporal order gets interrupted and new encounters consequently take place."[16] Frances is arrested for her violent attack on her manager and, as she is taken away in handcuffs, she casts Gloria, who looks at the scene from afar, a knowing glance. The camera then switches to a scene in which the pair, at another point in time but still in adulthood, are in bed together, locked in a lovers' embrace. The grainy, hand-held shots in this latter scene connote nostalgic longing, as the same camera setting had been used at previous points in the film to depict the teenagers' happiness in amongst the Nancy punk crowd.

The camera configuration implies an imagined return to adolescent fluidity in the present, which is to become a reality in the next scene when Frances is released from custody. Gloria, in this penultimate scene, waits anxiously outside the police station, and rushes to kiss her lover when she emerges. The moment critically apes the classic "reunion scene" of the romantic comedy genre, as a male paparazzi contingent snaps salaciously away at the lesbian embrace. This demonstrates the film's awareness of a hetero-patriarchal recuperation of the love story that it tells and it further separates *Bye Bye Blondie* from postfeminist representation that Negra and Tasker describe, citing examples such as the glamorized, Los Angeles-based series *The L Word* as corroboration, as "absolutely reject[ing] lesbianism in all but its most guy-friendly forms."[17] Prioritizing instead a queer "folded temporal order [...] in which beginnings and endings touch," the pair's reunion merges past and present time frames as the camera shifts to a grainy shot of a teenage Gloria and Frances dancing to punk music, before returning to the kissing couple in present-day Paris. This sets the stage for a queered version of "the future" in the final scene. While romantic comedies from *Four Weddings and a Funeral* (Newell, 1994) to *Sex and the City* conclude with a strictly dyadic reunion between the couple concerned, it is with *faux-husband* in tow that *Bye Bye Blondie*'s Gloria and Frances are chauffeured away (with the Eiffel Tower forming the backdrop to the film's parting tableau). The future that is implied for Frances and Gloria, having no truck with either heteronormativity *or* a homonormative equivalent, is an open-ended, uncertain one (emphasized by Pete Doherty's nihilistic song "Fuck Forever" playing in the background), which is filled with the possibility of alternative forms of kinship and love.

Conclusion

Bye Bye Blondie, we have seen, corrodes the parameter between adolescent and adult femininities and it unmoors the character of Frances in particular from the "appropriate, the decorous, and 'the natural',"[18] disrupting the chrononormative roles of wife and maternal television presenter that were earmarked for this character at the start of the film. Indeed, the restoration of queer girlhood is brought into sharp relief with a concluding reflection on the shifting significance of the title *Bye Bye Blondie* from the original novel to film. In the novel, "Blondie" refers to Gloria. Eric, Gloria's maladroit partner who induces the heroine's increasingly destructive behavior, assigns the affectionate nickname to his lover, in a reference to her hair color and, additionally, to the punk songstress of the same name. The novel's farewell to "Blondie," rather ominously, denotes the demise of Gloria's punk, adolescent-inflected freedom, as she is forced to return to Eric, their waning relationship notwithstanding: "[S]he was home, here, in her place, beside him. What she didn't know, however, was what they would need to do to make this living arrangement *minimally viable*" (my emphasis).[19] By contrast, "Blondie" in Despentes's film connotes Frances, not the raven-haired Gloria. Frances, it is implied, dyes her hair in later years, possibly for the sake of the television industry and its circumscribed definition of feminine beauty, as the adolescent Frances is pointedly brunette. Instead of bidding farewell to adolescence, then, as in the novel, it is *adulthood*, at least in its chrononormative guise, that is cast aside in the film. Girlhood recaptured in adult life serves to banish the omnipresent figure of "la bonne meuf" ("the good woman") in France, a figure that Despentes acerbically condemns in her feminist treatise, *King Kong Théorie* (Paris: Grasset, 2006). Frances, as a television presenter about to be demoted due to her aging status, recalls the "white woman, seductive but not a whore, married but not effaced, working without succeeding too much" disdainfully described by Despentes in this work.[20] Shedding the trappings of this ascription via queer rejuvenation, Despentes's rom-com, in sum, constitutes a "bye-bye" to "la bonne meuf."

Notes

1. Jordan Mintzer, "Bye Bye Blondie: Film Review," *The Hollywood Reporter* (March 29, 2012) online.
2. Despentes's documentary *Mutantes* (2009) could be compared to *Too Much Pussy, Feminist Sluts, A Queer X Show* (2010), directed by Emilie Jouvet and starring Wendy Delorme. Both focus on the importance of queer redefinitions of pornography on women's own terms free from patriarchal norms.

3. Diane Negra, *What a Girl Wants? Fantasizing the Reclamation of Self in Postfeminism* (London: Routledge, 2009), p. 5.
4. Sadie Wearing, "Subjects of Rejuvenation: Aging in Postfeminist Culture," in *Interrogating Postfeminism: Gender and the Politics of Popular Culture* edited by Diane Negra and Yvonne Tasker, (Durham, NC: Duke University Press, 2007), p. 278.
5. Elizabeth Freeman, *Time Binds: Queer Temporalities, Queer Histories* (Durham, NC: Duke University Press, 2010), p. 93.
6. Ibid., p. 3.
7. Lisa Downing, "*Baise-moi* or the Ethics of the Desiring Gaze," *Nottingham French Studies* 45:3 (2006), 54.
8. Virginie Despentes, *Bye Bye Blondie* (Paris: Grasset, 2004), p. 220, translation mine.
9. John Orr, "Stranded: Stardom and the Free-fall Movie in French Cinema, 1985–2003," *Studies in French Cinema* 4:2 (2004), p. 105.
10. Kathy O'Dell, *Contract with the Skin: Masochism, Performance Art, and the 1970s* (Minneapolis: University of Minnesota Press, 1998), pp. 33–34.
11. Negra and Tasker, "Introduction," *Interrogating Postfeminism*, p. 10.
12. For more on the interconnection between girlhood, queerness, and punk in the Anglo-American context, see Halberstam's and Freeman's commentaries on the Riot Grrrl movement at the dawn of the 1990s. Judith (Jack) Halberstam, *In A Queer Time and Place: Transgender Bodies, Subcultural Lives* (New York: New York University Press, 2005), pp. 170–174. Freeman, *Time Binds*, pp. 59–94.
13. Michèle Schaal, "Virginie Despentes or a French Third Wave of Feminism?," in *Cherchez La Femme: Women and Values in the Francophone World* edited by Adrienne Angelo and Erika Fülöp (Newcastle: Cambridge Scholars Press, 2011), p. 49.
14. Freeman, *Time Binds*, p. 40.
15. As Simon Foster notes on the film's use of flashback, "neither story [. . .] fully defines either the young or old protagonists in their own right," which this critic sees as a flaw. Foster, "Lesbian Love Affair a Little Light on Depth," http://www.sbs.com.au/films/movie/15184/bye-bye-blondie, accessed October 3, 2013.
16. Freeman, *Time Binds*, p. xxii.
17. Negra and Tasker, "Introduction," p. 21.
18. Wearing, "Subjects of Rejuvenation," p. 278.
19. Despentes, *Bye Bye Blondie*, p. 225.
20. Despentes, *King Kong Théorie* (Paris: Grasset, 2006), p. 13.

Part III

Sonic Youth: Girlhood, Music, and Identity

8

"Chica Dificil": Music, Identity, and Agency in *Real Women Have Curves* (Patricia Cardoso, 2002)

Tim McNelis

Youth films made in the United States typically focus on a white, middle-class, suburban coming-of-age experience. Any nod toward diversity tends to be a token gesture, and rebellious girls often conform to traditional gender roles by the film's end. Few films explore the experiences of Latina/o youth in the United States, although the number has grown in recent years.[1] Such films consider how ethnicity, class, gender, language, and sexuality form a space in which teens navigate the implications of a hybrid identity and deal with more complex issues than those of the average teen film protagonist. While scholars such as Charles Ramírez Berg[2] and Angharad N. Valdivia[3] have respectively provided excellent studies of Latina/os in film specifically and media more generally, little attention has been paid to the significant role film music plays in representing young Latina/os and constructing their complex and varied identities.

An interesting film to consider with regard to music's construction of hybrid Latina identity is *Real Women Have Curves* (Patricia Cardoso, 2002). This film tells the coming-of-age story of Ana Garcia (America Ferrera), a second-generation Mexican American who lives with her extended family in East Los Angeles. The film follows Ana's life as she is pulled by two opposing forces: the desire to go to Columbia University and the duty to fulfil the wishes of her family by working in her sister Estela's (Ingrid Oliu) dress factory. After Ana quits her fast food job on the last day of school, her mother Carmen (Lupe Ontiveros) insists that she goes to work in Estela's factory. Ana initially resists, complaining about the heat in the factory and the exploitation of the workers. However, her judgment is met with strong protest from the women who are proud of the work they do and think Ana is a snob. Ana ultimately learns to take pride in her work at the factory as she begins to take pride in her own body and mind.

Real Women is an independent film based on a stage play of the same name, written by Josefina Lopez, who also co-wrote the screenplay. According to Linda C. McClain, Lopez "drew on her experiences as an undocumented worker in her sister's East Los Angeles sewing factory, in which Lopez's mother and an older sister also worked."[4] In the film version, the focus was shifted from Estela and the factory to Ana and her experiences, and Carmen was turned into "a more antagonistic figure."[5] In addition, the play featured a more in-depth examination of immigration and citizenship issues.[6] As a film, *Real Women* does not abandon issues of immigration and citizenship altogether, but rather moves these issues from the foreground to the background, instead using them to modify challenges typically faced by (often white) teenage girls in mainstream youth films.

It is important to understand the relationship between identity and music in this film for a number of reasons. First of all, the focus on a Latina girl who does not fit the white stereotype of feminine beauty and yet has a high level of agency is very unusual in the world of teen films. In addition, her family background, elite education, and ambitions for college place her in an interesting cultural space that is partially constructed and commented on by *Real Women*'s soundtrack. The film uses a mix of Latin American musical styles to score Ana's experiences, and her hybrid identity parallels the hybridity of this music. Thus, the use of a variety of Latin styles in *Real Women* does not simply reinforce a generalized idea of Ana's ethnicity or the film's location in East Los Angeles. Rather, it foregrounds her existence in a mix of cultures. The songs that accompany important moments in Ana's story tend to be more modern fusions with elements of rock, reggae, and electronic music, and those that represent her parents are often more traditional in style. While I acknowledge that "traditional" is a relative and somewhat problematic term, I will be using it throughout this chapter to refer to identifiable musical styles that, despite being present in modern forms, were already established by the early- to mid-twentieth century.

As Steven H. Cooper and Adrienne Harris state, "the film brims with the complex mixes of speech patterns, accents, languages and cultures, the hybridity of modern and postmodern immigrant and urban life."[7] *Real Women* does not present difference from the white middle class as "Other," arguably due to the perspectives of the writer and director. Rather, Ana is presented as belonging to a mix of cultures. She is smart but is not a nerd. She has curves but is not undesirable. She is Latina but is not Other. Considering the Latina stereotypes historically presented in films, Ana's characterization is in many ways progressive.[8] She comes from a working-class immigrant family but is headed for higher education. Her class mobility suggests hybridity and empowerment, but this privileged path is not without its complications. Jillian M. Báez argues that "Ana places liberal American feminism at odds with the gendered and racialized ways of life" of the women working in the factory, and that "this marks a new kind of *Latinidad feminista*—one that demonstrates the social hierarchy and tensions between different generations within Latina/o communities."[9] Understanding this hierarchy is central to Ana's coming of age, and by the film's end she finally appreciates the lives of the women in the factory and the culture and history she shares with them. The songs in *Real Women* play a significant role in articulating Ana's hybrid identity and her eventual solidarity with the factory workers.

Just as music can be used to mark geographical location in cinema, it can also be used to mark the origin of bodies. An examination of the origins and hybridity of Latin American and Latino music can provide insight into the potential meaning these varied forms can bring to *Real Women* and other US films. Due to many centuries of migration to and from South and Central America, Latina/o identity is already complex and heterogeneous.[10] John Storm Roberts considers the European, African, and Amerindian elements contained in Latin American music:

> The resulting unity-in-diversity is extraordinary. Even the smallest country has its own clearly identifiable musical culture, ranging from the simplest folk idioms to national conservatory styles. Yet from another perspective, all represent versions of one cultural mix, even though not all its elements are equal, or even present, in every country [...][11]

This cultural mix representing the different countries of Latin America is just the beginning of the diversity, however. A closer examination leads to a fascinating history of musical migration. According to Alma M. Garcia, one of the most popular styles of music to cross the border was music from the north of Mexico, known as *música norteña* or *norteño*.[12] This genre "originated in the northern states of Mexico such as Nuevo León, Tamaulipas, and Chihuahua, and along the U.S.-Mexico border states, particularly Texas" and continued to evolve in the United States.[13] Roberts explains how *música norteña* originated in both Mexico and the United States, and that the term applies to "an ensemble, consisting of an accordion lead, a guitar and/or *baja sexto* (a type of 12-string guitar), and sometimes a double bass."[14] He goes on to say that this music "leans heavily on corridos and on dances like the polka, waltz, and schottische."[15]

Furthermore, both Roberts[16] and Garcia[17] state that German and Czech railroad builders introduced the accordion to the Texas/Mexico border region. Garcia also discusses the nineteenth-century introduction by German immigrants of dance music, such as the polka, that would later influence *música norteña*. Somewhat problematically, she refers to *música norteña* as a mix of two cultures—Mexican and German. This statement simplifies Mexican music, which is already a mix from many different cultures. Garcia later asserts that *música norteña* continues to evolve over time, on both sides of the border, as it absorbs elements of rock, pop, and techno.[18]

According to Roberts, the arrival of the waltz and the continued popularity of using three-fourths time in Mexican music are due to the strong influence of French culture in the eighteenth and nineteenth centuries, and it is even possible that the polka made its way to Mexico from France.[19] Roberts also states that Mexican music significantly incorporated Cuban (and thus African) elements from the middle of the nineteenth century onwards.[20] Thus, the history of Mexican music, as well as that of music from the rest of Latin America, is intimately linked to a history of immigration to and around the Americas.

The musical influences described by Roberts and Garcia from various parts of Europe and Africa, as well as those travelling around Latin America and the United States, result in an ever-changing set of hybrid musical forms that are at once separate and linked. Although there are obviously some distinct musical forms with origins in specific locations, Roberts asserts that much Latin American music is hard to categorize due to the many variations in form and subject matter, as well as the unclear origins and migration of musical styles.[21] The foregrounded tension between the traditional and the modern in *Real Women* reflects this hybridity of Latin American music and its tendency to evolve while retaining deep roots. The film's music, in its traditional and further hybridized modern forms, helps to construct identities that are as resistant to classification as the Latin music Roberts describes.

"Chica Difícil" ("Difficult Girl"), by Colombian alternative Latin rock band Aterciopelados, is the first significant song associated with Ana in the film. It begins after she refuses to miss her last day of school because of her mother's apparently feigned illness. The song bridges a cut to Ana slamming open the front door of her house and walking out, and continues to score her trip to school. "Chica Difícil" contains laid-back vocals, clean electric guitar, bass guitar, accordion, and light drums. The music has a shuffling, bluesy, lounge-jazz feel to it. The vocalist sings (in Spanish) about being a difficult girl who is worth the trouble, and explains how she is looking for a man who will do amazing things for her, but she insists she will not be easy to catch. For those who do not understand Spanish, the title and initial lyrics ("Soy una chica difícil") are fairly easy to comprehend (or at least to look up) and are arguably the most important words of the song with regard to Ana's character. Those who do understand will get the full meaning of the lyrics included in the film. These lyrics give a general impression of Ana's character: she is in fact difficult, but she is also a worthwhile person to know with plenty of positive attributes. Rather than simply being stubborn, Ana is an intelligent, demanding girl with strong opinions. Thus "Chica Difícil" sets up the exceptional agency that Ana has as the film's young, female protagonist, despite the somewhat comic quality the lyrics take on after the altercation between Ana and her mother.

The song follows Ana through her neighborhood and onto two buses, ending after it bridges a cut to her classroom in Beverly Hills High School. As the song plays, visuals alternate between medium-to-long shots of Ana and scenes of her surroundings, possibly from her point of view. As she walks to the first bus, Ana passes through her neighborhood, which is colorful, literally and figuratively, visually and aurally. After Ana is shown from behind passing bright flowers in her front garden, the view switches to a long shot of her from a high angle, with sneakers draped over a phone line taking up the lower left-hand corner of the shot. Children play in the street and her father's landscaping truck is visible in the driveway. Thus, the mise-en-scène signifies a working-class neighborhood. Ana waves to, but gets no reaction from, an old woman who sings "O Sole Mio" and slowly waves her arms as if she is performing in front of an audience.

On her way to the bus Ana passes two Latino guitarists in cowboy hats and matching shirts, as well as colorful murals on the fronts and sides of buildings. She finally stands at the bus stop in front of brightly painted ads for vegetables and a large painting of a farm on the front of a market. Her neighborhood is lively and cheerful, yet full of working-class people with complicated lives. Downtown Los Angeles looms in the background and a scruffy white man with a long beard and bin bag full of possessions sits at the bus stop. "Chica Difícil" may reflect the ethnicity of Ana and her neighbors, but it also constructs a clever yet difficult girl with a somewhat melancholic mood that is mirrored in her vibrant yet hard-working neighborhood.

As Ana gets off the first bus, an African-American man at the stop plays a flute. The flute blends perfectly into the song—in its jazzy style, key, and volume—to the point that one wonders if it is part of the recording. The flute is not in the original song, but it enhances the melancholic, contemplative mood of this instrumental passage. Thus, the boundaries between source music and dramatic score become blurred. We share Ana's point of audition through the source music as well as identifying with her subjectivity via the dramatic score. This underlines Ana's concerns about her relationship with her mother, the fact that she has to take two buses to school, and her desire to go to college despite serious doubts that it will be possible. Ana is not alone in her musical world; many people of different races, ethnicities, and religions appear on the same streets. Thus, the music informs the perceiver about Ana's ethnicity and personality, but it also connects her to the whole population of her city via characters who share the scenes, additional source music from the old woman who sings and the man with the flute, and the visible presence of downtown Los Angeles. This sequence foregrounds hybridity of music and identity, developing Ana's character and suggesting the evolution of her agency in the remainder of the film.

"Chica Difícil" pauses after bridging a cut to Ana's classroom and starts again after she quits her fast food restaurant job on the way home. She picks up a final pay check from her bitter boss who says, "You know, you can always just kiss my ass to get your job back." In response to her boss's comment Ana flings her hand up in the air as she walks out the door. The instrumental passage of "Chica Difícil" starts with this dismissive gesture as if Ana controls the music's entry. Mirroring the way she quits the job on her own terms, the reappearance of the song reinforces her agency in this matter and cements her determination for the rest of the film. The song later ends as Ana walks into her house and closes the door behind her. The fact that "Chica Difícil" begins as Ana leaves her house and ends as she returns suggests that her agency lies outside of this domestic space, which is traditionally coded as "feminine." Her life in this house is controlled by her mother, and the music locates her power in the outside world, foreshadowing her need to leave home.

Musically, Ana's future path is suggested by songs that mix a variety of contemporary popular styles, the influence of which has travelled beyond their countries of origin. These songs are associated with key coming-of-age moments depicted in the film. While "Chica Difícil" suggests something about Ana's personality, it also appears at a time when she is making important decisions and contemplating her future. Another featured song with an even more international feel is "Minha Galera" ("My Gang" or "My People") by Manu Chao, a French singer born to Spanish parents. The song's lyrics are in Portuguese, and Chao uses some Brazilian Portuguese phrases to reference Brazilian culture. A guitar and a keyboard playing a gentle reggae rhythm accompany the vocals.

"Minha Galera" plays when Ana is on her first date with Jimmy (Brian Sites), a white student from her school who comes from a wealthy family.

Before they meet, Ana walks her grandfather to a bar on the corner from which lively tejano music pours out into the street. John Koegel describes tejano as "the general term for contemporary Texas-Mexican popular music, [encompassing] many earlier and present-day musical styles to create a hybrid mix: polka, *ranchera*, blues, rock, jazz, *cumbia*, and so forth."[22] The tejano ends and "Minha Galera" begins with a cut to the restaurant where the date takes place, although the song's relationship to the diegesis is unclear—it bridges a few cuts and returns after a pause. The outside seating area of this restaurant is ornately decorated with cactuses, flowers, and a large statue of the Virgin Mary, adorned with several strings of Christmas lights and surrounded by mosaic tiling. Despite being multiracial, the hip, young, and seemingly affluent crowd contrasts with the more working-class Latino neighborhood from which Ana has just come. This adds to the impression that the stylized décor of the restaurant objectifies or even fetishizes Mexican culture with its collection of tacky religious icons.

The light reggae feel and Portuguese vocals of "Minha Galera" and the upscale but Mexican-themed restaurant place both Ana and Jimmy in a space somewhere between both of their usual worlds. For Jimmy, who comes from a wealthy, white family and has a narrow and sometimes vulgar knowledge of Mexican and Chicano/Latino culture, the restaurant may seem "authentic." However, the fact that the song is sung in Portuguese with a Brazilian slant by a French singer with Spanish ancestry complicates any notion of a fixed national/cultural identity that can be attributed "authenticity." For Ana, the restaurant has familiar if stylized iconography and presumably serves Mexican food. However, it may not have the kind of food she would eat at home and is probably not the type of restaurant where her family would eat.

Guitar and vocals are delivered in a poppy, quirky style, with Chao sometimes humming as if to mimic a kazoo. The eccentric, innocent feel of this song highlights the awkward interactions between Ana and Jimmy. The song then bridges a cut to the two teens walking through Ana's neighborhood until they reach the corner where Ana dropped off her grandfather. The song again jumps in volume, although more subtly, when Jimmy kisses Ana goodnight. The humming returns as the song bridges a final cut to Ana waking up in her bed and smiling in a dream-like state. A few scenes later, Ana visits her father at work to ask if he will lend Estela rent money so she can keep the factory open. He eventually agrees, and after she hugs him, "Minha Galera" returns. The song finally bridges a cut to Ana writing her personal essay for college applications, despite her parents' disapproval. Therefore, like "Chica Difícil," "Minha Galera" is connected with Ana's increasing confidence and agency.

The film's second Aterciopelados song, the low-key "Luto" ("Mourning"), enters the film when Ana and Jimmy decide to have sex for the first time. The song begins with a strummed acoustic guitar, soon adds a shuffling rhythm and melancholic vocals, and eventually incorporates squelching electronic flourishes. In this scene Ana seems self-conscious about the fact that her parents will not let her go to Columbia University despite already being accepted, and because Jimmy will be moving on while she stays and works in Estella's factory. Although it seems she will miss Jimmy, the "mourning" of the song's title suggests Ana's sadness over her loss of opportunity rather than her loss of Jimmy or the loss of her virginity. The idea to have sex is Ana's, and she makes a point of buying condoms beforehand. Her desire to have sex before Jimmy leaves is empowering, and once again, it is a more modern sounding song with contemporary international influences that accompanies her agency and colors her experience. The nonchalance with which Ana treats this first sexual encounter and loss of a boyfriend is atypically unsentimental for a teenage girl in cinema.

More traditional sounding Mexican and Latin American songs are generally heard when Ana is with her family or working in the factory. However, this is not simply a representation of ethnicity. "No le Hace" ("It Doesn't Matter") and "Tenemos la Culpa" ("It's Our Fault"), both by Banda Llaneros, are heard when Ana is being driven to the factory in her father's truck. It is not clear if the songs are emanating from the radio, but it seems more likely that this is the case with "Tenemos la Culpa."

In other cases tejano music flows from a local bar, and mariachis approach Jimmy to perform while he waits for Ana. The musical landscape of East Los Angeles is audible and visible in the streets. This mix of sounds blends traditional Mexican and other Latin genres with cross-border music and, in the case of "Aquí No Será" ("It Will Not Be Here") by Ozomatli, we hear the combination of a more traditional form with contemporary political lyrics. "Aquí No Será," which could be roughly described as a slow tango, plays three times in the film. The first two occurrences are during scenes in the factory and include only instrumental passages. The song first enters when Ana takes a bite of flan in defiance of her mother and bridges a cut to the steamy factory where all of the women are miserably hot and sweaty. After Ana removes her shirt to get some relief from the heat, her mother tells her that she looks terrible and asks if she is not ashamed. Once again Ana is defiant, insisting that there is more to her than her body and telling her mother that no one should criticize her for the way she looks. "Aquí No Será" returns when Ana and the other women start to remove more of their clothes to compare cellulite and stretch marks. Again the music is cued by Ana's actions—this time it starts when she unzips her jeans. Carmen eventually walks out in disgust, but the rest of the women are pleased with themselves. The women return to work in their under-wear, and Ana enthusiastically exclaims that they should finish the dress order that night. She then turns on the radio, from which blares the snappy "Que Rico el Mambo" ("How Good the Mambo") by Perez Prado. The women dance happily to the mambo while they work, feeling revitalized and comfortable in their own skin. In this instance, the music that accom-panies Ana's agency is of an older generation, but this makes sense in a scene where she finally bonds with the other women in the factory—thus finding pride as a young, working-class Latina with a body that defies the patriarchal expectations internalized by her mother.

To return briefly to "Aquí No Será," Victor Hugo Viesca explains the following about the local music scene to which Ozomatli belongs: "East Los Angeles is the center of a flourishing musical cultural scene with a renewed 'Chicana/o' sensibility [...] led by a collective of socially conscious and politically active Latin-fusion bands that emerged in the 1990s."[23] It is therefore appropriate that the band's music should amplify Ana's (re)connection with her own working-class Chicana identity. I will discuss the last appearance of "Aquí No Será" when I consider the film's ending.

Although Ana leaves at the end of the film with her father's blessing, her mother does not even come out of her bedroom to say goodbye. After she says farewell to her father and grandfather at the airport, there is a cut to Ana ascending from the New York subway near Times Square. She has adopted a more fashion-conscious style and the "feminine" walk encour-aged by her mother earlier in the film. As she surfaces, the instrumental "Strawberry Tango Parts 1 & 2" begins. The instrumentation is a mix of acoustic guitars, percussion, and syncopated low brass; the traditional genre of this song connects Ana to her home and family as she struts through Manhattan. After she has been walking confidently and survey-ing her surroundings, the music slows with some sustained minor chords strummed on guitar. When the song picks back up, the camera pulls away from Ana. The addition of melancholic strings then suggests an under-current of sadness and anxiety. Up to this point, the top half of the front of Ana's body is shown in a medium close-up tracking shot as she walks down the street, her face expressing a mix of excitement and apprehension. But once the camera pulls away, the perceiver is increasingly distanced from Ana; other characters pass between her and the camera, and she begins to blend into the crowded, unfamiliar city. As she approaches a corner, the camera continues to track backwards across the street, but Ana does not cross. Instead she looks around as if unsure of where to go, and as the pedestrian signal facing the camera flashes "DON'T WALK" in red, Ana turns the corner and walks off screen. The ambivalence of this shot is emphasized by the music, which slows to a few sustained, melancholic notes that seem to suggest Ana's sense of being alone in an unfamiliar and slightly menacing metropolis. A few final sustained electric guitar notes with a heavy tremolo effect add to the sense of unease as the scene fades to black.

This ambivalent ending and the following credit sequence suggest that Ana may have left something important behind—or perhaps that she has brought with her some of the problems of her past—and that her future will not be without complication. After the fade to black, there is a cut to a close-up of a radio. When a hand reaches into the shot and turns the radio on, the familiar "Aquí No Será" returns. The song continues over a montage of scenes (without Ana) that resemble those scored by "Chica Dificil" when Ana walks through her neighborhood early in the film. Brightly colored spools of thread, a running sewing machine, the neighborhood, religious icons, walking musicians, the family's parakeets, and the charismatic old woman who sings "O Sole Mio" at the start of the film, are all shown. While these scenes are cheerful, they are interspersed with shots of dirty bus windows and a tangled mess of phone lines, among other ugly aspects of life in Ana's old neighborhood. The mostly sentimental scenes tend to suggest nostalgia for a comfortable, vibrant community; the less beautiful images remind us of the hardships Ana faced in the past, and may still face in the future.

The inclusion of "Aquí No Será" further problematizes a nostalgic reading of the images. The song's lyrics, which seem to criticize the US government's support of El Salvador's violent military regime during the Salvadoran Civil War, only serve to amplify the dire mood of the song and end credit sequence. This adds to the feeling that Ana's old neighborhood is a somewhat tragic place, or perhaps the song's use is a critique of social inequalities such as those highlighted in the film. But at the same time, there is a definite air of nostalgia to these scenes, amplified by the inclusion of the song that previously accompanied Ana's ultimate bonding with the other women in her sister's factory.

Throughout *Real Women Have Curves*, Ana's hybrid identity and agency are intensely linked with music. On the journey I have traced from "Chica Dificil," through "Minha Galera" and "Luto," to "Que Rico el Mambo" and "Aquí No Será," Ana is transformed from the "difficult girl" of the initial song to the "real woman" of the film's title. It is significant that the film's title insists (in English) that real women have a body type more accepted of Latinas, since when we leave Ana she has changed from a *chica dificil* who existed in a mix of languages to a *woman* in the predominantly Anglophone context of college. It seems then that girlhood allows Ana to exist between cultures, exploring a "difficult" and different subjectivity, whereas within the context of becoming-woman her Latina identity constrains her body as "real" and grounded rather than ideal and mobile. Ana comes to accept her own body, both in terms of her size and her ethnic/socioeconomic background. The varying national origins of songs associated with Ana suggest a Pan-Latin solidarity that could connect Ana's struggles to those of other Latina/os, regardless of country of ancestry. However, the absence of songs with English lyrics suggests that her hybrid girl subjectivity still lies in her Spanish-speaking family life, rather than in the "real" (i.e., Latina) woman English-speaking context of her education. Overall, the use of music in this film insists on placing Ana's identity and agency within a complex cultural context, one which "Latina" both expresses, and like all labels, fails to sufficiently describe—one which transcends simplistic binaries of white or Other, immigrant or citizen, Mexican or American, girl or woman.

Notes

1. Examples include *Girlfight* (Karyn Kusama, 2000), *Crazy/Beautiful* (John Stockwell, 2001), *Quinceañera* (Richard Glatzer and Wash Westmoreland, 2006), *Don't Let Me Drown* (Cruz Angeles, 2009), *Down for Life* (Alan Jacobs, 2009), and *Love, Concord* (Gustavo Guardado, 2012).
2. Charles Ramírez Berg, *Latino Images in Film: Stereotypes, Subversion, & Resistance* (Austin, TX: University of Texas Press, 2002).
3. Angharad N. Valdivia, *Latina/os and the Media* (Cambridge: Polity Press, 2010).
4. Linda C. McClain, "*Bend It Like Beckham* and *Real Women Have Curves*: Constructing Identity in Coming-of-Age Stories," *Depaul Law Review* 54:3 (2005), 701–754 (733).
5. Ibid., 733.
6. Jillian M. Báez, "Towards a *Latinidad Feminista*: The Multiplicities of Latinidad and Feminism in Contemporary Cinema," *Popular Communication* 5:2 (2007), 109–128 (119).
7. Steven H. Cooper and Adrienne Harris, "Real Women Have Curves (2002)," *International Journal of Psychoanalysis* 86:5 (2005), 1481–1487 (1481).
8. For a discussion of Latino stereotypes in US cinema, see Ramírez Berg, *Latino Images in Film*.
9. Báez, "Towards a *Latinidad Feminista*," 120.
10. Valdivia, *Latina/os and the Media*, 19–21.
11. John Storm Roberts, *The Latin Tinge: The Impact of Latin American Music on the United States* (Oxford: Oxford University Press, 2009), 3.
12. Alma M. Garcia, *The Mexican Americans* (Westport, CT: Greenwood Press, 2002).
13. Garcia, *The Mexican Americans*, 98.
14. Roberts, *The Latin Tinge*, 21.
15. Ibid.

16. Ibid.
17. Garcia, *The Mexican Americans*, 98–99.
18. Garcia, *The Mexican Americans*, 99.
19. Roberts, *The Latin Tinge*, 16–17.
20. Ibid., 17.
21. Ibid., 5.
22. John Koegel, "Crossing Borders: Mexicana, Tejana, and Chicana Musicians in the United States and Mexico," in *From Tejano to Tango: Latin American Popular Music* edited by Walter Aaron Clark (London: Routledge, 2002), pp. 97–125 (107).
23. Victor Hugo Viesca, "The Battle of Los Angeles: The Cultural Politics of Chicana/o Music in the Greater Eastside," *American Quarterly*, 56:3 (2004), 719–739: 719.

9

Emotion, Girlhood, and Music in *Naissance des pieuvres* (Céline Sciamma, 2007) and *Un amour de jeunesse* (Mia Hansen-Løve, 2011)

Fiona Handyside

Céline Sciamma's *Naissance des pieuvres/Water Lilies* (2007) and Mia Hansen-Løve's *Un amour de jeunesse/Goodbye First Love* (2011), both made by young female directors, offer us insights into the heightened sensations and emotions of adolescent girlhood. Concentrating on a female protagonist who is aged around 15 at the start of the story, both films recount the bruising and painful experience of first love and its loss, and are part of a whole flurry of recent French films, from the art house to the popular, that consider girlhood and coming-of-age.[1] Both films make stunning and remarkable use of music on their soundtracks, and music is as much a vector of meaning and affect as mise-en-scène or dialogue. Rather than being "unheard melodies," to borrow Claudia Gorbman's now canonical phrase,[2] the music used by Sciamma and Hansen-Løve works to give form and expression to girls' emotions, but through a depersonalized register. The music is outside of the girls' worlds, usually non-diegetic, and is not the literal expression of their voice. Rather, it is a disembodied, non-identical expression of their feelings, and thus a paradox can be maintained, whereby the films simultaneously offer us insight into the heightened, disoriented sensations of the girls' encounters with intimacy, but allow the girls to retain their opacity and privacy.

Music is fundamentally linked to space in both these films. It expresses the liquid, shifting, precarious universe in which the girls operate, as their first experiences of sexual desire open them up to new pain and vulnerability. It thus functions to articulate feelings, intensities, and desires that can't be named by the girls themselves, translating their emotions and sensations into sounds that the audience, but not the protagonist, can hear. Music exists in the interstices between the private world of the girl, communicating her pain and also her overcoming of it, and the public spectacle of that process that forms the pull of the film for the sympathetically positioned spectator.

Music then comes to be the very tensions and contradictions of the girls' first experiences of sexual intimacy. As Lauren Berlant explains, while intimacy may seem to be among the most hidden and private of encounters, it has a public life: "the inwardness of the intimate is met by a corresponding publicness. People consent to trust their desire for 'a life' to institutions of intimacy." These institutions, such as schools, churches, therapists' clinics, and clubs, aim to manage the friendships and relations that form intimate exchanges. While the hope is for an unproblematic unfolding of the intimate relation, as Berlant continues, "romance and friendship inevitably meet the instabilities of sexuality, money, expectation, and exhaustion [...] since the early twentieth century these strong ambivalences within the intimate sphere have been recorded by proliferating forms of therapeutic publicity."[3]

These plays between private and public, proximity and distance, intimate and extimate, map neatly onto classic feminist theorizing of the role of music in film, particularly the generic form to which it is etymologically tied, melodrama. In the feminine mode of melodrama, music, alongside other non-representational elements (light, color, rhythm, and so on), becomes the vehicle of unspoken female emotion, and thus a way to navigate the punishing contradictions of patriarchal culture, which demands women bear total responsibility for the home but lack agency and full subjectivity. Sciamma and Hansen-Løve develop a politics of film form suited to a complex postfeminist landscape, in which, despite their more realist tone and feel, music is used in a way analogous to Hollywood melodramas from the 1940s and 1950s, to help female protagonists navigate contradiction (here, of gendered sexual norms). Both films pay close attention to the inception of sexual feelings, and their impact on the senses. As Emma Wilson explains, in *Water Lilies,* love is shown *and* felt to be lush and searing.[4] A similar dynamic is at work in *Goodbye First Love.* They create a politics of emotions, of affect, that communicates how it feels to be a girl in a society that still treats male and female sexual desire very differently despite the legal and social equality of men and women. This is especially the case in the French context, where the pressure for women to conform to narrow standards of beauty and behavior is taken for granted as part of "l'exception française": the idea that French society can achieve equality for men and women while preserving "difference," a catch-all term that defends beauty culture and sexual harassment, and sees any criticism of French sexual politics as "American" and against "rapports de séduction à la française."[5]

Part of the way they signal the cataclysmic impact of desire is through reconfiguring the soundscape, so that the girls' emotions become part of the very fabric of the film. Importantly, however, they also show their female protagonists surviving first loss, moving on, and the soundtrack is fundamental in taking us from pain and dissolution to tentative hope and reparation. As scholarship turns toward issues of postfeminism, it seems that feminist film scholars spend more time discussing plot and character than form. A good example of this is the neglect of film form in *Cinema Journal*'s "In Focus: Postfeminism and Contemporary Media Studies" issue, where the four (excellent) essays are primarily concerned with theme rather than aesthetics, as if the highly conventional form of many films associated with postfeminist culture precludes this kind of analysis.[6] In this context, contemporary French cinema provides a particularly welcome framework for assessing aesthetics as politics. In its unique ecosystem, French cinema provides a space for films about girls to thrive within an auteurist cinema that privileges stylistic flourishes. These films are alive to the very specific feelings of girlhood, its textures and emotions, and can use form to express the disjunctive, disturbing, but also profoundly touching intimacies of love and friendship. I turn first to the context in which Sciamma and Hansen-Løve produce this work, before going on to discuss in some detail how music works as an ambivalent thread, holding tensions together, in the films in question.

Before moving on to these topics, it is also worth briefly commenting on the significant antecedents to these French coming-of-age movies, which is the series of films made for the ARTE television channel in the 1990s. Chantal Poupaud collaborated with Pierre Chevalier, head of production at ARTE, and Robert Benayoun of IMA productions, to commission a series of nine feature-length films to be broadcast on television under the rubric "Tous les garçons et les filles de leur age." The only requirements were that the film took place during the period of the directors' own adolescence and featured a scene set at a party accompanied by music. Music was key then to giving the disparate films of the series cohesion, and it also worked as a temporal marker, signaling the time period of the director's own adolescence. The series thus articulates a particularly French inflection to the teen film. Poupard's decision to ask the directors to set the films in the period of their own adolescence, inviting a biographical relation to the subject matter, and the major stylistic and thematic differences between the films, from the unbridled urban violence of Olivier Dahan's *Frères* to the bitter-sweet melancholy of André Téchiné's *Les Roseaux sauvages*, demonstrates the overriding significance of the director in French cinema, whatever the genre of the film. Nevertheless, the presence of music as a guiding thread allows the films to highlight the importance of soundtrack in the French teen movie as the way to enable adolescent experience to be expressed.[7] Sciamma and Hansen-Løve both navigate within this terrain, providing films that contain stylistic, cinéphilic flourishes and autobiographical resonances that announce the presence of the director/auteur while incorporating music so as to enhance the emotional and affective intensity of audience engagement with the girls' subjectivity.

The Emergence of Girls' Cinema in France

While clearly they have both reached their majority and are therefore legally adult, Sciamma and Hansen-Løve can be labeled girls for two reasons. First, there is their relative youth in terms of the film profession, underlined by the autobiographical references within the relative contemporaneity of their films: *Water Lilies* is set in the New Town of Cergy-Pontoise where Sciamma grew up, in a rather timeless "present day"; Hansen-Løve had a relationship with a much older man, as does her heroine Camille, and the film is carefully set in the 1990s–2000s, using devices such as calendars and notes to signal the date. Unlike older directors, a reference to their own youth does not take these directors far into the past, unlike the directors of the ARTE series discussed above. Second, they occupy a position generationally associated in contemporary culture with girlishness, which is to say they are positioned to be constructed as what Sarah Projansky labels "discursive postfeminist daughters."[8] These are young women who grew up in an era that took feminism's gains for granted, and whose experiences of girlhood are within a context of legal, political, and educational equality for girls and women. Nevertheless, certainly in the French context outlined above, they are still subject to the pressures of beauty culture and sexual double standards.

The French cinematic landscape is uniquely suited to the creation of this girls' cinema. The French film industry has had an industrial bias toward the young from the days of the New Wave. Such association of French cinema and youth is now embedded in industrial support for the debutant film, from sources such as the CNC and the French film academy. Furthermore, French cinema routinely promotes young cinema in its prize structures. The Prix Jean Vigo, a prestigious award given for artistic originality and excellence, has long been geared toward newcomers (it was awarded to both *Le Beau Serge* (Chabrol, 1959) and *A bout de souffle* (Godard, 1960)). Sciamma and Hansen-Løve jointly won the Prix Louis Delluc for First Film in 2007, for *Water Lilies* and *Tout est pardonné/All Is Forgiven* (2007), respectively. The Césars, marketed as the French equivalent of the Oscars, has a category that does not exist at the latter ceremony—the *César du meilleur premier film*/César for best first film—which has been awarded under various nomenclatures since 1982 (the Césars began in 1975). Both Sciamma and Hansen-Løve received nominations for this award with their first films, *Water Lilies* and *All Is Forgiven*, in a landmark year (2008) when all five nominations were from films directed by women. Such a vibrant celebration of young female filmmaking was enthusiastically greeted in the mainstream film press. *Première*, a magazine far more focused on Hollywood cinema than its more upmarket equivalents, *Cahiers du cinéma* and *Postif*, nevertheless in August 2007 featured a remarkable dossier entitled "Girl Power" (in English in the original), which argued that renewal and diversity in French film would come from these girl directors. In a similar fashion, in *Studio* magazine's December 2007 issue, Béatrice Toulon published a report entitled "Girls' Time" [Le temps des filles], which reiterated the notion of a generational shift and an explosion of young female talent.[9]

In September 2012, in the wake of Cannes' failure to have a single female director in competition, *Cahiers du cinéma* had a special issue asking "where are the women"? Sciamma and Hansen-Løve both joined in the debate, with Sciamma in particular arguing it is important politically for Cannes to open up to younger filmmakers, as well as women. The production and industrial contexts that encourage youth cinema also open up the way to encourage female filmmakers. Both young people and women are faced with the prejudice of risk-averse Conglomerate Hollywood and require more diverse and pluralistic approaches toward the production and aesthetics of film. Indeed, cinema in France is an area of striking gender equality, in terms of crew salaries, audience figures (ca.52 percent of the domestic audience is female) and training. Between 1990 and 2008, some 40 percent of the overall intake at la Fémis, the prestigious state-funded French film school, was female, and it has achieved parity in its director strand. Given this institutional encouragement of gender parity, debutant films, and youth, the French cinematic landscape enables the emergence of a girls' cinema.

Céline Sciamma trained at la Fémis, graduating from the script-writing section. Her graduation script for *Water Lilies* was so well received by her graduating jury committee (which included filmmaker Xavier Beauvais), she secured funding to direct it as her first feature film. In contrast, Mia

Hansen-Løve consciously modeled herself after the New Wave generation, working as a film critic for the *Cahiers du cinéma* with the full intention of breaking into directing. Between them, then, Sciamma and Hansen-Løve are emblematic of two of the most important routes for becoming a director in France, and their relative openness to women as well as men. As such, they can be seen as representative of the emergence in the last decade of a girls' cinema in France—where girlhood is both subject matter and originating consciousness. It foregrounds a particularly French twist on the American teen movie genre, overlaying its interest in the struggle between the individual adolescent and the institutional structures of teen life (family/school/clubs) with a specifically cineliterate, visible authorial signature and a striking use of music.

Feminist Film Criticism: Music and Melodrama

Feminist film criticism emphasizes how music can be used to articulate female suffering and desire within the untenable contradictions and paradoxes of patriarchal culture. Within the "feminine" mode of melodrama, cinematic style, including music, has a privileged role as the expression of women's repressed discourse, as Tania Modleski succinctly explains:

> If women are hysterics in patriarchal culture because, according to the feminist argument, their voice has been silenced or repressed, and if melodrama deals with the return of the repressed through a kind of conversion hysteria [i.e., in its "excessive" stylistic markings, which symptomatically "appear" on the "body" of the film text], perhaps women have been attracted to the genre because it provides an outlet for the repressed feminine voice.[10]

Carol Flinn goes on to explain that music is said to give rise to this repressed voice and gain meaning. "Melodrama engages music and other non-representational elements (colour, texture, movement, melody and so on) [...] the genre deals with recognizable themes of everyday life, domesticity and intimacy, while at the same time, these themes receive dramatic and hyperbolically stylised expression."[11]

However, as Mary Ann Doane explains, while this configuration finds a particular symptomatic expression in the melodramas of 1940s–1950s Hollywood, these films "simply effect a historical specification of a more generalizable psychical configuration associated with patriarchy."[12] Doane's insight that the punishing experience of trying to live out these paradoxes, expressed as a highly coded aesthetic symptom, exists beyond the specific moment of the 1940s melodrama has great value for us when we come to analyzing the form of contemporary French girls' cinema. While these films generally have a more naturalist tone and feel, they use music in an analogous way to the Hollywood melodrama, finding this an element that is suitable to express the contradictions of living as a girl within a patriarchal system. Here, the contradictions are those of a postfeminist culture that, while it promotes agency and education for girls, still subjects them to a sexual double standard and policing of their sexual experiences in a way it doesn't to boys.

We see the girls navigating the complex terrain of sexuality, relations, and selfhood, managing their own desires while working through what it means to be a sexually desiring female and the pressures this places on identity formation. Both films suggest the contradictions and multiplicities of contemporary girlhood, but through different means. Sciamma has three central protagonists; Marie/Pauline Acquart, Anne/Louise Blachère, and Floriane/Adèle Haenel. The three girls all have strikingly different body types, with Marie skinny, gawky, and awkward; Anne chubby and clumsy; and Floriane slender, shapely, and conventionally attractive. Sciamma places the girls into the acutely body-conscious world of a synchronized swimming team, emphasizing the bodily discipline required in several scenes where we see the team practicing routines in unison, or where their armpits are inspected for stray body hair. Hansen-Løve shows us her protagonist Camille/Lola Créton changing through time as her film covers a period of around a decade. As we see her clothes, hairstyle, and bearing change, so we understand how the self itself is mutable: "The film can touch up against the fact of identity as non-self-identical, of the subject as shifting and ever transitional."[13] In this slippery terrain, music articulates the anxieties and confusions the girls repress in a postfeminist world that demands conformity to punishing double standards as the price of counting as a modern girl, in which she is expected to be sexual but not promiscuous, experimental but not lesbian, loving but not needy. *Water Lilies* deals mostly with the first two demands. It shows the conventionally attractive Floriane both enjoying the power of her ability to appeal to men, and negotiating barbed comments and criticism from her female peers, who accuse her of being a slut, and her manipulation of/possible attraction to Marie, who is overwhelmed with desire for Floriane. When the latter kisses her at a party then returns to flirt with François/Warren Jacquin, Marie realizes she is simply a play-thing for Floriane, and returns to her best friend, Anne, who has been abandoned by François in favor of Floriane. *Goodbye First Love* shows us 15-year-old Camille's desperation when her 19-year-old boyfriend Sullivan/Sebastien Urzendowsky leaves for a back-packing trip to South America. She plots his progress on a map with pins, trying to keep him close, but he stops writing to her and she attempts suicide. Gradually, however, her melancholia shifts, and she begins a new relationship with her architecture teacher and mentor Lorenz/Magne Håvard Brekke, yet her desire for, and attraction to, Sullivan, rekindles their relation eight years later. Once again, he breaks off with her, and Camille travels back to the Ardèche, where she once spent a holiday with Sullivan. She goes for a swim by herself.

Angela McRobbie claims that

> the new female subject is, despite her freedom, called upon to be silent, to withhold critique in order to count as a modern sophisticated girl. Indeed this withholding of critique is a condition of her freedom. There is a quietude and complicity in the manners of generationally specific notions of cool, and more precisely, an uncritical relation to dominant commercially produced sexual representations which actively invoke hostility toward assumed feminist positions from the past, in order to endorse a new regime of sexual meanings based on female consent, equality, participation and pleasure.[14]

These films provide some kind of way out of this impasse, both for their onscreen protagonists and via the very fact of their production by young female "girl" directors. These films show their protagonists participating in this "new regime of sexual meanings," as they consent to sexual activity and draw pleasure and agency from sexual relations. However, they also use music to enable a critique of the idea that this is unproblematic and not inflected by continued belief in gender difference. Music expresses tenderness, longing, hurt, salvation. While showing the difficulties and pressures in the new sexual norms girls are negotiating, these films use music to express the essential ambivalence of their subjects, poised between the external world of expectations concerning girls' sexual behavior, and their own private subjective experiences and feelings. Music articulates the shifting terrain of girlhood itself, enabling the simultaneous and paradoxical performance of sophisticated modernity and acquiescence and rebellious critique and rejection.

Water and Music

The films' scores are strikingly different, although their functions are very similar. In both films, music expresses the ability to break down distance between spaces, to erase rigid boundaries between private and public, and highlights the significance of water in the films' exploration of girls' intimacies.

Sciamma uses a commissioned electronic score by the cult French DJ ParaOne that contains no lyrics and, as Tim Palmer comments, "blends shrill, tinny electronic strings, distended minor-key treble slides often distorted by pitch bends, with intermittently off-beat rhythms, to create weirdly disjunctive accompaniment."[15] Used sparingly in a soundtrack dominated by the natural ambient noise of girls' chatter and rhythmic counting out of exercises, splashing water, and bird song, the music's strangeness and muffled quality expresses the cutoff and isolated underwater world of the girls. Philippe Azoury suggests that "the sound [...] conveys the aural qualities of the world of the deaf, an adolescence heard yet bottled-up and enclosed [...] a whole universe immersed like in a pool."[16] It accompanies moments in the film where the thresholds between soft and hard, liquid and solid, private and public, collapse.

As the credits begin, we hear the buzz of female voices over the image of an empty pool, signaling an immediate disjuncture between sound and image. As the initial credits finish, a repetitive, pulsating melody begins, accompanying the babble of voices (which we now learn come from the girls' changing room), and the music continues as Marie walks poolside. The applause of the spectators also pulses, fading in and out, as if we can hear what the swimmers hear, but the melody continues throughout. The extra-diegetic music navigates between the worlds both below and above water, suggesting a continuity of the hostile, strange, aseptic, but secretive and fascinating world of the pool beyond its confines.

The watery, liquid environment of the pool enables both the public display of, and Marie's private fascination with, Floriane's body, erasing rigid boundaries. She stands shyly at the edge of the pool until Floriane swims over and invites her in "to see better." We have a close-up on Marie's feet and legs as she climbs into the pool, making the transition from air to water, on top to underneath. The sequence cuts between Marie looking and images of the team, legs kicking furiously or arms wheeling, in contrast to their serene appearance above water. At one point, Marie swims in front of the camera, coming between us and our vision of the girls, so subtly the scene has shifted from being implicitly Marie's point-of-view to the disembodied perspective of the camera (Figure 9.1).

More generally, the music plays at moments where the film crosses the portal between the fantastical world of the pool and its enabling of reciprocity between Marie and Floriane, and the "normal" banal world of suburban Paris, such as in the key liminal spaces of the changing room and the showers, or when Marie and Floriane chat together about their different experiences of male attention (humiliating rejection or degrading lasciviousness, respectively) while sitting by the columns of Cergy's signature Axe-majeur.[17]

At the end of the film, there is a collapse of any distinct spaces. Marie confronts Floriane in the changing room, and they finally kiss. Floriane washes out her mouth and disdainfully leaves Marie behind. We then cut

Figure 9.1 *La naissance des pieuvres/Waterlillies* (Sciamma, 2007). Marie floats past the girls

from Floriane washing her mouth in the sink to Marie washing her mouth in the pool, and there seems to be no distinction between these environments. Marie jumps, fully clothed, into the pool, sinking into its depths. Floriane dances alone at the party. Anne comes to join Marie, and the two of them float together in the pool, and in the film's final shot, their faces are framed close together. The music plays over this whole sequence, enabling the seamless joining together of the spaces of pool, bathroom, and dance room, and moving us from Floriane's abusive rejection of Marie to the reassertion of the latter's friendship with Anne.

In contrast, Hansen-Løve's score consists of a series of pre-existing pieces of neo-folk music, with strong, catchy rhythms, harmonious melodies, and meaningful lyrics. Most significant is Johnny Flynn's beautiful *The Water*, a duet with Laura Marling where their voices blend together in harmony as they sing complex lyrics that speak of water as agent of life and sustenance but possibly as harbinger of death as well.

The song occurs twice in the film, the first time over a scene where Camille and Lorenz are driving through Paris at night after a date fairly early in their relationship. The music plays at a low volume so that we can hear the dialogue, a discussion about overcoming the past and possibilities for the future. As they fall silent, a medium close-up on Camille in profile with the car window behind her allows us to see the night sky and bright lights of the city, and the music increases in volume so that the car journey becomes a pause, an interlude, in the smooth realist flow of the film. The music carries on to the next scene, where Camille and Lorenz arrive back at her apartment, so that which could possibly have been diegetic music play-ing on the car radio is now signaled as definitely extra-diegetic. The music continues throughout the sequence, fading out as Camille chats, and finally she and Lorenz kiss, confirming the budding relationship. The image fades to black as the music continues, and then the film fades up to a bright sunlit building, and a shot on a notepad with a date in 2007 lets us know that the music has taken us over a four-year ellipsis. Hansen-Løve communicates the importance of the song in the fabric of the film, eliding its gentle, puls-ing rhythm and harmonious blend of voices to a sense of life continuing despite pain and loss.

The song plays again for the end credits of the film, where it plays over a shot of a river in the Ardèche, as Camille, alone, makes her way gin-gerly over rocks and pebbles to dive triumphantly into the water and swim, splashing through its green surface and drifting with its current. The cam-era lifts to a beautiful aerial shot, and we can make out Camille as a small figure on the river bank, and we see the water flowing and sparkling in the sunlight. Hansen-Løve explains the significance of music to her films:

> in my opinion, there's no music phase as such, it's an element among many that survives from the script-writing, through filming, to the editing process. What's important is that it has an organic relationship with the image [...] in any case, I don't work with a composer, because I like to change things, recycling, grafting pieces into my film, to produce something new. The rela-tionship between my film and a song is fundamental, because music is there to elevate and enlarge, not to simply comment on the images.[18]

Through foregrounding their scores rather than making them sub-servient to image, Sciamma and Hansen-Løve gesture toward a cinema that disrupts scopophilic regimes, refuses the subservience of sound to image, and that respects the autonomy and agency of its girl subjects' struggle for self-expression. Both films foreground a particular watery environment—a swimming pool, a river—and use this to express the fluid, shifting terrain that their girl protagonist inhabits. Music itself becomes expressive of this water, taking its fluidity and erasure of boundaries outside of the visual realm and into the very feeling of the film.

Notes

1. For example, *Et toi, t'es sur qui?/Just About Love?* (Doillon, 2007); *Bande de filles/ Girlhood* (Sciamma, 2014); *Lol (Laughing Out Loud)* (Azuelos, 2008); *La Vie d'Adèle—Chapitres 1 & 2/ /Blue Is the Warmest Colour* (Kechice, 2013); *Persepolis* (Satrapi, 2007); *Suzanne* (Quillévéré, 2012); *Tomboy* (Sciamma, 2010); *Tout est pardonné/All is Forgiven* (Hansen-Løve, 2007).

2. Claudia Gorbman, *Unheard Melodies: Narrative Film Music* (London: John Wiley and Sons, 1987).

3. Lauren Berlant, "Intimacy: A Special Issue," *Critical Inquiry* 24: 2 (Winter 1998), 281–288 (281).

4. Emma Wilson, " 'The Sea Nymphs Tested This Miracle': *Water Lilies* (2007) and the Origin of Coral," in *The Cinema of the Swimming Pool* edited by Christopher Brown and Pam Hirsch (Bern: Peter Lang, 2014), pp. 203–213 (212).

5. For a brilliant attack on this attitude, see Mona Chollet: *Beauté Fatale: Les Nouveaux Visages d'une aliénation féminine* (Paris: La Découverte, 2012). As Chollet points out, none of the classic crossover Anglo-American discussions of backlash and critiques of postfeminist beauty culture (Susan Bordo, Laurie Essig, Susan Faludi, Noami Wolf) has been translated into French. Meanwhile, popular books such as Mireille Guiliano's *French Women Don't Get Fat: The Secret of Eating for Pleasure* (New York: Vintage, 2007), and the fact that, internationally, French female actors are more likely to be known for selling perfume than their films, creates a transnational commodified image of beautiful French women as "a brand" for the French nation.

6. Yvonne Tasker and Diane Negra, eds. "In Focus: Postfeminism and Contemporary Media Studies," *Cinema Journal* 44:2 (Winter 2005), 107–126.

7. For further discussion of these films, see Olivier Davenas, *Teen! Cinéma de l'adolescence* (Paris: Moutons électriques, 2013).

8. Sarah Projansky, "Mass magazine cover girls: Some Reflections on Postfeminist Girls and Postfeminism's Daughters," in *Interrogating Postfeminism: Gender and the Politics of Popular Culture* edited by Diane Negra and Yvonne Tasker (Durham, NC: Duke University Press, 2007), pp. 41–72, (44).

9. Tim Palmer, *Brutal Intimacy: Analysing Contemporary French Cinema* (Middletown, CT: Wesleyan University Press, 2011), pp. 165–166.

10. Tania Modleski, "Time and Desire in the Woman's Film," *Cinema Journal* 23:3 (Spring 1984), 21.

11. Carol Flinn, "The 'Problem' of Femininity in Theories of Film Music," *Screen* 27:6 (Winter 1986), 56–73, (68).

12. Mary Ann Doane, *The Desire to Desire: The Woman Film of the 1940s* (Bloomington: Indiana University Press, 1987), p. 82.

13. Emma Wilson, "Precarious Lives: On Girls in Mia-Hansen-Løve and others," *Studies in French Cinema* 12:3 (2012), 273–284, (276).

14. Angela McRobbie, *The Aftermath of Feminism: Gender, Culture and Social Change* (London: Sage, 2008), p. 18.

15. Tim Palmer, *Contemporary French Cinema*, p. 39.

16. Philippe Azoury, "Pieuvres, comme un poison dans l'eau," *Libération* (May 19, 2007), online. http://next.liberation.fr/cinema/2007/05/19/pieuvres-comme-un-poison-dans-l-eau_93524

17. In its use of the striking architecture of Cergy-Pontoise, the film invokes an important intertext, Eric Rohmer's *L'Ami de mon amie/My Girlfriend's Boyfriend* (1987), which is also set in this New Town. Rohmer also uses the

swimming pool as a location that enables the development of female bonds, when he shows Lea and Blanche becoming friends during swimming lessons.

18. David Honnorat, "Interview de Mia Hansen-Løve, la réalisatrice d'Un Amour de jeunesse," *Vodkaster* (July 6, 2011), online. http://www.vodkaster.com/actu-cine/interview-de-mia-hansen-loeve-la-realisatrice-d-un-amour-de-jeunesse/693824

10

The Pleasures of Music Video Aesthetics in Girl Teen Film

Samantha Colling

What is "fun" about Hollywood girl teen film? What types of pleasure does this version of girlhood invite us to enjoy? The kinds of events and experiences created as "appropriately" fun for girls are generally part of a normative model that stresses femininity as a bodily characteristic and visibility as the girl figures' only access to power and pleasure.[1] In the romantic comedy/girl teen film *13 Going on 30* (Winick, 2004, USA), Jenna (Jennifer Garner) takes a shower, puts makeup on, looks through her wardrobe, and walks down a corridor. Though this does not sound like the stuff of spectacle, music video aesthetics are used to present these "everyday" activities in a mode that lends them excitement. Music video aesthetics combine image and music in a way that the two media collaborate: the visual takes on qualities of the music and the music is equally transformed by the visual. This combination of music and image is one way that the "stuff" of contemporary Hollywood girlhood is made to feel pleasurable. Like the magic of fairy tale, music video aesthetics make this version of girlhood more compelling than it may otherwise appear. As a consequence of the kind of spectacle that these aesthetics create, the dress, the walk, the dance move, the look, the lipstick, and so forth become more significant and captivating beyond their basic shapes.[2] Music video sequences in film are associated with the direct address of spectacle. Unlike the traditional score, composed after completion of the image track, this kind of sequence is identified with the use of prerecorded, popular, self-contained songs.[3] This chapter explores how music video aesthetics generate spectacle and the kinds of pleasure they aim to invite. Focusing on how pleasure is created and how these films aim to work on the body (not in spite of or because of ideology but as well as), we can understand *how* notions of fun (that sit in accord with postfeminist and neoliberal ideals) potentially *feel* pleasurable in millennial girl teen films.

Teen films can be defined by their thematic focus: coming-of-age narratives, rites of passage, and maturity as a narrative obstacle.[4] The types of girl teen films that I refer to here follow a Hollywood paradigm: these are mainstream films released between 2000 and 2010 in which girls are the protagonists. Robert Stam's discussion of genre suggests that analyses should also take into account how a subject is treated.[5] These are girl teen films in the "fun mode." They are structured around requisite moments that lead up to or make the girl figure the center of attention. These moments of visibility are presented as key forms of "girl fun" and include: makeovers and catwalks, singing and/or dancing, and (female "appropriate") sports. The spaces in which these spectacles take place are often sites of domesticity, regulation, or consumption: the home, school, mall, nightclub, or beauty parlor. Films such as *Bring It On* (Peyton, 2000, USA), *Mean Girls* (Waters, 2004, USA), and *The House Bunny* (Wolf, 2008, USA) are just some examples among many. In these films the subject of female adolescence is treated comedically with an emphasis on pleasure and fun.[6]

"Girl teen film," as I use it here, is a subgenre label that consciously identifies the generic genealogy and embedded relationship with the broader category "teen film" and provides the distinction that recognizes the films' girl-centered narratives. Although an awkward turn of phrase, girl teen film emphasizes the generic notion of girlhood that these films create. It does not suggest that the films' appeals are limited to teenagers or girls, or even that the characters explored are actually between the ages of 13 and 19. Girlhood is increasingly an indeterminate state—a moment of transition, suspended and made ever-flexible. Twenty-first-century girlhood has seen its boundaries stretched to include younger girls and young adults.[7] The girlhood that I refer to here is a concept. The girl is not an actual young woman but is an idea of female adolescence. The girl is a figure created by a set of discourses and girl teen films give us images and ideas of "girls." The kinds of moments given affective force in girl teen films in the fun mode are limited. That is not to say that the audio-viewer cannot enjoy experiences that I do not consider here, but those that we are invited to encounter are constrained by the Hollywood notion of "appropriate" girlhood.[8] This chapter explores what music video aesthetics are, what they do, and the kinds of pleasure they aim to create around gendered notions of fun. It begins by defining music video aesthetics, outlines the intimate public of girlhood that these films are a part of, and creates a framework that demonstrates the generic and gendered construction of spectacle. This framework is then applied to two girl teen films: the dance film *Make*

It Happen (Grant, 2008, USA) where we would perhaps expect to find music video aesthetics, and *13 Going On 30*, where the same stylistic devices are employed to make a spectacle of the "everyday."

Music Video Aesthetics

The kinds of pleasure that I refer to here are somatic. If aesthetics is origi-nally "anything that has to do with perception by the senses" then aesthetic pleasures can be described as those that connect with the body.[9] Following Virginia Postrel and Nigel Thrift I explore aesthetic pleasures thus:

> Aesthetics is the way we communicate through the senses. It is the art of cre-ating reactions without words, through the look and feel of people, places, and things. Hence, aesthetics differs from entertainment that requires cogni-tive engagement with narrative, word play, or complex, intellectual allusion [. . .] Aesthetics shows rather than tells, delights rather than instructs. The effects are immediate, perceptual, and emotional.[10]

Girl teen films do, of course, include pleasures connected to narrative or cognitive engagement. One obvious potential pleasure of girl teen films, for example, is their use of language and word play that engages with (or creates) contemporaneous adolescent vernacular.[11] Focusing on aesthetic pleasures, however, creates an opportunity to consider how this version of girlhood is designed to feel fun, as one aesthetically charged encounter among a myriad of others in an age where style is a part of everyday life.[12]

Music video aesthetics are one aspect of girl teen films that give moments of "fun" greater affective force and explain these moments' phys-ical appeals. Traditional Hollywood scoring fits image and music together in a way that aims to make the music "unheard."[13] In music video sequences in film, music makes the image and the image makes the music: both media are reliant upon and transform each other. In this particular way of com-bining music and visuals the differences between elements are not made visible but converge to create a general, coherent, and intense impression. Music video stylistics are made by an intermedia process that creates this distinct relationship between music and visuals. Yvonne Spielmann uses the term intermedia to describe a convergence of separate art forms.[14] She proposes that where multimedia forms cross borders and compare different media, each remains distinct. Intermedia, however, refers to an interaction and integration between different media that results in trans-formation: in their combination elements change to create a third aesthetic dimension that can be described as an *intermedia* aesthetic. Music video aesthetics create an audiovisual interaction in which music and image fuse and exchange. These sequences bring music to the fore to create an intense aural presence but the music does not work alone to generate impact, it is the combination of image and music that produces an audiovisual spectacle. The intermedia fusion of music and image, where both seem to respond and correspond to each other, creates distinct moments of spectacle.

In *Another Cinderella Story* (Santostefano, 2008, USA), for example, the Cinderella character is told to clean the house by her Wicked Stepmother. Introducing this music video sequence as a "cleaning number," the opening bars of a non-diegetic pop song begin the shift into a "supra-diegetic" space and the characters' movements become increasingly rhythmical.[15] The scene is cut around the beat of the music and movements are coordinated with rhythm and melody. Some shots do not abide by classical continuity but are cut to emphasize the rhythm of the song. Dusting, vacuuming, and polishing become dance moves that accentuate the beat of the music, whilst the music lends impact to the characters' gestures. Music and image work together to make cleaning "fun."

The collaborative relationship between music and image in film is nothing new. The use of prerecorded, popular music in films, however, is a relatively more recent practice that, since the 1970s, has become increasingly unexceptional.[16] The emergence of the pop-promo in the 1960s and the form's stylistic influence on films like *A Hard Day's Night* (Lester, 1964) is also a fairly recent development in the relationship between sound and image that has become progressively commonplace, more especially following the launch of MTV in 1981. This chapter does not explore a history of music in film, or compare the use of prerecorded popular songs to traditional scoring. Instead, I am interested in how this particular combination of music and image creates spectacle and the kinds of pleasures it aims to generate as a means to understand how girl teen films are designed to feel fun.

The Intimate Public of Girlhood

Girl teen films start from the premise that girls already have something in common. As Lauren Berlant proposes, cultural products aimed at a particular minority work from a presumption that consumers of particular "stuff" share qualities or experiences that are held in common.[17] Girl teen films aim to feel as though they express what is supposedly common among girls; making and repeating fixed desires, fantasies, and pleasures. Following Berlant, we can describe these films as part of the intimate public of girlhood. As Berlant describes: "An intimate public operates when a market opens up to a bloc of consumers, claiming to circulate texts and things that express those people's particular core interests and desires."[18] The intimate public of girlhood aims to feel as though it expresses what is ostensibly common among girls and in doing so it sustains the association of specific desires, fantasies, affects, and pleasures with girlhood.

Berlant describes the intimate public as a set of "porous constraints"; she suggests that the "motivating engine" of scenes within a "women's intimate public" is: "the desire to be *somebody* in a world where the default is being nobody."[19] The kinds of "fun" that girl teen films create are about the spectacle of the self. Being *somebody* in these worlds always involves the girl body and its visibility at the center. The use of music video aesthetics is one way that the films are designed to make this restricted version of girlhood feel exciting. As Berlant describes:

> the intimate public legitimates qualities, ways of being, and entire lives that have otherwise been deemed puny or discarded. It creates *situations* where these qualities can appear as luminous.[20]

The impact of music video aesthetics gives intensity to situations, trivialized by their connection to private, commercial, or institutional realms. The pleasures of music video aesthetics lend impact to "puny" and "discarded" aspects of femininity. By contributing the physical impact of music and dance, music video aesthetics make actions and activities seem fun and more significant than they may otherwise appear. Consequently, these films can feel like change, energy, possibility, choice, and freedom but what they create is a shift within parameters: a static movement.

The Impact Mode of Spectacle

In film all spectacles are not the same but sequences that create spectacle are often considered to be more striking or intense—displays occupying distinct spaces that aim to directly arouse the audience.[21] Within and between specific films and genres spectacles come in different forms. Usually associated with action and blockbuster cinema, the "impact spectacle" is an aggressive mode designed to encourage visceral reactions from its audience.[22] To create spectacles that aim for impact, action and blockbuster films employ particular presentational strategies. These stylistic devises render specific moments as especially intense. For example, through the use of rapid editing and movement toward camera, explosions in action films often build in intensity to create moments with increasing affective force.[23] In girl teen films very similar presentational strategies are employed but the things that these films make a spectacle of and the kinds of experiences that they create are restricted by traditional gender "norms."

The presentational strategies that make impact spectacles can be described as "post-continuity" techniques.[24] In *Post-Cinematic Affect* Steven Shaviro introduces the concept of post-continuity to make explicit the connections between contemporary cinematic presentational strategies, affect, and the body. Through reference to action and exploitation films, Shaviro suggests that cinema has now relegated continuity in favor of impact, with the aim of stimulating autonomic responses in the audio-viewer. Post-continuity techniques are used, he suggests, "towards a moment-by-moment manipulation of the spectator's affective state."[25] In the contemporary world, he suggests, the stylistics of image-based modes of presentation are used to engage full somatic participation.[26] Action films, Shaviro proposes, aim to create the same visceral involvement as that of a computer game.[27] Like computer games the stylistics of post-continuity are used to generate "user excitement."[28]

The "computer game" mode of post-continuity stylistics is evident in the boy teen film, *Never Back Down* (Wardlow, 2008). In common with the girl teen films analyzed here, *Never Back Down* is an exploitation film. Targeted at a male teenage audience, it was made with a relatively substandard budget and capitalizes on the increasing popularity of mixed martial arts in the twenty-first century.[29] When Jake (Sean Faris) joins a new high school, he becomes involved in an underground fight club. The kinds of physical experiences that boy teen films offer and those moments that gain affective charge through the use of post-continuity stylistics are determined by gender "norms." "Boy fun" is created as different from "girl fun." Jake's quest for maturity is explicitly tied to a set of physically aggressive challenges and the attainment of a stereotypical notion of manhood is achieved through physical prowess and emotional stoicism. The final fight sequence in the film uses a highly mobile camera and intense rapid editing with the aim of maintaining a constant sense of momentum. The camera is constantly in the thick of the action, close-up point-of-view shots work to create proximal intensity and flash frame whiteouts are used to generate the jar and clash of the fight. The exaggerated use of sound effects, of fists hitting bodies and bones breaking, adds to the overall rendering of the visceral impact of the fight. Used in this boy teen film context, where action and physical force are the main spectacle, post-continuity techniques are used to generate affects of a kind that respond to the aggression, force, and momentum of the fight.

In girl teen film the use of music video aesthetics—the specific combination of music and image—shifts the mode in which post-continuity techniques are employed. Music video sequences use the same post-continuity presentational strategies as those used in the impact spectacles of action cinema. However, these techniques are employed in girl teen films, not to generate the same user excitement as a computer game but stylistically and affectively to render the feelings created by music and dance.

The table provided below offers a basic breakdown of how the impact mode of spectacle works in girl teen films. As a means of illustration, the table compares (in a rudimentary way) the spectacles of action cinema to those of girl teen film. The comparison is made to demonstrate the generic and gendered construction of spectacle.

The table breaks the modes of spectacle down into three key areas: (1) *the Pro-filmic spectacle*: what is presented for the camera as spectacle; (2) *Presentational strategies*: the stylistic devises used to present spectacle; and (3) *Intended response*: the desired effect that the combination of the first two categories encourages—by this I do not mean to suggest what these spectacles *will* do, but what they *aim* to do (Table 10.1).

Make It Happen

As a means of illustration *Make It Happen* offers a standard example of girl teen dance film and music video sequence. Structured around set pieces of dance or burlesque, *Make It Happen* provides a narrative framework as motivation for each dance routine: having failed her audition to get into dance school, Lauryn (Mary Elizabeth Winstead) takes a job at burlesque club "Ruby's." The dance routines are integrated as club numbers or rehearsals, with each consciously employing a music video aesthetic, as director Darren Grant states: "each little dance routine was going to be like its own little music video."[30] Lauryn's first performance at "Ruby's" provides a typical example. The pro-filmic elements of this spectacle include the space of the nightclub, the stage in particular, and the body of the protagonist. The mise-en-scène of the sequence includes a highly stylized proscenium arch, strong backlighting, and saturated colors.

Initially Lauryn struggles to perform successfully. The diegetic music is a smooth jazz number, too slow for the character's style of dance. During this initial part of the scene, medium-length to long shots dominate to let the character's failure unfold. When the club DJ realizes Lauryn's predicament, he switches the diegetic track to the hip-hop/r'n'b based "Shawty Get Loose" by Lil Mama.[31] The contrast between the two songs is central to the narrative of the scene. The use of music underscores the juxtaposition between maturity and youth. The jazz track has a swing beat that maintains a slow tempo, its lyrical flow emphasizes a mature sophistication. "Shawty" uses louder dynamics, the tempo is faster, the use of syncopation adds to the sense of speed, and the rap in the song stresses beat rather than lyrics. When the music changes, the sequence shifts to use music video

Table 10.1 Mode of spectacle in girl teen films, Samantha Colling, 2014

	Pro-filmic spectacle		Presentational strategies		Intended response	
	Action cinema	Girl teen film	Action cinema	Girl teen film	Action cinema	Girl teen film
Impact spectacles	› Explosions › Car chases › Fighting › Running › Shooting › Parkour › Destruction › Elemental forces › Fetish objects (e.g., guns) › The body › Loud noises › Forceful music › Public sphere	› Shopping › Trying on clothes › Singing › Dancing › Laughing › Strutting › Applying makeup › Cleaning › "Girls' sports" › Parties › The body › Audience › Stage › Pop/hip-hop/r'n'b › Private/privatized public space	› Rapid editing › Movement toward camera › Cut on movement › Quick fire series of shots showing same action from varied angles › Highly mobile camera › Reliance on CUs › Shallow lateral space › Saturated colors › Strong backlighting › Intense sound › Intense special effects › Hasty cuts from falling to rising action (little use of establishing shots) › Rapid use of cross-cutting › Bipolar extremes of lens length	› Rapid editing › Movement toward camera › Quick fire series of shots showing same action from varied angles › Highly mobile camera › Reliance on CUs › Shallow lateral space › Saturated colors › Strong backlighting › Intermedia aesthetics: music &visuals › Hasty cuts from falling to rising action (little use of establishing shots)	› Shock › Surprise › Excitement › Exhilaration › Agitation › Astonishment › Desire › Tension › Tactile pleasure › Kinaesthetic empathy › Kinaesthetic sympathy › Kinaesthetic contagion	› Exhilaration › Excitement › Amusement › Astonishment › Admiration › Desire › Tactile pleasure › Kinaesthetic empathy › Kinaesthetic sympathy › Kinaesthetic contagion

aesthetics and following this change Lauryn manages to present a success-ful routine. Here, music video aesthetics create the spectacle and pleasures of a successful performance.

In *Make It Happen* music video, the aim of aesthetics is to render the experience of music and dance as much as to display it, and invite the audio-viewer to share in the joys of what it feels like to move to music. Michel Chion provides a way of thinking about sound that can be extended to the musical–visual relationship of music video aesthetics. Chion characterizes the verisimilitude of the film soundscape as a ren-dering of sensation, rather than as a reproduction of sound. In place of committing to straightforward representations of sound, the film sound-scape aims to embody "real-world," multisensory experiences.[32] As Chion explains: "The thing is that sound [...] must tell the story of a whole rush of composite sensations, and not just the auditory reality of the event."[33] Music video aesthetics create a specific rush of sensations, mutually con-structed by music *and* visuals that replicate the feelings of control and expansion related to dance.

From the moment that "Shawty" kicks in, the sequence in *Make It Hap-pen* is cut around the beat of the music. The intense sense of speed and immediacy emphasized by the tempo and syncopation of the track is met by the use of rapid cutting and close-ups. At points, the scene is cut around a series of seemingly disconnected close-ups—not revealing the flow from one move to another but accentuating the general pulse of music and dance.

In places, the sequence abandons continuity to stress the rhythms of the music and make a further spectacle of specific dance moves. Similar to displays of spectacular physical feats in action cinema, consecutive shots show the same move twice: first at 24 frames per second and then in slow motion and from differing angles. The sequence also aims to generate feel-ings of movement and alternation, echoing the configurations of tension and release central to music and dance. Dirty long shots (in which heads and shoulders obscure parts of the shot) from the diegetic audiences' per-spective act as counter-shots to those close-ups on stage in conjunction with the counterpoint between melodies and beat in the song. Together music and image create an audiovisual spectacle that renders the feelings and sensations of music and dance.

Music has the capability to create affective and emotional shifts. It can invite the body to take up specific modes of engagement.[34] Music and image together can similarly work on our bodies but their combination is potentially more intense. In *Make It Happen*, music video aesthetics aim to promote an embodied engagement with the pleasures of energy, tension and release, control, freedom and mobility connected to music and dance.

With a focus on rendering how the body feels as it moves with music, music video sequences encourage kinaesthetic contagion. Kinaesthetic contagion is a type of kinaesthetic empathy: an embodied experience of physical processes on display. Matthew Reason and Dee Reynolds describe kinaesthesia as referring to "sensations of movement and position [...] informed by senses such as vision and hearing as well as internal sensations of muscle tension and body position."[35] In its diffuse sense, kinaesthetic empathy is a mode of perception whereby another person or object's action is experienced in one's own body. I take an approach to kinaesthetic pleasures that focuses on how the audio-viewer is *invited* to respond to bodies and objects on display rather than make claims to how they *will* respond. A type of kinaesthetic pleasure, kinaesthetic contagion is a physically uplifting response to the general movement of the performance, dance, or object on display.[36] Exploring live dance, Reynolds suggests that the movement of the dance as a whole can affect us. That we may internalize movement and sense its processes in our own bodies, not just the movement of one dancer or single component of the dance but the movement of the whole piece.[37]

Music video aesthetics in girl teen film are used to encourage kinaesthetic contagion, not only with the body on display but also with how the dancing body is rendered by the fusion of music and image. These spectacles do not necessarily focus on the specific moves that the body makes but on generating the impact of how it feels to move to music.

In *Make It Happen* music video, aesthetics render the body in control and generate the impact of a successful dance routine. The number is constructed with a focus on generating what it feels like to dance rather than displaying the specific choreography of the routine. Music and visuals work to generate kinaesthetic contagion, not only with particular moves, but also with the back-and-forth, tension and release, shift and swing, of dance in general. The experience of pleasure in relation to music video aesthetics can thus have less to do with the dance itself than with the intermedia relationship that creates an encounter with music and dance.

13 Going on 30

Music video aesthetics can be applied to any sort of action to create a spectacular impact. Music video aesthetics can make even the most "ordinary" activities feel like music and dance without including dancing bodies at all. Music video sequences that do not involve dance routines can still create kinaesthetic pleasures. In the context of girl teen films these techniques are often used to create a spectacle around "unremarkable" practices of femininity.

13 Going on 30 provides an illustrative example of a music video sequence that utilizes music video aesthetics to make a spectacle of the "everyday." The film follows Jenna who makes a wish on her thirteenth birthday and wakes up the next morning as a 30-year old. The film is not strictly a girl teen film but more accurately can be described as a romantic comedy that includes many girl teen film elements: including a makeover and reveal structured by music video aesthetics. The film provides a useful example because it highlights the Hollywood version of girlhood in extreme. Like other body-swap film scenarios, stereotypes are played out to their zenith because it is the supposed contradictions between the mind and body (young mind in adult body) from which comedy is derived. Performed by an adult woman therefore, the Hollywood idea of what a 13-year-old girl is supposed to be is made stark.

The music video sequence begins when Jenna—13 in the body of a 30-year old—gets ready for a party. The loud dynamics of Whitney Houston's "I Wanna Dance with Somebody" signal that the spectacle has begun.[38] The pro-filmic aspects of the spectacle in this scene include, the domestic space of the flat, the body of the protagonist, and "everyday" commodity fetishes: clothes, accessories, and makeup. The use of music video aesthetics in this example lends impact to otherwise relatively "ordinary" activities and objects. The scene is a makeover and reveal that, without music video aesthetics, would simply show a character getting dressed and putting makeup on—lacking any of the necessary impact that surrounds moments of visibility in girl teen films. With the use of these presentational strategies, the makeover and commercial products that adorn the girl figure leave a physical impression on the body of the audio-viewer. Those facets that make up the intimate public of girlhood are made to feel pleasurable.

The music video sequence in *13 Going on 30* generates a sense of constant forward and upward movement. The movement of the music itself is uplifting but because the music does not work alone, the movement that the music is "doing" is intensified by its relationship with the image on screen.[39] Despite the lack of dancing bodies in this sequence, the combination of image and music invites the audio-viewer to enjoy the kind of kinaesthetic contagion that is experienced in response to the rhythm, energy, and movement of the scene as a whole. Kinaesthetic contagion is in reaction to the pulse of the entire sequence, rather than just the character's individual movements.

The scene begins by inviting the audio-viewer to adopt a familiar embodied watching position: a responsiveness to music and images that is similar to that offered by conventional music video. The music begins in combination with a graphic match between the front door of Jenna's apartment and the frame of the open bathroom door. The character emerges from billowing steam, reminiscent of the dry ice often used in music videos, making reference to a music video cliché. In combination the music introduction has a staggered entry of instruments—a buildup that gradually thickens the texture of the song. The visual-musical buildup acts as a transition point from classical continuity into the supra-diegetic space of the music video sequence, that aims to lead the audio-viewer into a mode of engagement that attends to the composite sensations of music and dance.

The sequence places a real emphasis on rhythm, with the aim of impacting upon the body of the audio-viewer. The synthesized handclap that opens "I Wanna Dance with Somebody" is layered with the cross-rhythm of a synth drum and piano that uses a repetitive, syncopated rhythm based on one note. This lack of melody at the beginning of the sequence places full weight on beat and rhythm. Composer Howard Goodall explains that rhythm is the element of music that reacts most immediately with our bodies—it is the component of music that most directly impels us to move.[40] In this sequence beats explicitly hit on the cut or in reference to movement in shot and the audio-viewer is invited to enjoy the kinaesthetic contagion of the musical and visual beat that the aesthetics create (Figure 10.1).

A little further into the sequence, synth horns join in with an emphatic glissando (a slide up in pitch), which is echoed in Houston's vocals ("Woo!"). The accompanying image works as an onomatopoeic imitation of the exhilaration and upward movement of the song. The aural and visual

Figure 10.1   *13 Going on 30* (Winick, 2004). Onomatopoeic visuals

movement on screen implies movement beyond what we see—in combination music and image suggest an exhilarated "jump." All of the synthesized instruments and visuals have a high and bright color tone—even the bass is bright. The elements work together to generate an *upbeat*, creating energy infused, ascendant movement. The flow of musical and visual movement invites the audio-viewer to experience the immediate pleasures of this energized, upward motion.

   The construction of the sequence also mirrors the configurations of tension and release fundamental to music and dance by emphasizing call and response. Houston's vocals and synthesizer use call and response throughout the verse and the visuals correspond to the motion of the synthesizer to answer the vocals. This call and response maintains a sense of momentum, echoing the back and forth of dance. Visually and aurally, the sequence as a whole also uses an ascending/descending/ascending pattern. As the song moves into its first verse and the visuals shift to a new location, the dynamics become quieter and the pitch lower. In combination the camera tracks smoothly and the protagonist's body movements become relatively more fluid. At the end of the sequence, the chorus kicks in with a horn slide. In combination the front door of the apartment opens and the camera tracks back and jibs up the protagonist's body as she struts down the corridor toward the camera. The quieter dynamics in the verse and visuals previous to this moment provide the necessary contrast that highlights the spectacle of the chorus and strut down the corridor. The buildup between verse and chorus/makeover and catwalk, provide the necessary impact for the big reveal by rendering the tension and release of music and dance. Through these techniques the dress, the makeup, and the walk become something spectacular.

Conclusion

Girl teen films use post-continuity techniques that are usually associated with blockbusters and action cinema as a means of creating impact. These music video aesthetics invite the audio-viewer to experience the specific kinaesthetic pleasures of music and dance. Without necessarily presenting human bodies dancing, these sequences themselves dance: rendering the sensations and pleasures of movement, tension, and release fundamental to music and dance. Through the use of music video aesthetics, this version of girlhood becomes meaningful, significant, and compelling, maintaining the association of specific desires, fantasies, affects, and pleasures with girlhood. "Girl fun" is limited, not only around the specific moments and "stuff" that creates the intimate public of girlhood but also around the kinds of pleasures and affects that it aims to generate. Lauryn's dance and Jenna's makeover feel like the energy, freedom, and possibility of music and dance but, part of the intimate public of girlhood, they only create a set of "porous constraints." These moments feel like transformation but they are restricted by gender "norms." Nonetheless, understanding how music video aesthetics are designed to feel fun explains why we might sometimes choose to go along with this version of girlhood.

Notes

1. See Rosalind Gill, *Gender and the Media* (Cambridge: Polity, 2007).
2. For an exploration of the ways that the detail of fairy tale makes objects appear more significant than they would otherwise seem, see Jessica Tiffin, *Marvelous Geometry: Narrative and Metafication in Modern Fairy Tale* (Detroit: Wayne State University Press, 2009).
3. Teen film has developed with a distinct relationship to popular music and the music industry. The use of popular music in teen film is industrially recognized as both a selling point for movies themselves and a key to lucrative ancillary markets. In the Hollywood context aesthetic appeals do of course have economic imperatives at their basis. This chapter, however, maintains a focus on the kinds of pleasure these films aim to generate. For an analysis of the economic influence of popular music in teen film, see: Andrew Caine, *Interpreting Rock Movies: The Pop Film and Its Critics in Britain* (Manchester: Manchester University Press, 2004); Kay Dickinson, "Pop, Speed and the 'MTV Aesthetic' in Recent Teen Films," *Scope* 2001, online at www.nottingham.ac. uk/film/journal/articles/pop-speed-and-mtv.htm; Thomas Doherty, *Teenagers and Teenpics: The Juvenilization of American Movies in the 1950s* (Philadelphia: Temple University Press, 2002); John Mundy, *Popular Music on Screen: From Hollywood Musical to Music Video* (Manchester: Manchester University Press, 1999); John Mundy, "Television, the Pop Industry and the Hollywood Musical," in *Film's Musical Moments* edited by Ian Conrich and Estella Tincknell (Edinburgh: Edinburgh University Press, 2006), pp. 42–55.
4. Catherine Driscoll, *Teen Film: A Critical Introduction* (Oxford: Berg, 2011).
5. Robert Stam, *Film Theory: An Introduction* (Maiden: Blackwell, 2000).
6. In film this treatment of girlhood is especially recognizable in the clean teen films of the 1950s and 1960s (e.g., *Gidget* [Wendkos, 1959, USA] or *Beach Party* [Asher, 1963, USA] but this version of girlhood can be identified as part of Cinderella's legacy, a history that reaches back to the eighth century for which we do not have space to cover here.
7. See Catherine Driscoll, *Girls: Feminine Adolescence in Popular Culture and Cultural Theory* (New York: Columbia University Press, 2002); Juliet Schor, *Born to Buy: the Commercialized Child and the New Consumer Culture* (New York: Scribner, 2004); Catherine Grant and Lori Waxman, *Girls! Girls! Girls! In Contemporary Art* (Bristol: Intellect, 2011).

8. In this chapter I place particular emphasis on the relationship between music and image and for this reason the term spectator seems inadequate to describe the individuals addressed by film. Instead I use Michel Chion's term audio-viewer as a means to highlight and more accurately convey the kinds of sensorial experiences that these films aim to achieve. Michel Chion, *Audio-vision: Sound on Screen* translated by Claudia Gorbman (New York: Columbia University Press, 2004).

9. Stephen Regan, *The Politics of Pleasure: Aesthetics and Cultural Theory* (Buckingham: Open University Press, 1992), p. 5.

10. Virginia Postrel, *The Substance of Style: How the Rise of Aesthetic Value Is Remaking Commerce, Culture, and Consciousness* (New York: HarperCollins, 2003), p. 6. Nigel Thrift, "The Material Practices of Glamour," *Journal of Cultural Economy* 1:1 (2008), 9–23, (10).

11. See, for example: Nico Lang, "40 *Mean Girls* Quotes That Make Everyday Life Worth Living," http://thoughtcatalog.com/2013/40-mean-girls-quotes-that-make-everyday-life-worth-living/

12. see Virginia Postrel, *The Substance of Style*, p. xiv; Nigel Thrift, "The Material Practices of Glamour."

13. Claudia Gorbman, *Unheard Melodies: Narrative Film Music* (London: BFI, 1987).

14. Yvonne Spielmann, "Intermedia in Electronic Images," *Leonardo*, 34:1 (2001), 55–61 (57).

15. Rick Altman, *The American Film Musical* (London: British Film Institute, 1989).

16. Ian Inglis, *Popular Music in Film* (London: Wallflower, 2003), pp. 1–7.

17. Lauren Berlant, *The Female Complaint: The Unfinished Business of Senti-mentality in American Culture* (Durham, NC: Duke University Press, 2008), p. viii.

18. Ibid., p. 5.

19. Ibid., p. 13 and p. 3.

20. Ibid., p. 3 [italics in original].

21. Warren Buckland, "A Close Encounter with Raiders of the Lost Ark: Notes on Narrative Aspects of the New Hollywood Blockbuster," in *Contempo-rary Hollywood Cinema* edited by Steve Neale and Murray Smith, (London: Routledge, 1998), pp. 166–177, (170); Tom Gunning, "The Cinema of Attrac-tions: Early Film, Its Spectator and the Avant-Garde," in *Early Cinema: Space, Frame, Narrative* edited by Thomas Elsaesser and Adam Barker (London: BFI, 1990), pp. 56–62, (59).

22. David Bordwell, *The Way Hollywood Tells It: Story and Style in Modern Movies* (Berkeley, CA: University of California Press, 2006), p. 158; Geoff King, *Spec-tacular Narratives: Hollywood in the Age of the Blockbuster* (London: I. B. Tauris, 2000), p. 95.

23. See King, *Spectacular Narratives*, p. 114.

24. Steven Shaviro, *Post Cinematic Affect* (Winchester: Zero Books, 2010), pp. 118–126.

25. Ibid., p. 118.
26. Ibid., p. 8.
27. Ibid., p. 104.
28. Ibid., p. 120.
29. See Thomas Doherty, *Teenagers and Teenpics* on teen film as a mode of exploitation film.
30. Anon, "The Art of Original Filmmaking: Make It Happen," *The Writing Studio*, online at http://www.writingstudio.co.za/page2366.html.
31. Lil Mama, Shawty Get Loose, Jive Records (2008).
32. Michel Chion, *Audio-vision*, pp. 107, 109.
33. Ibid., p. 113.
34. Tia DeNora, *Music in Everyday Life* (Cambridge: Cambridge University Press, 2000).
35. Dee Reynolds and Michael Reason, *Kinesthetic Empathy in Creative and Cultural Practices* (Bristol: Intellect, 2012), p. 18.
36. Kinaesthetic contagion can be connected to Jennifer Barker's notion of muscular empathy (Jennifer M. Barker, *The Tactile Eye: Touch and the Cinematic Experience* (Berkeley, CA: University of California Press, 2009). Barker extends Linda Williams body genre categories to suggest that the audio-viewer's response is a type of embodied mimicry, not just of the characters but also of the film itself. Williams' body genres catch the audio-viewer in mimicry of what they see characters perform onscreen: pornography creates arousal; horror creates fear; melodrama creates tears (Linda Williams, "Film Bodies: Gender, Genre, and Excess," *Film Quarterly*, 44:4 (1991), 2–13.). Barker broadens this idea to propose that audiences' responses can be triggered by the "film's body." In a similar vein Reynolds draws on Vivian Sobchack's work as a means to explore the affects of live dance and the audience's experience of the "dance's body" (Dee Reynolds, "Kinesthetic Empathy and the Dance's Body: From Emotion to Affect," in *Kinesthetic Empathy in Creative and Cultural Practices* edited by Dee Reynolds and Michael Reason (Bristol: Intellect, 2012), pp. 122–136; Vivienne Sobchack, *Carnal Thoughts: Embodiment and Moving Image Culture* (Berkeley, CA: University of California Press, 2004)).
37. Dee Reynolds, "Kinaestheitc Empathy and the Dance's Body"; Vivienne Sobchack, *Carnal Thoughts*, p. 129.
38. Whitney Houston, I Wanna Dance with Somebody, Arista Records (1987).
39. Tia DeNora, *Music in Everyday Life*, p. 107.
40. Howard Goodall, How Music Works—Rhythm (2006), online at http://www.youtube.com/watch?v=ZZJPnAer7EM.

Part IV

Extraordinary Girlhoods

11

Where's Girlhood? The Female Child Killer in *Where's Mary?* (Tony Hickson, 2005)

Lisa Downing

In December 1968, in Newcastle-upon-Tyne, 11-year-old Mary Bell was found guilty of manslaughter by reasons of diminished responsibility after having strangled to death two younger boys, Martin Brown (aged four) and Brian Howe (aged three). Unlike other near-contemporary murder cases that had shocked the nation, such as the child-killings dubbed "the Moors Murders" in Manchester three years earlier, Bell's crimes would not go on to inspire very much fictionalized representation, nor would they provide the fodder for lucrative true crime publications or "biopics."[1] The aberrant fact of a female child having killed other (male) children seems to have silenced the usual cacophony of lurid speculations and adaptations that follow murder cases, as if people simply did not know *what to say* about a killer who was both so young and, crucially, female. The only prominent books to be published about Mary Bell in the years following her trial would be Gitta Sereny's two serious and impressive studies of Bell's childhood and psychology, the latter revealing the physical and sexual abuse she claims to have suffered at the hands of her mother.[2] Almost 40 years after the trial, in 2005, Tyneside actor and filmmaker Tony Hickson released a puppet animation short, *Where's Mary?*, which is the only extant filmic treatment of the case to date. It tells the story of Bell's childhood, culminating in two murders. The film makes numerous explicit references to details of the Bell case, and includes in its narration paraphrased versions of the contents of notes written by the young murderer. However, the fictionalized victim's names, and in one case sex, are changed in the film

(Martin and Brian become Jimmy and Sally), so that the film straddles the genres of biographical account, on the one hand, and cautionary fable with a universalizing reach, on the other, as befits its folkloric visual aesthetic. The film is at once oppressive and whimsical, a hybrid of children's puppet theatre and psychological noir.

When news of the film's release was announced, an outcry arose from the surviving relatives of Bell's victims, who considered the forthcoming film "sick."[3] Mary Bell herself, released from prison in 1980, and granted lifelong anonymity in 2003, also objected to the film via her legal representative on the grounds that it could lead to her identity being uncovered. Despite the film being a puppet animation—and therefore inherently incapable of revealing the real Bell's new identity—Hickson was sent a warning copy of the injunction that prohibits publication of Mary Bell's new name.[4]

The very title of Hickson's film, "Where's Mary?," is suggestive of a prominent and unusual feature of the Mary Bell case: the difficulty of locating Bell herself amidst the events that unfolded in 1968. It draws attention to the numerous ways in which the young killer was made invisible and silenced—the paucity of representations of the case, the absence of any official investigation into her motivation and background, and the fact of her being locked away at the age of 11 and denied a voice (except the one that Sereny would later give her via their interviews and the published biographies). Unlike other killers, who retain a strong, if antagonistic, relationship with press and public (again, Myra Hindley and Ian Brady, the Moors Murderers, are obvious examples), Mary Bell seemed to come out of nowhere and then to disappear into further obscurity. Psychological investigation into Mary's mental and emotional state and critical analysis of the cultural meanings of her crimes were apparently deliberately ignored by a public seemingly too traumatized by the coexistence in the diminutive figure of Mary Bell of violent killing and girlhood. Biographer Sereny writes: "unprecedented in a country famous for its murder trials and literature, the public not only resisted but rejected the case of Mary Bell. 'I don't want to read about it,' people said. 'It's too horrible.'"[5] Indeed, the reception that greeted the announcement of Hickson's film suggests the same imperative to silence expressions of curiosity about, or analysis of, this case in the twenty-first century. It is almost as if it would be *bad luck* as well as bad taste (or "sick," in the words of Martin Brown's mother) to do otherwise. It also, thereby, suggests a quasi-superstitious suspicion of the process of representation itself.

Ironically, perhaps, given the response to Hickson's film and the overwhelming impression that to make entertainment out of this particular case would be beyond the pale, journalists of the time used a filmic reference made by the judge at Bell's trial to describe Mary in the press.

Mr. Justice Cusack dubbed Mary a "bad seed" after the title of Mervyn LeRoy's popular 1956 adaptation of Maxwell Anderson's play about an evil, murderous little girl who drowns a classmate and attempts to kill her mother. This reference removed Mary from the realm of disturbed child and served instead to mystify her as an innately evil or demonic entity, someone who was, to quote variously prosecutor, judge, and press, "a freak of nature," "evil born," "wicked," and "terrifying." As well as reflecting her crimes, these impressions were arguably reinforced by her assertive, precocious, and "un-childlike" behavior in court.[6]

In my recent book, *The Subject of Murder,* I demonstrated that while "murderer" is a readily understandable and available, indeed overdetermined, subject-position for adults (especially adult males) in our culture, there are very limited discursive means for talking about the child who kills.[7] In order to do so, one needs either to evoke the failure of the ideal of "childhood innocence," itself a nineteenth-century Romantic invention, or else to fall back on a pre-seventeenth-century tendency to view children as harbingers: morally weak, and therefore innately susceptible to evil (Cusack's "bad seeds").[8] A class-based analysis reveals that class "murderer" and class "child" do not intersect; they are constructed as mutually exclusive. As soon as a young person kills s/he gives up membership of class child (which is currently defined by both innocence and the absence of agency) and enters an indeterminate realm of ontological and taxonomical confusion.

The discursive difficulty of representing the underage killer is especially true in the case of *girls* who kill, since innocence and monstrous evil born of weakness are also the incompatible dual faces of otherness that accrue to the feminine in our cultural unconscious, as psychoanalytic feminist film critic Barbara Creed has argued. Creed shows how girlhood is a prime locus on which fears about threatening female sexuality and feminine violence come to rest, particularly in the film genre that best thematizes cultural anxieties—the horror genre. Taking *The Exorcist* (Friedkin, 1973) as an example, Creed shows how pervasive and contradictory cultural ideas about girlhood innocence and feminine evil find particularly baroque expression in the same iconic (possessed) female figure, 12-year-old Regan, who goes from innocent adolescent to demonic magus, "tries to fuck her mother" and "murders two men."[9] The gothic conceit of demonic possession literalizes the kind of unspeakable junior evil that killer-of-males Mary Bell too was held to personify. Our cultural projection of qualities of innocence and passivity onto childhood, and girlhood in particular, denies young girls the capacity to express violent actions or emotions, rendering these so unintelligible as to be apparently explicable only in extravagant terms that belong properly to the realms of superstition and theology.

In what follows I will consider, via a detailed analysis of Hickson's film, how *Where's Mary?* and the publicity that it attracted articulate the cultural difficulty of representing the "non-child" that is the murderous girl.

"Let Me Tell You a Story without a Beginning, a Middle, or an End . . . "

Thus begins the hypnotic, voiceover narration of *Where's Mary?*, which opens on a stark black-and-white image of the rod marionette that represents Mary, framed in a shadowy setting with a moon and the silhouette of trees visible in the background. Just as the idea of a story without a beginning, middle, or end suggests a rejection of straightforward chronology or periodization, so we are told that Mary lived "a long time ago" and "in the forest with the bears and the wolves," in keeping with fairy-tale conventions of (imprecise) historical distance and darkly Romantic settings. The film has a very particular visual appearance and is technically designed to emphasize light and shade. Hickson shot on special black-and-white Fomapan film stock, which has been made in the Czech Republic using the same method since the 1950s, and he used two lights in filming to maximize the contrast.[10]

The film's brooding and crepuscular aesthetic is inspired by Robert Wiene's *Das Cabinet des Dr. Caligari* (1920) and the work of the Czech filmmaker Jan Svankmejer.[11] According to Hickson, "There is a tradition of using puppets to tell dark and sinister fairytale stories in the Czech Republic and that is something which inspired me."[12] The Tyneside-born filmmaker's decision to tell a Tyneside-based story by borrowing from an Eastern European aesthetic, film stock, and narrative tradition dislocates the specificity of the Bell case to some extent, rendering it independent of historical and geographical circumstance and situating it as part of broader cultural fantasy and lore. Hickson explains that he came to be interested in the case as a boy because his grandmother had attended Bell's trial at the Crown Court and would tell him about it on her return home in the evenings. Since this same grandmother had entertained him with ghost stories and fairy tales, the figure of Mary Bell and her story became intertwined with the same, darkly fantastical, qualities as the fictional tales. For a while, Hickson believed that Mary Bell herself was a character from a fairy tale; a supernatural "baddie."[13] The significance of this goes beyond the personal or individual circumstances of the young Hickson's apprehension of the case, and tells us something about the function of the murder narrative in our cultural imagination. Demonized, sensationalized murderers resonate as folkloric heroes and antiheros; the stuff of melodrama and mystery.[14] Moreover, the fact that Hickson heard the story of a child who killed children when he himself was a child, and that he chose to retell the story via the medium of children's puppets, contribute to the striking dissolution of the division between what we too readily assume to be "adult" content and "children's" content. Just as we find it hard to understand a child who kills because of our perceptions of *what a child is*, so we assume that children could not partake of violent impulses and pleasures, even as we feed the most lurid and frankly terrifying content to young children in the form of fairy tales. (Many of Grimm's tales in their original forms, for example, are famously replete with abuse and violence.) *Where's Mary?* exposes the hypocrisy of serving tales of mutilation and violence to children, while assuming that children themselves are not capable of understanding or feeling the urge to be destructive (a misperception that Melanie Klein's findings about the homicidal rage felt by toddlers should have dispelled over half a century ago[15]). The evocation of the fairy-tale tradition also implicates all of us who enjoy the barely disguised violence of this tradition in the consumption of the Mary Bell case.

The film is particularly interested in incongruity and juxtaposition, both in terms of its shadowy visual aesthetic, and in the way in which it holds in tension the archetypal fairy tale and the specificity of the Bell case. We are told that "the forest has all changed. And the bears have all gone now. And the only wolves are the ones that live in the shadows in the darkest corners of our minds." The slippage between fairy-tale wolves and the ones we carry in our minds suggests the disconnect between the ambivalent fantasy pleasure of fiction and the reality of Bell's traumatic life and grisly crimes. With this narrative voiceover signpost, we move visually from a woodland setting to a starkly urban one, with the screen filled with images of vertiginous, imposing buildings that are again reminiscent of the German expressionist aesthetic (Figure 11.1).

In terms of plot, the film documents the escalation of a young killer's journey into violence. We are shown Mary "playing" with a cat before kicking it down a well, and the ironic voiceover tell us that "even serial killers start small," echoing the commonly reported offender-profiling truism that many murderers of this type begin by torturing and/or killing animals. The eeriness of the film lies in the simultaneity of the sometimes whimsical appearance of the puppets and childlike tone of the voiceover ("What's Mary doing? She's pushing it down the well! Oh no! Mary is very naughty") and our knowledge that these events have a shocking and tragic real-life referent. Yet, this form is also particularly appropriate to conveying the uncomfortable reality that violent acts may signify differently to a child (and that acts of everyday banal violence and the "ultimate crime" of murder are not comfortably categorically separate but instead lie on a continuum, implicating us all). The idea of Mary's actions being

Figure 11.1   *Where's Mary?* (Hickson, 2005). Mary in the forest (with the bears and the wolves)

"children's games going too far"[16] is evoked throughout the film. As with the cat, Mary's encounter with her first human victim "Jimmy" is framed in terms of "playing a game." Jimmy's murder is narrated in the following words:

> Look at little Jimmy. He's so happy dancing and playing about in the street. But what's this? Mary wants to play with him. He doesn't like Mary's game. And soon the game comes to an end.

In perhaps the most disturbing and melancholic sequence of Hickson's film, shot in Mary's bedroom, allusions are made to the hidden horrors that may motivate Mary's acts. The voiceover announces "Mary sits alone at night, thinking. She looks from her window. She writes in her diary: 'Beware: I kill so I may return.'" At this juncture, true crime references intrude deliberately into the fictionalized space. On a note that she left in the nursery classroom of her murdered victim, Mary Bell scrawled "I murder so that I may come back."[17] A skeletal face that appears in the window in front of which the Mary puppet is positioned embodies the "visions of the past" and "shadows" announced in the voiceover. This allusion, as so many others in the film, works at both the level of the fantasy/horror narrative (evoking the ghosts and demons that are the *dramatis personae* of fairy tales) and as a reference to the all-too-real past abuse that, according to Sereny, haunted Mary and was posited as a potential cause of her crimes. Much like the "wolves and bears" that are staples of dark fairy tales and yet, as the voiceover tells us, that only really "live in the shadows in the darkest corners of our minds," fiction and fact are made to coexist uneasily in the diegetic space.

As most of the film is shot in unrelentingly stark black and white, as discussed above, the cut to a section in garish color (an animation approximation of Technicolor) presents a striking surprise, a variation on the visual theme of contrast that has previously been achieved via gradations of shadow. Hickson explains:

> The colour section was shot on Kodak reversal, the same stock they use for home movies. The camera was a 1950s clockwork Bolex H16. I was trying to get a very "magic lantern" feel to it.[18]

It is in keeping with the film's uneasy, jarring aesthetic that this almost joyous color sequence, announced by the voiceover exclamation, "Ah, the long summer days!," should follow the "visions of the past" sequence, which is the darkest and most introspective of the whole work. The jump into color announces the entry of skipping Sally, a blonde, smiling, butterfly-chasing girl-puppet who will be Mary's second victim. The shots of Sally are counterpointed with a soundtrack of a whimsical, tinkling, musical-box-like tune, inducing pathos via the juxtaposition between innocence and menace. Sally stands for "the ideal child" as constructed by the cultural imaginary,[19] an archetypal girl—sweet, nurturing, gentle—who seems fated to play the role of victim in this "funny game." " 'I like butterflies. They're so delicate and fragile; just like dreams,' " the narrator tells us, voicing Sally, before adding with sinister undertones: "Sally is very delicate also." The obvious contrast between the taller, imposing, dark-haired Mary marionette and her innocent blonde victim visually recalls a representative trend noted by commentators on children who kill other children, such as Bell, and such as Robert Thompson and Jon Venables, the 10-year-old murderers of James Bulger in the United Kingdom in 1993. The trend in question is for the media and public to polarize the players in such tragic dramas as "our children," who might be victims and who need protection, and those "non-children" who commit the un-childlike acts to the degree that they are rendered wholly other beings, who could not, possibly, be "ours."[20] Sally, who is substituted in Hickson's narrative for Brian Howe, presents a visually effective "anti-Mary"; she is the ideal girl; the "natural" child (Figure 11.2).

Figure 11.2 *Where's Mary?* (Hickson, 2005). "Child" and "non-child"

In correspondence with Tony Hickson, I asked why he chose to change the two victims' names and the sex of the second victim. He answered that this gave him more creative freedom when developing the story: "I felt that if I used the real names, people would expect me to stick to the actual story."[21] Yet, media descriptions of the victims in *Where's Mary?* are noteworthy. Despite having obviously watched the film (since they fairly accurately recap the depicted events leading up to the murders), several journalists who commented on the adverse reaction to the production of *Where's Mary?* committed the faux pas of writing that the film "shows Bell killing four-year-old Martin Brown and Brian Howe, three"[22] or that "the film ends with the deaths of Martin Brown and Brian Howe."[23] The journalists' erasure of the very pronounced changes that Hickson so deliberately made to the identity of the victims depicted in his film is striking. Hickson is aware that his creative decision with regard to the introduction of Sally changes the gendered meaning of Mary's crimes somewhat:

> When the trial was on, there was a lot made of the fact that she was a girl that only killed boys. I remember my Grandmother telling me that all the people in the public gallery, 90% of which were women, felt she was more evil because she killed boys rather than girls.[24]

Part of what was so unbearable about the case for the surrounding culture, then, was that the perpetrator was a girl who killed boys, a "monstrous feminine" figure (or, alternatively, an unloved and abused daughter), who plucked beloved, nurtured, valued boy-children from the streets. It may well be the enduring resonance of this gendered transgression committed by Mary Bell that explains why the journalists persist in seeing Martin and Brian where, in actuality, we find only the fictional Jimmy and Sally.

Concluding Remarks

The film ends with shots that pan over Mary, alone again. Her arms and hands are outstretched, having strangled Sally, and the film has returned to black-and-white in stark contrast to the Technicolor sequence that has preceded it. The narrator announces, in tones that are both elegiac and prophetic, "Sally and Jim have gone now. And so has Mary. But beware; she may return." This very obviously harks back to Hickson's earlier paraphrase of Mary Bell's note: "Beware: I kill so I may return." The implied threat that Mary "may return" is resonant and multiply suggestive. In many ways, the structure of the film's narrative is cyclical. Just as we are told at the very opening that it has no beginning, middle, or end, so the suggestion is allowed to persist that the enduring, aberrant other personified by Mary Bell, the murderous girl, the non-child, will never go away. Fairy tales have been so susceptible to Jungian analysis in literary criticism over the years because they deal precisely in archetypes, appealing to persistent cultural fears and feeding on the fantasy of an eternal return.

Second, the threat contained in Mary's note about murdering so that she can return has, in a way, been confirmed by Hickson's film. If part of what killers do, with both their crimes and the words they leave behind, is to craft a legacy of infamy, of being unforgettable, *Where's Mary?* announces precisely the unwelcome news that Mary is *here*; that what she means to us has not gone away, despite the public's (and even the now-released, legally renamed Mary Bell's) attempts to forget. Hickson's film is received as an unsolicited resurgence of attention that must be paid to a hated figure that our culture has been so determined not to discuss.

Yet I would argue that, like the symbol of the repressed that she is, Mary and everything she signifies *must keep returning*. Taking seriously Hickson's disturbing portrayal of a girl with an aberrant, shadow-filled childhood, who did not conform to the saccharine and dehumanizing projections of what an "ideal girl" is supposed to be, encourages us to reconsider the symbolic and ethical violence we do to all children, and especially to girls, by placing expectations of unalloyed sweetness on them and thereby setting them up as victims rather than as agents in scripts of cultural dominance.

By requiring innocence and lack of agency from the young, we deny those who fall into class "child," despite all evidence to the contrary, their capacity for the more destructive and unsavory aspects of being human, and we thereby do violence to their personhood more generally. To paraphrase the title of another fictional work about an underage killer, I have been arguing, via a reading of Hickson's film and its instructive media reception, that we really do need to talk—and to keep talking—about Mary.[25]

Notes

1. The Moors Murders case, for example, provoked a glut of true-crime and semi-fictionalized books, with Emlyn Williams's bestseller *Beyond Belief: A Chronicle of Murder and its Detection* (London: Hamish Hamilton, 1968)—published the year of Bell's trial—being the most famous and successful. Various made-for-TV films and series about Hindley and Brady have followed, such as the two-part *See No Evil* (Menaul, 2006) and *Longford* (Hooper, 2006). Similarly, fact and fiction are blurred in such books as Gordon Burn's account of the case of the Yorkshire Ripper, *Somebody's Husband; Somebody's Son: The Story of Peter Sutcliffe* (London: Faber and Faber, 1984) and the film *Peter, Portrait of a Serial Killer* (Kite, 2011). Gordon Burn also treated in true-crime format the killings committed by the Wests in *Happy like Murderers: The Story of Fred and Rosemary West* (London: Faber and Faber, 1998) and Julian Jarrold directed the acclaimed TV drama about the Wests, *Appropriate Adult* in 2011. There is simply no Mary Bell equivalent.
2. Gitta Sereny, *The Case of Mary Bell: A Portrait of a Child Who Murdered, with New Preface and Appendix* (London: Pimlico, 1995 [1972]); Gitta Sereny, *Cries Unheard: The Story of Mary Bell* (Basingstoke and Oxford: Macmillan, 1998).
3. June Richardson, mother of Martin Brown, was quoted in a Newcastle newspaper as saying: "The person who is doing this [Hickson] is sick. The whole thing is wrong." J. Diffley and J. Picken, "Mary Bell Film Fury," *Evening Chronicle* (August 16, 2005), pp. 1–3 (1). She goes on: "The puppets look sick [...] Anyone who helps him [Hickson] is sick." (p. 2).
4. See Diffley and Picken, "Mary Bell Film Fury," pp. 2–3.
5. Sereny, *The Case of Mary Bell*, p. 185.
6. Quoted in Sereny, *Cries Unheard*, p. 11. At her trial, Mary spoke up for herself and asked questions, unlike her co-defendant, Norma Bell (no relation), who was acquitted of any involvement in the two murders. Norma appeared demure, timid, and afraid in court and thereby gained the sympathy of the jury, partly, one can assume, by dint of her conformity to the norms of girlhood femininity.
7. Lisa Downing, *The Subject of Murder: Gender, Exceptionality, and the Modern Killer* (Chicago and London: University of Chicago Press, 2013).
8. See Philippe Ariès, *Centuries of Childhood*, trans. Robert Baldick (New York: Vintage, 1990); Chris Jenks, *Childhood* (London: Sage, 1996); Gill Valentine,

"Angels and Devils: Moral Landscapes of Childhood," *Society and Space* 14:5 (1996), 581–599.

9. Barbara Creed, *The Monstrous Feminine: Film, Feminism, Psychoanalysis* (Abingdon and New York: Routledge, 1993), p. 31.

10. Personal correspondence with Tony Hickson, February 16, 2014.

11. Ibid.

12. Hickson cited in Diffley and Picken, "Mary Bell Film Fury," p. 2.

13. Personal correspondence with Tony Hickson, February 16, 2014.

14. See Downing, *The Subject of Murder*.

15. The Austrian-born British psychoanalyst (1882–1960), the first of Sigmund Freud's adherents to work with children rather than adult patients, developed a theory of human aggression based on her observations that young children appear to display, in almost entirely un-sublimated form, what Freud called "death drive" and to routinely feel homicidal rage against parents and other children.

16. Personal correspondence with Tony Hickson, February 16, 2014.

17. Gitta Sereny, *The Case of Mary Bell*, p. 113.

18. Personal correspondence with Tony Hickson, February 16, 2014.

19. Alison Young, *Imagining Crime* (London: Sage, 1996), p. 142.

20. See Alison Young, *Imagining Crime*, p. 142 and Lisa Downing, *The Subject of Murder*, pp. 173–81.

21. Personal correspondence with Tony Hickson, February 16, 2014.

22. See Diffley and Picken, "Mary Bell Film Fury," p. 1.

23. K. Donald, "Film on Mary Bell Sparks Legal Row," *The Journal* (Tuesday August 30, 2005), p. 7.

24. Personal correspondence with Tony Hickson, February 16, 2014.

25. I refer to Lionel Shriver's celebrated novel *We Need to Talk about Kevin* (New York: Counterpoint, 2003) made into a film by Lynne Ramsay in 2011.

12

Performing History: Girlhood and *Sib/The Apple* (Samira Makhmalbaf, 1998)

Margherita Sprio

Contemporary Iranian Cinema, and its specific use of children as nonprofessional actors in particular, asks important questions that raise a specter from the past both in terms of cinematic history and in relation to the history of girlhood on screen. In an earlier essay, I looked at the way that reenactment was being utilized in contemporary Iranian cinema[1] and I argued that this acting style was linked to the politics of performance known to us through Italian Neo Realism.[2] In this essay I will look at *Sib/The Apple* (Samira Makhmalbaf, 1998) in relation to the wider issues of reenactment and performance in cinema but more specifically at how girlhood is explored in the film. In addition to this, my argument will reconsider Laura Mulvey's earlier writing about Iranian cinema, in which she states that "there is a politics of representation at stake, but also a politics of cultural specificity at a time of encroaching cultural homogenization."[3] This chapter will examine how can these ideas engage with the performance of girlhood onscreen and how might an analysis into this assist an understanding of contemporary transnational modernity.

If, as Roland Barthes and Annette Kuhn claim in their respective accounts of photography, the ability to act oneself in front of the camera comes from the desire to recognize oneself, then how might we understand the performance of girlhood on screen in Iranian cinema?[4] Based on "real events," the parental consent given on behalf of their young daughters in *The Apple* was presumably given with the assumption that the girls in the film would be able to perform themselves—to literally act out their girlhood. A normative understanding of the importance of photographic archives, still images that help to construct family histories and identities, forces us to think through an ethical dimension in relation to moving images and to documentary film practices in particular—what is at stake for young girls, whose childhood is being documented on film for it to be subsequently scrutinized by the world? Whilst agreeing with Azadeh Farahmand that the representations of children in recent Iranian cinema are "informed by sentimentality and an obsessive romance with children's supposed innocence, purity and beauty," this idea is made even more complex by the girls in *The Apple*.[5] With reference to Farahmand, Gow states that Iranian cinema is framed within the context of pandering to a "humanist framework" and he argues that this framework is promoted by the impact of international film festivals.[6] I would agree with Farahmand's assertion that due to the international success of earlier films such as *Where Is the Friend's House,* (Kiarostami, 1987), subsequent representations of children have greatly differed from earlier representations of the 1970s and early 1980s where the films tended to be much grittier (films such as *Yek ettefāq-e sādа/A Simple Event* (Saless, 1973) or *Davandeh/The Runner* (Naderi, 1985)) in their portrayals. Children as symbols of humanism can be traced back to iconic art films such as *Ladri di biciclette/Bicycle Thieves* (de Sica, 1948) and the "*Apu*" trilogy (Ray, 1955–1959).[7] What children brought to these films, although often historicized as helping to define a new reality, in fact implied the existence of other realities beyond the diegetic world of the film. *The Apple* also functions in this way and Hamid Dabashi's claim that the director is part of a post-ideological generation of filmmakers should be seen within the context of Makhmalbaf being part of a generational shift that enables a vision of reality with no claim to a monopoly on truth, an insistence on the particular, and no patience for the universal.[8]

Engaging with an approach that sees cinema as intrinsically transnational and global from its outset, it is important to reference that in the West there is a long tradition of child performers in both early theatrical and cinematic productions and *The Apple* can also be seen within the context of these earlier genres as well as within a specific Iranian cinematic tradition. As the work of Anne Varty shows us, the use of children in theatrical performances in Victorian Britain for example, was very widespread.[9] If a professional theatrical company did not train the children to perform, then they were commonly taught to perform by their parents.[10] Interestingly, in this earlier historical period the use of young women and girls in particular forced them to be in "the double bind in which society held them, idolized on stage, spurred off stage."[11] Their protection became guarded through the *Prevention of Cruelty to Children Act* passed in

Liverpool 1883, and this legislation marked a change whereby the parents' authority over the performance of their children was no longer unchallenged.[12] There is a key resonance here with the relationship between the girls, the parents and the wider civic authorities in *The Apple* that will be explored later on in this chapter. Another important issue to consider about this earlier period of child performers is the extent to which the professional training that young children were given was in order to render them capable of rendering performances of spontaneity, naturalness, and playfulness, all of which conform to existing notions of ideologies of childhood, and which points to the paradox at the heart of capturing an "authentic performance" onscreen.[13]

Importantly there is also a long tradition of the use of reenactment in early cinema and the collapsing of the boundaries between notions of naturalism, humanism, and "acting" is significant right from the very early beginnings of cinema, such as in the work of the Lumières brothers. They filmed the delights of bourgeois family life, including such footage as them feeding their baby in the garden, which Vicky Lebeau relates to a general Victorian delight in "child-watching," and in which the power and appeal of the camera is linked to its ability to document natural and spontaneous movement (so that the young child here becomes linked to the "authentic" natural movement of trees in the breeze, who can't possibly know they are being captured on film, and a cinephilic delight in witnessing such movement).[14] *La Sortie de l'Usine Lumière à Lyon* (Workers Leaving the Lumière Factory in Lyon) (1985) focused on their factory workers leaving the factory and while the single take of factory doors opening, workers pouring out, and a solitary dog crossing the screen, documents one evening in Lyon, it also propels us into asking questions about the power relations between those in front of the camera and those behind it. The well-historicized reactions of the factory workers knowing that they were being filmed whilst "being themselves" is a key consideration in relation to the idea of performance: can we truly "be ourselves" on camera? Leaving infancy and coming into self-consciousness would seem to preclude such a possibility, or at least complicate it.

Films such as Flaherty's silent film *Nanook of the North: A Story of Life and Love in the Actual Arctic* (1922) and Humphrey Jennings's *Fires Were Started* (1943) both engage with the blending of real and fictional inside the film world that is key in this discussion of *The Apple*. Whilst they are very different films from very different cinematic traditions, both films promote the debate on the nature of filmic realism and the question of performances inside the filmic space in reenactment and the complexities of performance by non-actors.[15] *The Apple* is not a straight documentary, nor is it a docudrama: it is a reenactment, by the original participants, of a "true story" and thus offers a means to reflect on what it means to self-consciously perform a girlhood coming-of-age story outside of the dominant global narratives of modernity, progress, and luminosity associated with Western girlhood, and promoted as a desirable global development goal for all, with girls frequently presumed to be catalysts for social change.[16] I am not aiming here to debate the rights and wrongs of this broader politics, but rather to ask what kind of cinematic realism emerges in relation to the "true story" of *The Apple*, and how this claim to truth therefore poses ethical questions. *The Apple* is an 84-minute narrative film that compresses 11 days of "real life" and poses these questions of authenticity and performance within the context of a story about a very particular experience of girlhood. What knowledge of Iranian girlhood is being offered to international audiences? To what extent are we encouraged to see this performance of girlhood as "authentic," and to what extent can we understand Makhmalbaf's film as a highly codified generic intervention in which a coming-of-age story is packaged for a film festival audience raised on sentimental and humanist accounts of childhood in general and girlhood in particular?

Daily survival in *The Apple* is made difficult for the two girls who form the central protagonists of this compelling film made by Makhmalbaf when she herself was only 17 years old, a quite remarkable fact. She became interested in the story when she saw the sisters in a welfare center on television and went there and asked their father, other family members, and the social worker assigned to the family (Azizeh Mohamadi) if they would re-perform earlier aspects of their lives for a film that she wanted to make about them. The film begins with hand-held video footage and then changes to 35mm film—this was because the director could not quickly get hold of a film camera but did initially have a video camera and hence the immediacy of reportage and documentary truth is encapsulated from the very beginning of the film. The improvised film reenacts the events of the previous days in the real life of a poor family in Tehran in the late 1990s. The 11-year-old twins are not allowed to participate in modern everyday life, as they are literally encaged inside the family home. The metal-barred front door is kept locked at all times and the two girls (Zahra and Massoumeh Naderi) are not socialized and so cannot walk or speak properly. Although this is not to assume that they cannot communicate as they can and do with each other and with their parents. Thus their experience of girlhood has been shared between the twin sisters alone and always together. This film is also an original intervention into the childhood of female twins—the reenactment of the "coming of age" that the young women provide us with is one that is unique in cinematic history. This is not a film that mythologizes childhood and neither does it offer a reparative formula. It never easily fits into the normative codes associated with American films that can sentimentalize the maturing of young girls on the screen.

The narrative comprises a reenactment of the lives of these two sisters whose parents do not ever let them leave their locked caged existence within their home. Concerned neighbors expose their imprisonment and social services intervene and force their parents to allow them a childhood outside of this confinement. I want to consider this film in relation to how young girls function in contemporary Iranian films, how this function links to earlier periods of film history, but also what it might help us to reconsider in terms of a transnational experience of seeing girls in film.

Children are often central protagonists in Iranian cinema, so what is it that the child's performance brings that is of significance and that distinguishes it from what the adult performer brings? With this question, I wish to stress my specific interest here, which is in relation to the context of the girl who reenacts events that she had previously experienced. This is a mode of "acting," or the "acting out" of girlhood (growing up on the screen) that I would like to think of as a performance that goes on to shape the child's lived experience. As well as Makhmalbaf, who is of a younger generation, other Iranian filmmakers such as Abbas Kiarostami, who has also used reenactment in his films (for example, *Close-Up*, 1990) cite their work as being inspired by "reality," indeed in an interview Kiarostami states that he has done nothing *but* depict reality in his work.[17]

The depiction of children in Iranian cinema has a long history and cannot be confined to this century's generation of filmmakers. As Hamid Reza Sadr explores, in part the current trend for utilizing children comes out of the confines of the pre-revolutionary film industry, which saw major actors and actresses stopped from working, and sex, singing, and dancing banned.[18] One of Kiarostami's early experimental films, *Nān o Kūcheh/Bread and Alley* (1969), depicts an 11-minute journey of a small boy who has to try to navigate a barking stray dog whilst walking through an alley. This film was made through the government organization The Centre for Intellectual Development of Children and Adolescents and this organization was very instrumental in both the utilization of children in cinema and supporting early innovators such as Kiarostami. It went on to produce his film *Khane-ye doust kodjast/Where Is the Friend's House* (1987) and other films, all of which had children, and other non-professional actors, as central protagonists. This trend for using non-professional child actors was in part due to the success of these films outside of Iran but they were also often hugely successful within Iran. The first Iranian film to be nominated for an Oscar, *Bacheha-ye Aseman/Children of Heaven* (Majidi, 1997), is about the poverty experienced by two siblings who have to share a pair of shoes in order to get to school. For Reza Sadr,

Non-professionals were themselves, they were subtle and genuine, their lives resembling their characters' lives. Their plain acting combining the authenticity of everyday unattractiveness ... their faces had significance, the impressions of an intense inner life.[19]

Makhmalbaf is part of an extraordinary Iranian "new wave" of female filmmakers that are putting women's, and often "girls'," experiences at the center of their films. This group also includes her younger sister, Hana Makhmalbaf, who made the gripping film *Buddha Collapsed Out of Shame* in 2008 when she, herself was aged 14.[20] This film deals with its central female protagonist Baktay trying to get herself to school despite the many impeding attempts of those that try to stand in her way. They are part of a significant group of women filmmakers such as Mania Akbari, Mahnaz Mohammadi, Manijeh Hekmat,[21] and Niki Karimi, whose very desire to place female experience onscreen has at times become linked to political feminist activism: Mohammadi was imprisoned for five years in June 2014 for creating "propaganda against the Iranian regime."

Important to consider in this context of representation of girls and women by female Iranian filmmakers are the wider implications of the phenomenal success of films such as *Women without Men* (Shirin Neshat, 2009). Slightly earlier and much applauded films by Jafar Panahi such as *The White Balloon* (1995) and *The Mirror* (1997) have both seen young girls as the central characters of the narratives, with the former seeing seven-year-old Razieh go to extraordinary lengths in order to convince her mother to buy her a gold fish and the latter about six-year-old Mina who has one arm in a sling, making her own way home through the streets of Tehran after her mother has forgotten to pick her up from school. A fascinating aspect of *The Mirror* is the way that midway through the film the "actress," Mina Mohammad-Khani suddenly removes her sling and announces that she is tired of acting and now wants to go home! Authenticity and the performative collide to create a different version of realism—as I go on to show, a realism that forces the spectator to reconsider performance, "truth telling," and historical fact.

Such aspects are compellingly interwoven in *The Apple* in which Makhmalbaf asks a family to reenact their traumatic experience of coping with girlhood and the outside world. The family attempt to keep the girls "safe," a position that is itself interpreted as abusive, and points *in extremis* to the broader contradictory pressures of contemporary girlhood, which is simultaneously called upon to be innocent and empowered, idealized and knowing. The narrative is made all the more compelling by the fact that the mother, whilst often in the background of the drama, is blind and has her face and body covered in a chador throughout the entire film.

The parents' 11-year reluctance to allow their daughters out into the world is broken by complaints to the local social services by neighbors and their actions force an external gaze onto the family. A social worker is assigned to encourage the parents to allow the girls to go outside of the home and the narrative of the film presents us with the ethical dimensions of her worthy attempts at bullying the family into modernity set against the parents' desire to follow their own parental beliefs. The father explains that he fears his daughters will mix with boys and that he can foresee what the consequences of this would be. Indeed many young boys seem to inhabit the local neighborhood and the scenes in the film illustrate their fascination with the young girls when their ball falls into the same family courtyard that the girls are allowed to look into but are locked out of. Perhaps their ball falls accidentally as is common to many children who "play"—and yet within this scenario, we have to constantly remind ourselves that both the girls and the boys are self-conscious in their actions, since they are in fact reenacting their "original" lived experience.

There are many complex scenes in *The Apple* in relation to girlhood and modernity and there are some extraordinary moments when, for example, one of the girls sees her own reflection in a plastic mirror for the first time. This scene is made all the more extraordinary when we recognize the fact that she is also learning to see herself in front of the film camera. However, this fascinating moment with the mirror (an object that she quickly disregards) is forever thwarted by the knowledge that we are in fact watching a knowing performance and not seeing "the captured" moment as it "originally" happened in front of the camera. But what is at stake here and does fidelity to performance really matter? All performance is authentic and no single original experience lasts forever—in the film, the girls are able to bring resourcefulness to acting out their truth that one would often associate with adult maturity and Method Acting in particular.[22] An ability to draw from past experience is often cited as the reason that an actor is able to create an "authentic" performance—the children in *The Apple* are able to illustrate their original experience in a way that would be different from an actor learning to play a role.

Some of the most poignant moments in the film's narrative are in the sequences between the girls and other children—the other children in the film act as foils for the girls' difference. Normative interactions become scrutinized; they encounter a boy selling ice cream in the street, the neighbor's boys that climb over the wall in order to regain their ball, a boy leads the girls into the center of Tehran via a plastic jug tied to a string, and finally, toward the end of the film, they learn to "play" with other girls. (The latter performers were in fact the girls' cousins in their "real" lives but in the film they are acting as recently acquired affluent friends.) The girls' "authentic" entry into the modern world of the child is performed here as spectacle—the children are all "acting out their original experience" for the camera or at least a remembered version of it. For Reza Sadh, ordinarily children liberate plots by introducing non-professional actions—generally loafing around on the street or in rural areas.[23] They are unencumbered by the burden of acting techniques and unlived emotions. However, in *The Apple*, the children are being asked to re-perform the exact events that had once already happened. Since many censorship regulations prevent the display of adult emotions, much of what is witnessed through the simplicity of the girls' actions whilst out "playing in the streets" of Tehran is understood by a mature spectator. The empathy expected from these scenes is perhaps consciously aimed at adults and yet it was a female teenage filmmaker who directed us toward these emotions. The fact that Makhmalbaf herself is a young woman does posit the notion of identification in such a way that is unusual when discussing any feature-length film in film history.

In *The Apple*, the relationship to the girls is complicated by the fact that the children, their parents, and nearly everybody else in the film perform the entire version of events in front of the camera over a period of 11 days. Their lives are filmically condensed and with their approval. The filmmaker became interested in the story at the point that it got television media coverage and she immediately approached the father—hence the family's enforced entry into modernity was a mediated one right from the outset. The literal poverty experienced by the family in the film is matched by the emotional poverty performed throughout the film's narrative. For example, the opening frames make this apparent through the caged girl's hand attempting to pour water through the metal-barred door onto a dying plant. It remains unclear whether the filmmaker offered the parents money in order to participate in the making of the film, and they do not appear to make any stipulations about the objectives of the film, although the father does say that he sees this opportunity as a way of being able to give his version of the "truth" of his lived experience.

Like other "reality-based" systems of contemporary media, we might already be asking what happens to the girls and indeed their family once the cameras disappear and what are we to make of this system of actuality and performance? Filmmaking as a moral medium is an even more complex idea in the digital era given the range of possibilities now on offer in relation to making both still and moving images. The ethical implications are wide-ranging and the director has spoken about the role that she took as that of onlooker rather than the storyteller and she insists that the protagonists within the film "were all performing themselves."[24] She had to make little intervention because she could not have known their life story as well as they did. She felt that as a director, she could direct the performers and their actions, but that she could not have told them how to perform who they were in front of the camera because only they could do this in an authentic manner. To authentically be yourself in front of the camera is a very significant idea here particularly in relation to the girls and their performance. Their lack of access to any media platforms including seeing themselves in photographs is integral to how we begin to formulate a relationship to their on-camera "acting." Together with this, it is important to consider how one knows oneself other than through an experience of the world? A "child-like state" acts as a contradiction in *The Apple* whereby the young girls are in a continuous state of emerging maturity both in front of and away from the camera.

How much does a particular incident, actually happening "live" in front of the camera, aid in creating a modality of emotional intensity precisely because it is happening in front of the camera? The family's only access to any form of media was at the point at which they entered into it as the main object of its gaze. Their ability to navigate the power of the camera must be considered in relation to this, even though the director insists that the film was a collaborative endeavor that was improvised, constructed, and directed together. Until they experienced the outside world, these girls had not even viewed television, and had no history of themselves as subjects outside of their parental control. Play-acting in front of the camera came to them through the film director since no other photographic records or family videos of them had previously existed. Although a particularly Western and prescriptive way of thinking about the construction of childhood, the photographic record is still a very strongly resonating way of thinking through who we become and how the experience of growing up in front of the camera impacts on our later sense of selves.[25] What impact did this live narrative have on the sisters and what might have become of them without the presence of Makhmalbaf's camera?

Continuing with the idea of "play" and "play-acting" in particular, when the sisters are let out "to play" for the first time by the social worker, they immediately retreat back into their home and it takes them some time to understand the potential of play. Their return and the social worker's insistence that they stay away from their home and "play" like other children happens on three separate occasions (one cannot help wondering on how many other occasions it actually happened in "real life"). The spectator is asked to reconsider their own place in the world and the film forces identification with the assumptions about other girls (regardless of location) of a similar age who might be engaging with play time. How much does a normative code of how childhood is understood through the gaze of the camera impact on the spectatorial experience of watching *The Apple*? After all we were all once children and we all once played. Childish treats are culturally inscribed—significantly the sisters have to be persuaded that eating ice cream is an act of pleasure—its taste is something culturally determined and they are not used to its texture and are not aware that it will melt. The girl's ill-fitting shoes, with holed socks give this performance of authenticity a unique and haunting power. As spectators we know that these "events" actually happened and that the director picked out lived moments from the sisters' lives that she felt would aid an understanding of who they were and how their girlhood had been shaped, but she also takes rather universal signifiers of girlhood—ice cream, shoes—that encourage audiences to empathize with the girls and possibly further alienate them from the parental perspective.

Was this film an important political reportage and well-intended object of performance for a filmmaker who, by her own admission, was an onlooker into a story that fascinated her as well as many other middle-class Iranians in the late 1990s? The family had limited resources in every sense and in the film the father (Ghorban Ali-Naderi) says that he had only ever been educated for four winters. Nonetheless, the anguish and anger that he performs, the dishonor that he felt he had received through the original news of their story being exposed through the media offers up all kinds of additional questions about the performance of girlhood and the problem of imposing a mono-cultural perspective.

The Apple is a film that critiques the politics of the past for the present generation, although Makhmalbaf claims that nobody is to blame and "that it is the story of a nation that buries its women alive."[26] The intergenerational conflict exhibited here highlights an example of overprotective parents versus the assumed powerlessness of girlhood. As spectators we are witnesses to a narrative that shows us the "liberation" of the girls from parental control and we see them instructed into modernity.[27] For Dabashi, *The Apple* becomes a devastating condemnation of the mind-numbing oppression of women, not just in Iran, but everywhere.[28] The father in the film makes the distinction between the boys whose ball falls into their courtyard and what could happen if those same boys got close to his daughters, hence his justification for locking the girls up. He would be personally dishonored as would the name of his daughters so the question is raised—for whose sake are the girls being kept away from the outside world? Importantly, how might this very form of parental control be understood when it is the parents who grant permission for the children to reenact their original experience through making *The Apple*? In the same way that the girls are retracing an original experience, so are their parents. Are the girls reacting to their parents' request to perform to order or are they actually remembering an original experience as they attempt to re-perform it? This brings to mind Cesare Casarino's essay about Pasolini's documentary *Comizi d'Amore/Love Meetings* (1965) where the film director asks children about sex. For Casarino, the children let their bodies show that they are reciting, that they are on stage, and that their words are encased by quotation marks in the first place … they know that the questioning adult knows that they know the truth.[29]

In *The Apple*, life does not mirror art but art is created in order to speak about girlhood to a transnational audience. This is an audience that is familiar with the popularity of the representation of childhood via film festivals through the previously mentioned works of the Apu trilogy and the traditions of Italian neo-realism. In *The Apple*, the performance of girlhood is both within its narrative and outside of it. One can only imagine the consequences of having one's childhood made into a film that then goes on to have such international interest. The film carefully frames the sisters' entry into modernity as a form of release, it is a rite of passage for them and we the audience have been witnesses to an "authentic" portrayal of this journey. Their performances cannot be scrutinized along traditional parameters usually given to other child "actors" and yet neither can we discount the specifically controlling power of the camera. This version of "an authentic performance" of girlhood reveals itself as containing within its very construction the falsity of its premise. The work of art here performs the same act of modernity that the parents seem so against and Makhmalbaf's film enables a local story to become globalized and the very qualities and nature of girlhood itself to be performed in such a way that they come to seem universal. However, what are the girls being released from is an easier question to answer than what are they being released into.

Notes

1. M. Sprio, "Filmic Performance, Authenticity and *The Apple*," *Widescreen* 1:1 (2009), pp. 1–9.
2. I would wish to link it more to the Italian movement in terms of its politics rather than French New Wave as discussed elsewhere, for example in Christopher Gow, *From Iran to Hollywood and Some Places in-Between, Reframing Post Revolutionary Iranian Cinema* (London, I. B. Tauris, 2011).
3. Laura Mulvey, "Afterword," in *The New Iranian Cinema—Politics, Representation and Identity* edited by Richard Tapper (London: I. B. Tauris, 2002), p. 261. This is an extended essay originally given as concluding remarks at a conference held at UCLA in 1999.
4. See, for example, Roland Barthes, *Camera Lucida*, translated by Richard Howard (New York: Hill & Wang, 1980) and Annette Kuhn, *Family Secrets: Acts of Memory and Imagination* (London: Verso Books, 1982).

5. Azadeh Farahmand, "Perspectives on Recent (International Acclaim For) Iranian Cinema," in *The New Iranian Cinema—Politics, Representation and Identity* edited by Richard Tapper (London: I. B. Tauris, 2002), pp. 86–108.

6. Christopher Gow, *From Iran to Hollywood*, p. 49.

7. The Apu Trilogy is a trilogy consisting of three Bengali films directed by Satyajit Ray: *Pather Panchali (Song of the Little Road), Aparajito (The Unvanquished)*, and *Apur Sansar (The World of Apu)*. The films, completed between 1955 and 1959, were based on two Bengali novels written by Bibhutibhushan Bandopadhyay: *Pather Panchali* (1929) and *Aparajito* (1932). Using very limited funds and an "non-professional" cast and crew, the trilogy was a milestone in Indian cinema and remains one of the finest examples of Parallel Cinema, part of the Indian New Wave Realist movement. The three films went on to win seven awards from the Cannes, Berlin, and Venice Film Festivals.

8. See Hamid Dabashi, "The Perils and Promises of Globalisation," in *Close Up—Iranian Cinema Past, Present and Future* edited by H. Dabashi (London: Verso Books, 2001), p. 267.

9. Anne Varty, *Children and Theatre in Victorian Britain: All Work and No Play* (London: Palgrave, 2008).

10. Ibid., p. 29.

11. Ibid., p. 200.

12. Ibid.

13. Ibid., p. 37.

14. Vicky Lebeau, *Childhood and Cinema* (London: Reaktion, 2008), p. 13.

15. *Nanook of the North,* while usually theorized in terms of it being the first feature-length documentary, arguably blurs the boundaries between fiction and documentary to the extent we could see the film as what goes on to be known as "docudrama." The film follows the struggles of Nanook, his wife Nyla, and their baby, Cunayou, as they travel looking for food in Québec, Canada. Flaherty employs different filmic devices that include some aspects of the film being scripted whilst other parts are "pure documentary," that is, captured as they happened. It is impossible to know the extent to which the family acted out for Flaherty's camera, rather than simply being recorded spontaneously. Similarly, Jennings in *Fires Were Started* uses both reconstructed and documentary footage to explore the lives of firemen during the London Blitz.

16. See, for example, projects such as Nike's Girl Effect campaign. Proponents of this campaign argue that investing in a girl's health and education will increase her family and her country's economic prosperity, and use commanding statistics to back up their claims. For example, the Nike Foundation (2011) argues, "when an educated girl earns income she reinvests 90 percent in her family, compared to 35 percent for a boy." See Lyndsay M.C. Hayhurst, "Girls as the 'New' Agents of Social Change? Exploring the 'Girl Effect' through Sport, Gender and Development Programs in Uganda," *Sociological Research Online* 18:2 (2013), pp. 1–8.

17. Farah Nayeri, "Iranian Cinema: What Happened in Between," *Sight and Sound*, 3:12 (1993), 28.

18. Hamid Reza Sadr, "Children in Contemporary Iranian Cinema: When We Were Children," in *The New Iranian Cinema—Politics, Representation and Identity* edited by Richard Tapper (London: I. B. Tauris, 2002), pp. 227–237.
19. Ibid., p. 237.
20. Hana Makhmalbaf also starred as the child in *A Moment of Innocence* directed by her father Mohsen Makhmalbaf, 1988.
21. Manijeh Hekmat was also the producer of *The Girl in the Sneakers* (1999), which is another important film to consider here.
22. Inspired by theatre director and actor Constantin Stanislavski, Method Acting involves a set of techniques that actors use in order to "become" the person that they are acting. In his quest for "theatrical truth," Stanislavski's teaching method involved asking students to make personal identifications with the characters that they are playing. This "method" went on to inspire the actor and acting teacher Lee Strasberg in America and it has gone on to have a lasting impact on American acting.
23. Hamid Reza Sadr, "Children in Contemporary Iranian Cinema," p. 233.
24. Samira Makhmalbaf spoke about this during the Q & A session of the premiere of *The Apple* at The London Film Festival in London, Leicester Square, UK, October 1998.
25. The prevalence of photographic images of children in the West is underlined by the amazing statistic that half the photographic film processed in the United States features young children. Vicky Lebeau, *Childhood and Cinema*, p. 12.
26. Hamid Dabashi, "The Perils and Promises of Globalisation."
27. The proceeds of the film were used to pay for the girls' subsequent education.
28. Hamid Dabashi, "The Perils and Promises of Globalisation."
29. Cesare Casarino, "Can The Subaltern Confess?," in *The Rhetoric of Sincerity* edited by Ernst van Alphen, Mieke Bal, and Carel Smith (Stanford, CA :Stanford University Press, 2009), p. 138.

13

Girlhood in a Warzone: African Child Soldiers in Film

Kate Taylor-Jones

Since early 2000, UN edicts and NGO awareness-raising campaigns have resulted in the increasing global visibility of child soldiers. Their lives have been presented in both fictional and documentary formats in films such as *Blood Diamond* (Zwick, 2006), *Innocent Voices* (Mandoki, 2004), *Soldier Child* (Abramson, 1998), *Ezra* (Aduaka, 2007), *War Child* (Chrobog, 2008), and *Kassim the Dream* (Davidson, 2008). However, in the act of making visible the realities of the child soldier, what has too frequently happened is that the life and experiences of the girl has been ignored in favor of her male counterparts.[1] Girls constitute as much as 40 percent of all child soldiers,[2] yet they are infrequent focal points, with a large majority of films centering on the male experience. This chapter will examine how these complex female figures have been inflected in the fictional cinematic space and debate why the presentation of the girl soldier has, to date, been limited and constrained by dominant gender narratives related to girlhood, childhood, and the global North's engagement with Africa. Whilst there have been several documentaries made on child soldiers (both feature-length and short), there is not enough space here to fully engage with both formats (since overall there are some key areas of divergence) and I am keen to avoid the sin of generality. Hence, this chapter focuses on the fictional space and on films that have been made by international filmmakers and distributed globally.[3] Therefore, these cinematic engagements are from the point of view of outsiders to the situation rather than those local to the region. The three films to be examined here are notable for being the only fiction films to date that directly place the African female child soldier at the center of the diegesis. This positive fact aside, *Rebelle/War Witch* (Nguyun, 2012), *Johnny Mad Dog* (Sauvaire, 2008), and *Feuerherz/Heart of Fire* (Falorni, 2009) all respectively maintain the common narrative elements that have become key markers in the child soldier tale as told to an international audience. These specifically narrative elements, as this chapter will explore, become the defining element of the girl solider narrative as it has been told on a global scale. The three films discussed here all had international cinematic release and are available worldwide via DVD in a variety of languages, hence their applicability in the discussion of global engagement with the girl solider as opposed to seeing them set inside any specific national cinema discourse.

This chapter's methodology is drawn from debates on the political and sociological discussion of how the West has engaged with, and processed, the experiences of child soldiers[4] rather than an approach that concentrates on the aesthetic or formal qualities of the films as individual creative texts. This chapter will explore how dominant notions of girlhood are inflected and reinforced via these film texts and debate how the films conform to a "very specific perceptual and cognitive comprehension of the world."[5] Whilst an intensive textual examination of aesthetics and content may result in possible readings that imply empowerment and development inside that specific filmic space, this chapter holds that where a film's narrative clearly confirms to popular global narratives, the films themselves become cultural communicators of the status quo rather than revolutionary texts. As this chapter will examine, the genuine aim of these films to give an account of the experiences of a girl ultimately fails since they are unable to escape the globalized trope of "innocence lost." Like literary narration, a point this chapter will touch upon later, film can influence viewing positions of the recipients via the construction of the narrative text alongside its visual and auditory engagements. As Bordwell comments, film stories are constructed according to the specifics of the medium "in order to achieve specific time-bound effects on a perceiver."[6] I am not here arguing viewers to be perceived as passive but rather this chapter is engaging with the fact that these films are aimed at a specific globalized, Westernized audience that is seeking to have its own world position ratified and consolidated via this viewing experience. This chapter focuses on examining how narrative is used, not to challenge prevailing ideals or to give these girls a voice, but rather to present easily digestible narratives that confirm to dominant representational global trends with regard to this female figure. The girls, aged between 8 and 14, are either kidnapped (Komona in *Rebelle,* Lovelita and Laokolé in *Johnny Mad Dog*) or sold (Awet in *Heart of Fire*) into an armed guerrilla unit. Once there, they are threatened with violence, raped (or rape is attempted), and profoundly abused. Although violence, rape, and torture committed by—and on—children is an undeniable global horror, narrative definitions of childhood, namely, innocence, choice, and free-dom, are brought into play in a process whereby the children's own sutured experiences are most often disregarded. Thus in these films, the uphold-ing of governing narratives of childhood (from the viewpoint of a global North-led adult point of view) are favored over the reality of the child's lived experience.

David M. Rosen comments that there have been three key influences in the recent conceptualization of child soldiers: "changes in the nature of warfare in the postcolonial era, the emergence of the small-arms trade, and the *special vulnerability and innocence of childhood* (my emphasis)."[7] Jean and John Comadroff's arguments about a "globalisation of childhood"[8] are highly pertinent here. There is a tendency "to speak of youth as a trans-historical and trans-cultural category,"[9] in short, an envisioning that the perceived innocent and carefree time of childhood is a *global* narrative. As Lisa Downing notes in her chapter in this book, children have tradi-tionally been defined as both innocent and lacking in agency. In agreement with this approach the representational sphere has been generally homoge-nous with regard to portraying child soldiers and all three films keep to the prevailing narrative of childhood as interrupted/lost innocence rather than seeking to complicate the discourse. As a result, the films place strong emphasis on the ages of the girls and the inappropriateness of the respec-tive roles they are being asked to undertake. In *Rebelle*, the narrative of Komona is presented to us in subtitles charting her age at various intervals as she moves from the roles of solider, to wife, to widow, to sex slave, and then to mother. In *Johnny Mad Dog,* Laokole's clear status as child via her physical immaturity is challenged through her role as carer for her disabled father, younger brother, and the baby she will later adopt—a parental role she is forced to assume. In the same film, Lovelita/Fatumata will be taken from the roadside stand where she is working and forced into a role as soldier and lover of Johnny (the titular character) despite her young age.

Awet (*Heart of Fire*) will be denied food and a weapon due to her sta-tus as child (at one point she is given a wooden gun rather than a real weapon); nevertheless she will ultimately be expected to kill and function in battle as an adult solider. Throughout the film the visuals support this reading. The camera frequently places Awet in long and medium shot to allow us to clearly see the height difference between her and the older child recruits. When she is asked to kneel down beside the old automatic rifles they are being expected to use, we can clearly see how much smaller and younger she is than the rest. She manages to escape the massacre of her unit at the end of the film by hiding inside a suitcase as a further indica-tion of her small stature when compared to the older children and adults (Figure 13.1).

Figure 13.1   *Feuerherz/Heart of Fire* (Falorni, 2009). Awet (pink dress at the front) is clearly smaller than even the other child recruits

Henry Jenkins suggests that the "dominant conception of childhood innocence presumes that children exist in a space beyond, above, outside the political"[10] and as Emma Wilson notes, for many years innocence has been a "dominant fantasy"[11] with regard to filmic presentation of the childhood experience. The notion of the child as apolitical and unable to fully understand and engage with wider issues *as an adult* results in the child soldier becoming a contradiction in terms. Responsibility for their very existence as simultaneous child and soldier is thereby passed onto the adults who recruit and manage them.[12] The narrative of the child as lacking in agency and thus not being responsible for their own actions is therefore preserved via a sustained illustration of adult abuse and failure. For Komona (*Rebelle*), adults will either be the source of her abuse—such as the commander who forced her to kill her parents, the solider who rapes her, the Great Tiger in whose name they all fight—or are unable to help and protect her. Komona's parents will be killed at the film's opening (yet will return to haunt her). Her uncle by marriage, "the butcher," will try to aid her, but Komona's nightmares will spur her to nearly kill a woman and force her to leave the sanctuary of his village. In *Heart of Fire*, the failures of the adults that surround Awet to protect her ensure that we never condemn her actions. Her mother abandons her in a suitcase; her father sells her to the army; and the army officers refuse to acknowledge her vulnerability as a child and fail to shield her from the ensuing violence. Adults in *Johnny Mad Dog* are either unable to protect the girl from her fate or are highly active in the recruitment, repression, and mistreatment of children and non-combatants. The child soldier therefore remains sutured to the narrative of the innate innocence of, and "right" to, a carefree childhood via this adult failure, since the child is, by extension, ultimately not responsible for the actions she undertakes.

Innocence, as it specifically relates to girlhood, becomes an even more powerful tool when the bio-politics of sexuality enters the discourse. Sexual activity would seem to immediately call to account the notion of "childhood as innocence." To this end, sexuality inside the films tends to be clearly demarcated as rape and abuse rather than teenage promiscuity—the *bête noir* of the modern world. Women and girls are often focused upon as the symbolic bearers of ideas of nationhood and or ethnic identity due to their reproductive abilities and their roles in the social communication of group identity. Therefore, rape and enforced breeding are seen as emblematic acts against a wider social, national, or cultural group.[13] Girlhood therefore enters into the *symbolic* rather than opening up the option of *embodying* the national moment. As symbols of a national identity rather than citizens of the nation, the girl solider presents a series of complex and negative connotations. As the embodiment of rape, abuse, and unwanted (and usually illegitimate) children, girl soldiers become highly marginal figures that function as symbols of rupture and dissent rather than individual agents of nationhood. This can be seen most clearly in *Johnny Mad Dog*. The aim of Laokolé is to avoid sexual slavery (or death) and she is placed in marked comparison to the character Lovelita. Fatumata (renamed Lovelita by Johnny) is the archetypal girl soldier. Johnny recruits her for reasons related to lust; he sees her at a market stall and demands she join his unit. Although he dismisses her initially as a "fucking dogo girl," he attempts to charm her and make her "his woman." The sex, when it occurs, is clearly presented as survival-sex in that Lovelita has either the option of passively accepting Johnny or being unavoidably raped. Visually this scene is arresting for the sheer lack of emotion shown in Lovelitas' face. The camera is positioned in close-up and focuses on her breasts, her expressionless face, and Johnny's hands around her throat (Figure 13.2).

In the novel by Emmanuel Dongala, *Johnny Chien Méchant* (Paris: Serpent à plumes, 2002), Lovelita has a more established back-story and is a more active character. However, in the film, her main function is twofold. First, she allows Johnny a chance to tell his tale of woes (becoming a soldier at ten, having no family) as possible reason(s) for his vicious behavior; and second, her subsequent murder by fellow soldiers allows the audience a chance to see Johnny show an actual emotional response to a death. Lovelita in this way does not function as a character in her own right but the means through which we come to understand and engage further with the lead male protagonist.

Figure 13.2 *Johnny Mad Dog* (Sauvaire, 2008). Lovelita is left with little choice but to accept Johnny's advances

Her sexual activity with Johnny places her in direct contrast with Laokolé who fights him off; moreover, Lovelita's violent demise clearly reasserts the female child-soldier narrative of the need to remain pure or face death. Lovelita, as living testimony of rape and abuse, is not allowed to survive the duration of the film and enter into the postwar moment whilst Laokolé's status as "pure virgin" allows her to move beyond the warzone and live. In her book *Feuerherz/Heart of Fire* (Germany: Droemer Knaur, 2006), by which the film is "inspired," Senait Mehari clearly articulates she was raped. However, the film *Heart of Fire* avoids including child rape as part of the narrative. As the site of identification within the film, Awet is required to remain above the war narrative to function as a symbol for potential peace and the innate innocence of children, and rape leaves a negative cultural stigma that is globally recognized and, alas, upheld.[14]

The only consensual relationship we see in any of the films takes place in *Rebelle*. Here the sexual acts of Komona and Magician are bound inside the institution of marriage and always conducted off screen. Their young ages aside, the film seems to need to ensure they are adult at the moment of implied coitus and the Magician's search for the white chicken, whilst offering a respite from the harrowing events of the opening and ending of the film, seems to imply that via his quest he earns the "right" to marry his lady in a classical romantic style. We never actually see Komona and Magician engaging in intercourse. Once they arrive in the village they both wash, a further indication of the cleanliness that this marriage is affording them both when compared to their previous states of existence in the rebel camp, and seem to return to an almost childlike state. They learn to press oil, play on the village seesaw, and Komona cradles Magicians head in her lap as they lie on the grass together but we never see any sexual activity. Thus the boundaries of innocence and sexual permissiveness are safely maintained. In a final act to demonstrate their love and commitment for each other, she kneels down next to him as he awaits his death but is unable to stop herself been dragged away from him before he is slaughtered. Her rape at the hands of the commander who murders Magician and takes Komona for his bush wife is not only a violation of the rights of a child but also an act against the sanctity of marriage. In her widowhood and subsequent enforced sex slavery and unwanted motherhood, Komona is further debased as she is made the site of national shame as an example of some of the worst excesses of the war.

In the construction of the postwar nation state, the girl soldier becomes the site through which national shame is most articulated; those highly marked wartime bodies present a postwar problem. As stated, around 40 percent of the child soldiers are female; however, the number of females engaging with demobilization and reintegration programs number less than 5 percent. These girls are missing for a variety of reasons, most (if not all) of which are directly related to gender. The stigma of sexual activity, whether by choice or by force, whether real or imagined, results in social and cultural exclusion. Richard Clarke comments, "in contexts of entrenched gender discrimination, and in situations where a girl's 'value' is defined in terms of her purity and marriageability, the stigma attached to involvement in sexual activity . . . can result in exclusion and acute impoverishment."[15] The emphasis on rape and sexual violence has been the dominant marker in the Western imaginations of the girl soldier and yet, although this aspect is undoubtedly important, it seeks to obscure the multiplicity of roles that girls and women play inside the war environment. When the traditions of virginity, marriage, and respectable motherhood have been destroyed via warfare, the futures and fates of these girls are left in the balance—indeed, rendered valueless. Value, as bequeathed by purity, has been removed (whether in actuality or merely in perception) and as in so many conflict zones, traditional notions of honor and shame result in the women losing "respect and support" from their respective communities[16] and being removed from the national postwar rebuilding and reconstruction process. Whilst inside the filmic texts itself there are clear nods and engagement with the notion of female agency and empowerment, what the films are failing to do is situate any real discussion of the actual lives and experiences of these girls. Take for example, the ending of *Rebelle*. Komona has buried the few remains she has managed to find of her deceased parents and given birth on her own in the abandoned village. She makes her way to the roadside where eventually a truck filled with people allows her to board. Once onboard an older woman offers to hold her baby to let Komona sleep. The last shots of the film are of her staring out into the surrounding countryside and gradually settling down to sleep as the truck drives off. The music that closes the film is Eme N'gongo Lami, an adaptation of an Angolan song by "world fusion" group Tanga who specialize in a mixture of jazz, latin-jazz and electronica.[17] Komona has acted as narrator throughout the film; at the end she is silent and unable to offer any insight into her future or her fate as the voices of the male musicians take over. Likewise Laokolé is left silent. The end shot is of her crying as she points a gun at the prostrate Johnny. Her future, and that of the child she has adopted, will remain un-discussed in the film text. This open-ended engagement allows the audience to read their own thoughts and considerations into the stories but, ultimately, fails to reflect the complexities that face these girls after the war is over.

These girls will be condemned on the basis of their specifically gendered engagement with the armed conflict and this is something that the films refuse to tackle. Girlhood is not compatible with aggression and there is particular contempt in the Western world for girls (usually girls of color) who are marked as "dangerous" and embroiled in often gang-based violence.[18] Women (and the "feminine" as it applies to both genders) are stereotypically associated with peacefulness, life-giving, and the need to be protected—direct counterpoints to the "masculine" process of war, killing, and "protecting." Violence is stereotypically reflected as masculine, both materially and narratively, and the girl who actively embraces violence ruptures a construction of girlhood as the site of non-active aggression.[19] Therefore, these films function as what Catherine Belsey casts as a declarative text, "imparting 'knowledge' to a reader whose position is thereby stabilised by a privileging narrative which is to varying degrees invisible."[20] As David Rodowick notes, these often diegetically sealed texts therefore assume a normative status in their transmission of this knowledge.[21] This normative status in terms of the films being discussed here, results in texts that do not seek to rupture commonly held narratives of childhood or gender that we receive in the global North, but rather, seek to confirm them. The girls must reject violence in order to sustain the narrative of the innate non-aggressive stance women are required to take. Awet's admiration for Ma'aza will be undermined once she sees the horror of war. Ma'aza's own support of violent revolution and warfare will lead to her own death and all of those children and adults who followed her, a point that the film clearly emphasizes in clear support of Awet's own non-aggressive stance. We see Komona kill on many occasions but mostly these acts are represented as justifiable as, for example, when she kills her parents with a rifle, it is to prevent the fate of being hacked to death with machetes. She will kill government soldiers to save her own life (and is haunted by them afterwards, illustrating her innately "good" nature), and her murder of her rapist (and killer of her husband Magician) is arguably justified since it is the only way she could escape the rebel camp and the endless abuse she suffers. These non-typical gender roles the girls have taken, however, will be safely resolved by the films' conclusions. Motherhood, in the case of Laokolé and Komona, becomes the method though which they are asked to move forward with their lives. Laokolé adopts an orphan child (despite her own young age) and Komona finally embraces the child born of rape. Awet returns to a suitable space of childhood once more as she moves to Germany with a distant relative.

These positive endings mask the realities that face the real-life counter-parts that are negated in favor of a tale that can be sold to audiences. Case studies indicate that, contrary to popular presentation, most child soldiers are neither abducted nor forcibly recruited.[22] However, this is the path to military life that we are primarily shown. Even in the most negative situations, agency can be developed; in short, "there is evidence for agency and resilience masked by the label vulnerable, though all are marginal as childhoods."[23] Therefore the question becomes: how can we articulate the dynamic of repression and abuse whilst acknowledging and supporting agency? Inside the narratives of the respective films there is acknowledgment of an agency of girlhood: Laokolé kills (or at least badly injures) Johnny; Komona castrates her rapist utilizing her own body (via a razor inserted in a fruit, which is then inserted inside her vagina); and Awet will walk away from the army to a new life in Europe. What Howanna calls "tactical agency" is hereby shown, it may be "sporadic and constrained"[24] but it does allow a person to service the immediate scenarios that surround them. However, these moments of agency and self-preservation will be subsumed inside the wider narratives of innocence interrupted and the need for outside engagement.

Empirical studies have found that girl soldiers have very mixed feelings about their time in the military environment.[25] The placement of girls as faultless, passive victims of a patriarchal, repressive, and militaristic society is a narrative that undermines and rejects the multiple and myriad roles women play in warfare whilst simultaneously ignoring the complexities of their individual experiences. Films such as *Rebelle* and *Heart of Fire*, although focusing on a specific, fictionalized girl, often reflect dominant narratives rather than attempt to portray their complexities. In *Johnny Mad Dog* the strong and active female voice of the book is denied and she primarily operates as a means though which the male is offered a possibility of (denied) redemption. Johnny's distress at Lovelita's murder is the second time we see him clearly debating his actions (the first time is when he allows Laokolé to escape when he corners her in a stairwell). The female in this sense operates as either the focus through which Johnny will discover his humanity or as the site of his worst excesses (such as his brutal rape of a female reporter). Unlike the book, the film diminishes Laokolé and leaves her almost silent; her actions and thoughts are left to the audience to speculate at. Whilst the novel allows her free reign to debate the causes, effects, and rationale of the war, the film's continual focus on the vicious Johnny as site of interest removes the narrative of the female soldier almost completely. She is reduced to being part of the process by which the male can articulate and enact his subjectivity. The film changes the children's ages, making Johnny and Laokolé younger, and the consistent emphasis in the film for Johnny's ability to feel emotion maintains the notion of the child as ultimately seeking redemption and care. The film leaves open whether Laokolé kills Johnny, whereas the book makes it clear that she has murdered him without regret. Whilst comparison with the book may seem to some an approach that does not always easily fit for some, no amount of camera angles can achieve the sense of self-aware subjectivity that the filmic rendition of Laokolé is denied. Whilst I am not a subscriber to the approach that sees the film as lesser in comparison to their literary originals, the loss of Laokolé's narrative power in this case is a loss of a female subjectivity that weakens the film as a potential site of female empowerment.

Rebelle, more than any other film discussed here, allows the audience to see the multiple roles Komona plays inside the rebel/soldier camp, yet it ultimately resorts to the three specifically gendered roles she plays—sex slave, wife, and daughter—as her most defining elements. Jenkins' previously cited comment—that childhood is outside the political—ignores the fact that girls can be, and are, politically active. Awet has a strong sense of Eritrean politics; Laokolé is highly intelligent and cognizant of the world around her; and Komona quickly realizes that the key reason they are fighting is related to natural resources rather than ideology. However, these small moments of realization are overtaken and minimized in favor of the continual emphasis on the construction of the child soldier as both a "helpless object manipulated locally by adult malevolence"[26] and a figure who needs to be rescued by adult humanitarianism. As Kristen Cheney notes, "African children are commonly made objects of the political motives behind aid agendas, local and global,"[27] and therefore the child soldier serves broader political purposes related to a transnational humanitarianism that is too often grounded in a narrow set of Western values and practices.[28]

Jenkins asks the question about "what the figure of the child means to adults"[29] and, in this agenda-making content, the girl soldier will be used to uphold the narratives of development, gender, and politics that the global North expects. The number of films focusing on child soldiers that are aligned with and presented by NGOs and charities working in this field is relatively significant: *Soldier Child* was utilized by Amnesty International in their awareness-raising campaigns; *War Child* was the platform for launching the aid organization Gua Africa; *Kassim the Dream* has links to a variety of aid agencies and NGOs on its official website; and *They Fight Like Soldiers They Die Like Children* (Reed, 2012) is in conjunction with the Roméo Dallaire Child Soldier Initiative. This is not to deny the genuine desire to provide aid, which is central to these projects, but rather to raise the complex global bio-political dimensions of conflict representation that come to bear on the girl soldier. She must endlessly play the role of innocent victim, the ravaged girl-child, the enforced mother and the abused recruit in order to sustain global narratives of inequality and global development (or lack of). As Martins notes, the figure of the child soldier has been used as a trope by the global North, as a key figure, that allows for "the ultimate denial of an independent History for Africa and the reassuring confirmation of western paternalism and supremacy."[30] In *Heart of Fire*, Awet will leave Eritrea for Europe and the film clearly implies that her life will be significantly better outside her African homeland by the addition of intertitles stating the number of child soldiers operating in the world today and the current status of Eritrea.

This impartation of a presumed highly situated knowledge, whilst simultaneously failing to challenge the dominant representational geopolitical frame, can be seen across modern cinema and is often articled as "awareness raising." For example, abused women, starvation victims, and armless children have become tropes across a variety of formats and yet this has not served to make us more aware in a culturally or historically specific way. As Michael Shapiro notes in the current age of mass media dissemination, "cinematic technology brings remote battle venues into view all over the globe."[31] These situated and intimate images of global warfare have become common within endlessly recycled fields of international reference. It is into this discourse that the girl soldier is cast. Locations are varied, *Heart of Fire* is clearly set in the Eritrean-Ethiopian war (1998–2000) and *Johnny Mad Dog* is ostensibly set in 2003 in the end of the Liberian civil war. *Rebelle* is set in an unnamed sub-Saharan African nation but was filmed in the Democratic Republic of Congo and the music is Angolan therefore linking the film to these two respective conflict regions. Yet these locations are secondary to the individual tales of the children. We learn nothing about the respective conflicts and the move to homogenize reduces all third world women and girls to a conceptualization as passive victims who require international interventions and aid.[32]

This problem, whereby film becomes a tool of global politics, becomes evident when juxtaposed against the original book on which the *Johnny Mad Dog* was based. The aims and objectives of the film *Johnny Mad Dog* (to keep a constant structure of childhood innocence corrupted and to present the perceived traumas of an African existence) is not found in the book *Johnny Chien Méchant*. As already mentioned, in *Johnny Chien Méchant* the narrative interchanges between the words of Laokolé and Johnny. The book, via Laokolé's inner monologues, is highly critical of the United Nations' powerlessness; the uncaring nature of the international rescue mission, which only saves the non-African citizens caught up in the conflict (they even run over Laokolé's friend in their haste to leave); the foreign primatologists who place the life of a gorilla over the lives of African citizens and the problematic racial, economic, and gendered narratives that the war highlights.

Intriguingly, when these films are compared to recent productions examining, for example, the plight of sex trafficking victims, some curious changes can be noted. Emma Wilson focuses on films that are able to produce a "seizure of emotive response," where adults suddenly *feel* like children. In her examination of *Lilya 4 Ever* (Moodysson, 2002), Wilson notes how a distanciation is rejected in favor of a sense of the emotive, "to reattach us to child experience, to make its affect and range of sensation present for us."[33] The images of childhood interrupted in films such as *Johnny Mad Dog*, *Heart of Fire*, and *Rebelle* work against this reading. Just as we are expected to experience an affective response to the European children's plight, conversely, in the context of Africa we are in fact encouraged to maintain our distance, to ensure our position as "other" in these narratives of suffering. This is not a vision of girlhood that we are expected to identify with; rather we are being asked to sit outside the narrative in our position as the outsider who could (if we so wished), affect a change via global humanitarianism. The visual style of all three films is similar. The shots are mostly in long and medium with a few close-ups to focus on the faces of the specific girl as we see her struggle through the horrors around her. The camera rarely takes her point of view and when it does it is serving a narrative purpose rather than an affective one. We take Laokolé's point of view only once in the film as we see her watch Johnny murder a young boy he has captured and accuses of being a government spy. This scene functions, not to aligned us with the affective experiences of Laokolé but as a narrative plot to establish the beginning of the "relationship" between her and Johnny. The below image is taken from *Rebelle* and is an example of one of the visualizations of Komona's ability to see the souls of the dead, the fact that will earn her the moniker and status of *sorcière de guerre* or war witch. As we can see, even when we enter Komona's internal imagination we are expected to keep a suitable distance and the aim is not to develop for us a range of sensations but to position us outside the events taking place (Figure 13.3).

The call in girlhood studies to hear the girl would seem to meet with constant deaf ears when faced with the transmission of the tales of former

Figure 13.3 *Rebelle/War Witch* (Nguyun, 2012). Komona faces the souls of the dead in *Rebelle*

child soldiers. Susan Mckay and Dyan Mazurana note that "the roles played by girls in fighting forces have long been ignored by government, military, multilateral agencies, community leaders and NGO's."[34] Girl soldiers are required to perform the same roles and tasks as boy soldiers (carry, fight, cook, etc.) with the added burden of gender-specific violence (rape and sexual slavery) and the consequences of this (HIV/Aids, pregnancy, social stigmatization). The girl therefore becomes doubly marginalized both inside the film text and in the wider cultural sphere. Whilst the films discussed here are not without merit, they ultimately render passive the girl "objects" who are examined by a Western gaze "which seeks to confirm its own agency and omnipotence to ward off its own insecurities."[35] In short, child soldiers are "exoticised, decontextualized and essentialised."[36] Presented for humanitarian consumption, the girl therefore operates as a site of local shame and global tension. Rather than allowing the possibility of the self-articulation of active agents, the films discussed (and many others like them) leave her silent inside the vicarious dynamics of benevolent paternalism and the national symbolic imagination.

Notes

1. This lack of attention is also reflected in film scholarship that has seen a very limited engagement with the visual representation of child soldiers and, as of writing this chapter in 2014, there have been no studies focusing solely on the filmic girl soldier (as compared to adult female) despite her increasing visibility on the global stage.

2. Mark A. Drumbl, *Reimagining Child Soldiers in International Law and Policy* (Oxford: Oxford University Press, 2012), p. 8.
3. Kim Nguyun (*Rebelle*) is Canadian, Jean-Stéphane Sauvaire (*Johnny Mad Dog*) is French and Luigi Falorni (*Heart of Fire*) is Italian.
4. See David. M. Rosen, *Armies of the Young: Child Soldiers in War and Terrorism* (New Jersey: Rutgers University Press, 2005), Jean Comadroff and John Comadroff, "Reflections on Youth from the past to the postcolony," in *Child and Youth in Postcolonial Africa* edited by Alcinda Honwana and Filip De Boeck (Tenton NJ: African World Press, 2005), pp.19–30 and Alicinda Honwana, *Child Soldiers in Africa* (Philadelphia: University of Pennsylvania Press, 2006)
5. Torben Grodal, "Film Narrative," in *Routledge Encyclopaedia of Narrative Theory* edited by David Herman, Manfred Jahn and Marie-Laure Ryan (London: Routledge, 2005), pp. 168–72 (169).
6. David Bordwell, *Narration in the Fiction Film* (Madison: University of Wisconsin Press, 1985), p. xi.
7. David. M. Rosen, *Armies of the Young*, p. 9.
8. Comadroff and Comadroff, "Reflections on Youth," p. 19.
9. Ibid.
10. Henry Jenkins, *The Children's Culture Reader* (New York: New York University Press, 1998), p. 2.
11. Emma Wilson, "Children, emotion and viewing in contemporary European film," *Screen* 46:3 (2005), 329–334 (329).
12. Honwana, *Child Soldiers in Africa*, p. 2.
13. See Cynthia Enloe, *Bananas, Beaches and Bases: Making Feminist Sense of International Politics* (Berkeley, CA: University of California Press, 1990), and Nira Yuval-Davis, *Gender and Nation* (London: Sage Press, 1997).
14. This could also be due to the legal situation that has subsequently emerged vis-à-vis the book on which the film is based. The author has been accused, both in the media and in court, of fabricating elements of the book, including the fact that she was a child soldier and raped in the camp. This chapter cannot comment on the validity of either side and is taking the film specifically as a fictional account.
15. IRIN "Analysis: Girl Soldiers Face New Battle in Civilian Life" (February 12, 2013) http://www.irinnews.org/report/97463/analysis-girl-child-soldiers-face-new-battles-in-civilian-life
16. Nira Yuval-Davis, *Gender and Nation* (London: Sage, 1997), p. 110.
17. As Tim McNelis notes elsewhere in this collection, questions of authenticity in "world music" complicated ideas of fixed national or cultural identities. In this case, the music serves to remove us from a specific and localized situation into a broader international debate.
18. Meda Chesney-Lind and Katherine Irwin, *Beyond Bad Girl: Gender Violence and Hype* (London and New York: Routledge, 2008) and Christine Alder and Anne Worrell, eds. *Girl's Violence: Myths and Realities* (New York: SUNY Press, 2004). In terms of wider work on women, girlhood, and violence in the media, see also the work of Drew Humphries, *Women, Violence, and the Media: Readings in Feminist Criminology* (Lebanon, NH: Northeastern Press, 2009), Hilary

Neroni, *The Violent Woman: Femininity, Narrative and Violence in Contemporary American Cinema* (New York: SUNY Press, 2005) and Cynthia Carter and C. Kay Weaver, eds. *Violence and the Media* (Maidenhead: Open University Press, 2003).

19. See Cynthia Enloe, *Bananas, Beaches and Bases* and Véronique Pin-fat and Maria Stern, "The Scripting of Private Jessica Lynch: Biopolitics, Gender and the Feminization of the US Military," *Alternatives* 20:1 (2005), 25–53.

20. Catherine Belsey, *Critical Practice, 2nd edition* (London and New York: Routledge, 2002).

21. David Rodowick, *The Crisis of Political Modernism: Criticism and Ideology in Contemporary Film Theory* (Urbana and Chicago: University of Illinois Press, 1988), p. 12.

22. Mark A. Drumbl, *Reimagining Child Soldiers*, p. 13.

23. Philip Kilbride, "A Cultural and Gender Perspective on Marginal Children on the Streets of Kenya," *Childhood in African*, December 2:1 (2010), 38–47.

24. Alicinda Honwana, "Innocent & Guilty: Child-Soldiers as Interstitial and Tactical Agents," in *Child and Youth in a Global Era* edited by Alicinda Honwana and Félix De Boeck (Oxford: James Curry, 2005), p. 96.

25. See Harry G. West "Girls with Guns: Narrating the Experience of FRELIMO's 'female detachment'," *Anthropological Quarterly* 73:4, Youth and the Social Imagination in Africa, Part 2 (October 2000), 180–194, and Angela Veale, *From Child Soldier to Ex-fighter, Female Fighters, Demobilisation and Reintegration in Ethiopia* (Pretoria: Institute for Security Studies, 2003) and Chris Coutler, *Bush Wives and Girl Soldiers* (Ithaca: Cornell University Press, 2008).

26. Mark A. Drumbl, *Reimagining Child Soldiers*, p. 6.

27. Kristen Cheney, "Deconstructing Childhood Vulnerability: An Introduction," *Childhood in African*, December 2:1 (2010), 4–7, p. 5.

28. See Julia Pacitto and Elena Fiddian-Qasmiyeh. "Writing the 'Other' into Humanitarian Discourse: Framing Theory and Practice in South–South Humanitarian Responses to Forced Displacement," *Refugee Studies Centre: Working Paper Series No.93* (2013) http://www.rsc.ox.ac.uk/publications/writing-the-other-into-humanitarian-discourse-framing-theory-and-practice-in-south-south-humanitarian-responses-to-forced-displacement [Accessed: July 23, 2014].

29. Jenkins, 2.

30. Catarina Martins, "The Dangers of the Single Story: Child-soldiers in Literary Fiction and Film," *Childhood* 18:4 (2011), 434–446 (440).

31. Michael J. Shapiro, *Cinematic Geopolitics* (London and New York: Routledge, 2009), p. 16.

32. Jasbir K. Puar, "Nicaraguan Women, Resistance and the Politics of Aid," in *Women and Politics in the Third World* edited by Hed Afsher (London and New York: Routledge Press, 1996), p. 74.

33. Emma Wilson, "Children, Emotion and Viewing," 334.

34. Susan Mckay and Dyan Mazurana, *Where are the Girls? Girls in Fighting Forces in Northern Uganda, Sierra Leone, and Mozambique: Their Lives During and*

After War (Montreal: International Centre for Human Rights and Democratic Development, 2004), p. 11.

35. Erica Burman, "Innocents Abroad: Western Fantasies of Childhood and the Iconography of Emergencies," *Disasters* 19:3 (1994), 238–253 (28).

36. Myrian Demov, "Child Soldiers and Iconography: Portrays and (Mis)representations," *Children and Society* 26: 4 (July 2012), 280–292 (283).

Daddy's Little Sidekick: The Girl Superhero in Contemporary Cinema

Martin Zeller-Jacques

Since the turn of the Millennium, Hollywood-produced superhero movies have dominated US and global box offices. This cycle of films, beginning with *X-Men* (Brian Singer, 2000) and continuing to the present day, has provided three of the ten highest grossing films of all time (*The Avengers* [Joss Whedon, 2012]; *Iron Man 3* [Shane Black, 2013]; *The Dark Knight Rises* [Christopher Nolan, 2012]);[1] earned a new cultural respectability for superheroes through Christopher Nolan's *Dark Knight* trilogy (*Batman Begins* [2005]; *The Dark Knight* [2008]; *The Dark Knight Rises*); and established new models of transmedia synergy with Disney/Marvel's Cinematic Universe of films, TV shows, games, and toys. The contemporary superhero cycle has failed, however, to have very much to say about or to women. In many of these films, women remain confined to roles as victims, love-interests, sidekicks or, at best, team-mates. Male superheroes still vastly outnumber female superheroes, and it remains exceptionally rare for a female superhero to be the central character in one of these films. (*Elektra* [Rob Bowman, 2005] and *Catwoman* [Pitof, 2004], both critical and commercial failures, remain the two recent exceptions.) Even rarer than the adult woman superhero, however, is the figure of the girl superhero.

Despite appearing extensively in both live-action and animated television,[2] girl superheroes remain a rarity in contemporary superhero cinema. Yet superhero comics are full of heroic girls. Some are prepubescent adventurers, saving the world behind their unknowing parents' backs (Julie and Katie of Marvel's *Power Pack*[3]); some are precocious teens trying to live up to the ideals of heroes they may never even have met (Batgirl, in any number of incarnations); some are beings of cosmic power, capable of bending the world with a thought (Jenny Quantum of *The Authority*[4]); and some are teenage savants, with maturity and bravery that puts their older teammates to shame (Kitty Pryde of *The X-Men*[5]). Some are daughters, sisters, mothers, and lovers (Stephanie Brown/Spoiler/Batgirl III is almost all of these); some are aids sufferers (Mia Dearden/Speedy II) or rape survivors (Starfire of *The New Teen Titans*[6]); and some are knowing parodies who pastiche the conventions of their medium (Hit-Girl from *Kick-Ass*[7]). Nor are these obscurities plucked from alternative titles and publishers, but in nearly every example above, they are mainstream characters published by one of the two major comic-book companies (DC and Marvel) that provide the source material for most current superhero cinema.

One of the chief reasons for this lack of girl superheroes is the more general lack of representation of superheroic children and adolescents in cinema. Since at least 1954, when Frederick Wertham testified on the effects of comic books on children before the Senate Judiciary Sub-committee on Juvenile Delinquency,[8] fears about the corruption of youth have pervaded the reception of superhero stories. Wertham accused superheroes of promoting everything from homosexuality to vigilantism to race-hatred, and drew attention to what he saw as the sexualized appearance of the young sidekicks who populated comics at the time: "Robin is a handsome ephebic boy, usually shown in his uniform with bare legs.... He often stands with his legs spread, the genital region discreetly evident."[9] The queasy sense that there is something suspect about grownups who bring children along on their morally questionable nighttime excursions continues to shape contemporary superheroic narratives, with comics like Frank Miller's *All-Star Batman and Robin*[10] and Mark Millar's *Kick-Ass* offering satirical deconstructions of these relationships. Meanwhile, superheroic cinema has tended to avoid these characters altogether, as part of a cycle-wide drive toward real-world verisimilitude, which has seen many of the outlandish elements of superhero comics sidelined in the attempt to seek mainstream audiences.[11] One result of this trend is that, even where the comic-book originals of some characters were children, their cinematic incarnations have been adults, as in the reimagination of Robin in *The Dark Knight Rises* and of Bucky Barnes in *Captain America* (Joe Johnston, 2011).

Amid this scarcity of superheroic representations of children in general, and girls in particular, it has been left to superhero films that stand outside of the mainstream comic-book-inspired worlds to address stories of powerful girls—often from a position that pastiches or critiques conventional superhero narratives. Pixar's *The Incredibles* (Brad Bird, 2004) and independent black-comedy *Super* (James Gunn, 2010) offer two such treatments of girl superheroes (though still not as the central characters). However, the most sustained and explicit representation of a girl superhero has come from the superheroic pastiche, *Kick-Ass* (Matthew Vaughn, 2007) and its sequel, *Kick-Ass 2* (Jeff Wadlow, 2013). The story of an ordinary teenager who becomes a superhero for no particularly compelling reason, only to become embroiled in the adventures of Big-Daddy and Hit-Girl, two "real" superheroes attempting to take down a local mob-boss, *Kick-Ass* is both a parody of and a loving tribute to superhero comics. The film gained notoriety in part because of its representation of the girl superhero, Hit-Girl, which broke a number of previously unspoken taboos around child superheroes and foregrounded the problematic aspects of this type of character. The representation of Hit-Girl troubles the lines between hero and victim and between protection and abuse, dramatizing the costs and compromises of empowerment for a girl in a world that is powerfully defined by patriarchy, as embodied in the overbearing figure of Big Daddy.

The girl superhero, like other female action stars before her, is a figure with tremendous transgressive potential. She is an avatar of a culture that "has embraced virtually superheroic ideals of young femininity . . . [and in which] girls are repeatedly told they can do anything, be anything."[12] Yet in practice, the girl superhero remains constrained both by her femininity and by her youth. Yvonne Tasker has argued that "The female action hero offers a fantasy image of (proletarian) physical strength showcased within narratives that repeatedly seek to explain her (and to explain her away)."[13] Tasker sees the transgressive power of the adult female action hero as limited in several crucial ways. These characters are either masculinized, presented as inauthentically feminine through their appearance and behavior; essentialized, presented as hyper-feminine by being constituted as protective mothers and/or sexual spectacles; or othered, presented as the junior partners to more narratively central male characters. While these dynamics remain visible in the treatment of a contemporary girl superhero like Hit-Girl, they take on a different character when filtered through the lens of her adolescence. While Hit-Girl is relatively untouched by the hyper-sexualization of women, which is a part of many action films, and of the superhero genre in general,[14] she is contained in different ways. The narratives of *Kick-Ass* and *Kick-Ass 2* set out to explain Hit-Girl in ways that limit her transgressive potential. *Kick-Ass* is particularly concerned both with Hit-Girl as spectacle and Hit-Girl as daughter, with the first aspect of her representation carrying a tremendous transgressive charge and the second working to contain it. *Kick-Ass 2* is more concerned with Hit-Girl as "girl," focusing on discourses of natural or essential subjectivity, which contrast two patriarchally determined subject positions—normative girlhood and superheroism—in ways that fundamentally limit Hit-Girl's agency.

Kick-Ass: Transgression and Containment

Hit-Girl is a character designed to make us uncomfortable. The pint-sized assassin combines signifiers of heightened, but conventional, girlhood (the kilt, the lilac color-scheme of her costume, the broad, easy smile) with the traditionally masculine signifiers of the action hero (brutal violence; a lack of emotion; copious swearing). In crossing the (socially constructed) lines between child and adult, girl and woman, criminal and hero, Hit-Girl forces us to examine the pleasures we take in the superhero genre, and our wider cultural assumptions about gender and age. Yet, ultimately, within *Kick-Ass*, she is constructed as a "good daughter" who fulfils her father's wishes and then retires into a "normal life." In this way the film contains Hit-Girl's transgressive potential within a normative discourse of girlhood as temporary and developmental, rather than destabilizing conventional gendered social constructions.

The film derives much of its transgressive charge, and much of its humor, from the incongruous spectacle of Hit-Girl's superheroic performance, which sees her adopting adult roles and behaviors that appear alternately ridiculous and frightening, depending on the context. This led to profound discomfort among some critics, who regarded her appearance and behavior as sexualized.[15] However, the sexualization of Hit-Girl (which is, at most, only arguable), is part of a wider discourse within the film that concerns her lost childhood and premature adulthood. Hit-Girl exists in an uneasy space between child and adult, exhibiting both arrested and premature development, and empowerment without agency—she is simultaneously a dangerously precocious child and a stunted and emotionally traumatized woman. In the film's own terms, Hit-Girl always remains overdetermined by her relationship to her father, the first superhero, Big Daddy. Big Daddy is the progenitor of her identity, her skills, and her purpose as a character, and throughout the film she progresses from existing as her father's tool, an extension of his purpose, to fighting her own battles (albeit still in his name), and then finally, to a normative teenaged existence under the guidance of a new, more normative father.

When we first meet Hit-Girl, she is out of costume, and identified not as a superhero, but as a little girl undergoing a strange and disturbing ritual under the careful guidance of her father. The pair stand facing each other in a deserted concrete wasteland, her father holding a gun by his side. Looking nervous, she admits, "Daddy, I'm scared." He gently calms her, tells

Figure 14.1   *Kick-Ass* (Vaughn, 2007). Hit-Girl: incongruously deadly

her there's nothing to worry about, and then shoots her in the chest. This startling moment of violence establishes the tenor of their relationship—a combination of tender, even excessive, closeness between father and daughter and a training regime that appears to cross the line between rigorous and abusive. In the strange, symbiotic world of Big Daddy and Hit-Girl, a day spent learning how to take a bullet is capped off with ice cream sundaes; twin butterfly knives are the perfect birthday present; and homework consists of a pop-quiz on firearm specifications and John Woo movies.

Hit-Girl's first in-costume appearance shows her at her most arresting and powerful. She is an avatar of motion, all flips and jumps as she slices her way through a room full of thugs to the incessant trilling of The Banana Splits, by the Dickies. Incongruously cute in her purple wig and matching kilt, she smiles broadly while removing her blade from the body of a drug dealer, then stares down the camera and sneers, "Okay you cunts, let's see what you can do now" (Figure 14.1).

The whole image is both ridiculous and frightening, a little girl playing at being a grown-up action hero, but with very real results. Aligned with the wannabe superhero, Dave/Kick-Ass, the audience is encouraged to wince at the casual brutality with which Hit-Girl dispatches her opponents. Yet the combat ends with an abrupt reminder that Hit-Girl is, ultimately, just a girl—and that her agency extends no further than her father's gaze. Stopping to talk to a terrified Kick-Ass, she is nearly taken by surprise by a gangster she has overlooked before he is felled by a sniper's bullet. The shot then cuts to a sniper-sight view of Hit-Girl, and then to the face of Big Daddy, manning the rifle from a nearby rooftop. She is visibly shaken as he admonishes her to keep her back to the wall, and her girlhood resurfaces in her apologetic use of his dual moniker, Daddy. Hit-Girl, the scene tells us, may take on aspects of masculine power, but ultimately she derives her real power from the patriarchal oversight of Big Daddy.

Figure 14.2   *Kick-Ass* (Vaughn, 2007). First person shooter game perspective in *Kick-Ass*

Through the remainder of the film, this father–daughter dynamic remains relatively static. We learn about the origin story Big Daddy has concocted for his daughter through a self-drawn comic-book detailing his incarceration, her mother's suicide, and the reasons for their vendetta against the mobster, Frank D'Amico. Concern about Big Daddy's parenting style is given voice by his former partner, Marcus, who still serves with the police. Accused of stealing his daughter's childhood, Big Daddy asserts that he is merely "making it into a game." Indeed, his claim seems to be supported by Hit-Girl's playful over-performance of her role. Her tough guy sneer and constant swearing, though certainly backed up by genuine skill, are nevertheless laughable, drawing attention to the incongruity of a little girl beating up adult criminals (or perhaps to the adolescent absurdity of the whole superhero conceit) (Figure 14.2).

This ludic aspect of Hit-Girl's persona finds its fullest expression in her second fight-scene, as she attacks group of thugs in the process of setting fire to Big Daddy and Kick-Ass on a live webcast. Much of the scene is filmed from a perspective familiar from first-person-shooter videogames, as Hit-Girl works her way through her opponents armed with a pistol and knife. Once he realizes that she is pinned down, Big Daddy begins shouting commands to her, effectively taking control of his daughter in the same way that a gamer controls an avatar.

Even in her final fight-scene, Hit-Girl remains an instrument of her father's will. Although urged by Dave/Kick-Ass to give up and seek shelter following the death of Big Daddy, Hit-Girl convinces him that what her father really would have wanted was for them to finish off the mob boss who ordered his death. The film further subjects Hit-Girl to her father's determination by eliding several of the problematic elements of its comic book source. In the comic book, Big Daddy's origin story is revealed to be an elaborate lie; rather than a police officer avenging the destruction of his family, he is a deranged comic-book fan who has kidnapped his own daughter in order to live out an elaborate fantasy—a revelation that is likely to remove any remaining sympathy the audience might have for his actions. Yet, even after learning of his deception, Hit-Girl remains loyal to her father, and once she has dispatched the last of the mobsters, allows herself a brief moment of vulnerability, removing the mask that completes her superheroic garb and leaving only Mindy McReady, who turns to Kick-Ass with blood on her face and tears in her eyes, and asks, "Would you give me a hug? My daddy just died." The Hit-Girl of the film offers no such stark moment of loss, presenting instead only determination to avenge the death of her father, and celebration at her eventual success. Effectively, she leaves her girlhood behind, becoming the apotheosis of the superheroic fantasy that her father instigated—a story that leaves much less room to question the motives and methods of the patriarch who has dominated her life.

Perhaps paradoxically, this moment of transformation doesn't see Mindy permanently become a superhero, but just the opposite. Having proven that she can function effectively as a hero, Mindy retires her Hit-Girl identity and assumes a life as an ordinary school-girl under the watchful protection of her father's former partner, Marcus. Mindy's transgressive behavior as Hit-Girl is constructed as temporary and aberrant, something to be left behind as part of her journey toward fully developed subjectivity—even if that subjectivity remains constrained within the confines of another controlling father–daughter relationship.

Kick-Ass 2: It's Biology, Bitch

The second Kick-Ass film sees Hit-Girl negotiating her own girlhood in more complex ways, balancing the expectations of her new father figure, Marcus, those of other girls at her school, and those of her role as a superhero. Early in the film she attempts to balance superhero training with Dave/Kick-ass and keeping Marcus happy. With Dave she takes on the role that her father once occupied for her, training him in martial arts and teaching him to take a bullet. With Marcus she plays the shy little girl, camouflaging her nighttime exploits with a baby-pink bedroom and reserved manners. However, Marcus soon discovers that she is continuing her activities as Hit-Girl and forces her to promise to stop for the sake of their newly constituted family. This establishes the central dilemma of *Kick-Ass 2*, as Mindy/Hit-Girl tries to decide between two identities, each of which is heavily determined by its relationship to a powerful patriarchal figure. Both of these choices are presented as, in their different ways, natural or authentic for Mindy—yet the "choice" to be Hit-Girl is finally both more important and more attractive. In presenting this as a choice between competing discourses of authenticity, the film really presents it as no choice at all; in the film's terms she cannot *really* be *both* Mindy *and* Hit-Girl, and so one of the discourses must be proven false. In this way *Kick-Ass 2*'s representation of Hit-Girl corresponds to more general representations of feminine adolescence in late-modernity, wherein "performances of feminine adolescence ... most often figure as a definitive failure of subjectification (of coming to be a coherent self-aware subject)."[16] Yet whereas conventional constructions of girlhood would, as the first film does, position Mindy's Hit-Girl identity as experimental, temporary, and inauthentic, in opposition to her normative, feminine identity as Mindy McReady, *Kick-Ass 2* makes the opposite choice. While there is a suggestion of something transgressive at work here, this still confines Mindy to an identity chosen for her, and does so at the cost of total alienation from society.

Kick-Ass 2's portrayal of high school, and with it, normative girlhood, as a world of cliques and cruelty owes much to films like *Mean Girls* (Mark Waters, 2004) and *Heathers* (Michael Lehmann, 1988). Through this narrow field of representations, girlhood is presented as vapid, shallow, and meaningless—ultimately, even, as morally bad. Unlike the heroines of similar "mean girl" films, Hit-Girl is never exposed to alternative groups within the school that might provide her with healthier friendships—instead, the alternative established by the film is total individualism, confirmed by the complete rejection not only of the popular clique, but of high school, adolescence, friendship, and family. In this way, *Kick-Ass 2* redoubles the ideological force of these earlier films, which, as Kelly and Pomerantz argue, "privilege projects of individual but not collective empowerment."[17] Yet we might also argue that *Kick-Ass 2* draws attention to the costs of such specific, personal empowerment, showing Hit-Girl having to flee the city by the close of the film.

Brooke, the leader of the clique of "mean girls" at Mindy's school, provides the film's exemplar of normative girlhood, a construction that relies upon the familiar "double-entanglement"[18] of postfeminism, combining a pronounced neo-conservative discourse of natural, biological femininity with the valorization of female agency and choice, though only when expressed through hyper-sexualization:

> Mindy, I'm gonna give you a chance that the rest of the girls in our class would kill for. Don't you want to walk out the door every day in skintight clothes, knowing that everyone worships you? Don't you want to sneak out at night, raise a little hell and show the world what a strong, independent woman is capable of? Don't you want to belong?

While Brooke is oblivious both of the tensions between independence and belonging within her own position, and of the fact that Mindy is already raising plenty of hell, Mindy herself is easily convinced that she has things to learn from Brooke. Her susceptibility is constructed as the result of a general lack of feminine influence in her life—the child first of one father, then of another, Mindy has been taught to be Hit-Girl, but never to be *a* girl. The things Mindy may be missing are viscerally demonstrated when Brooke and her friends play her a music video by the boy-band, Union J.

The sequence cross-cuts repeatedly between the girls and the video, Mindy's befuddlement at her friends' excitement gradually turning into uncontrollable arousal at the chiseled jaw-lines (and even more chiseled torsos) of the band. A quick, thumping bass-beat begins as part of the music but gradually resolves into the sound of a rapid heartbeat as the camera zooms in on Mindy's face as her whole body tenses. Gasping and flushed, Mindy's erotic awakening elicits satisfied smirks from her new friends. "You may not dress like us or talk like us," Brooke tells her, "but when it comes to boys we're all pretty much the same . . . It's biology bitch."

While Mindy's attempts to integrate herself into normative girlhood are constructed as natural through the discourse of biological essentialism, her identity as Hit-Girl is simultaneously constructed as natural, but through the alternative discourse of individualism. Throughout the film Mindy oscillates between her new father, Marcus, who tells her, "Hit-girl: that's not who you are," and Dave/Kick-Ass, who argues, "It doesn't matter if you're wearing a mask or makeup. [Hit-Girl]'s who you really are." The construction of Mindy's Hit-Girl persona as innate, of course, ignores its patriarchal construction—as we have already seen, Hit-Girl is both literally and conceptually the progeny of Big-Daddy. Even when she finally articulates to Marcus her preference for her superheroic role, Mindy's reasons for doing so are so conflicted as to be barely coherent:

> I know you see me as this little girl, but I'm not. You're right, Daddy did take my childhood away, but I'm not so sure that was a bad thing. He gave me a gift, a gift that I can't escape, no matter how hard I try. And I don't need to spend the next four years of my life trying to figure out who I am, because I already know. I'm Hit-Girl.

Describing her role of Hit-Girl as both a gift and a burden, as something both essential to her identity and the result of something being taken from her, Mindy/Hit-Girl makes an apparently paradoxical choice. Choosing to refuse the process of social maturation to be found in high school, and to remain *Hit-Girl*, an identity that, in the terms of the first film, was constructed as temporary and transitional, Mindy elects to sustain a kind of permanent adolescence. In doing so, she rejects all social structures in a way that both displays and punishes transgression.

Mindy/Hit-Girl's transgression is at its most spectacular not in her superheroic guise, but in her Mindy McReady persona. After all, we are now used to the sight of Mindy slaughtering criminals and there is little suspense or surprise around her ability to do so. The question of how she will negotiate the less obvious evils of high-school politics is where the film places its real narrative emphasis. After Brooke and her friends ritually humiliate Mindy by arranging a "date-dump," in which her supposed date drives her to a field and publicly abandons her in front of dozens of classmates, Mindy plots a spectacular vengeance that is explicitly constructed as a unification of the two types of girlhood with which she has been struggling throughout the film. Following the paradoxical advice of Dave/Kick-Ass to "Beat them at their own game . . . by being yourself," Hit-Girl puts on a glamorous dress, does her hair and makeup and goes to the cafeteria to publicly confront Brooke and her friends.

The film toys with tropes of the teen genre, whereby Mindy's newly revealed beauty, confidence, and aplomb should win her acceptance, but instead takes a short-cut. First declaring to Brooke that, "It doesn't matter what costume I wear, yours or mine. I'm a superhero. It's who I am. [And] you're an evil bitch," Mindy then lightly taps Brooke and her friends with an electronic wand, which triggers a decidedly non-magical transformation. Mindy's "sick-stick" causes uncontrollable vomiting and diarrhea, violently rupturing the carefully controlled boundaries of Brooke's femininity and revealing it as a performance through a series of emetic outpourings.

However, this transgressive rejection of the discourse of normative girlhood as biological and essential comes with a serious price. By the close of the film, Mindy's refusal to conform to socially normative behavior leaves her estranged from her new father and on the run after killing several criminals in the film's climactic battle. Effectively, she has become exactly like her first father, Big Daddy, a social outcast, living off the grid without family, friends, or any personal identity beyond her costume. *Kick-Ass 2* ultimately settles on the bleak assertion that the only choices for Mindy are either mindless conformity or stark individualism.

Future Girls?

The chief impression left from an analysis of the representation of girl superheroes in the two *Kick-Ass* films is one of contradiction. Issues of performativity are central to the superhero genre, yet the films rely on discourses of authenticity to describe Hit-Girl's girlhood, while personal choice and empowerment are consistently framed by the guiding hand of a patriarchal presence. Ultimately, while these films pastiche the representative conventions of the superhero genre, they restrict the representation of superheroic girls far beyond that which is found in comics, the originary medium of superhero stories. In doing so they point to the contradictory discourses that impinge upon the lives of actual girls, who like Mindy McReady, must balance cultural assumptions about their nature, cultural expectations about their behavior, and cultural hopes for their futures. As the Hollywood's superheroic film cycle continues to develop, we may yet see more progressive, hopeful, or simply more varied representations of superheroic girls. As yet, however, the superhero film's definitive statement on the girl superhero remains conflicted and contradictory.

Notes

1. boxofficemojo.com/alltime/world [Accessed: December 20, 2013].
2. Superheroic girls based on existing comic book characters have featured, for instance, in *Batman: The Animated Series* (Fox, 1992–1995); *Birds of Prey* (WB, 2002–2003); *X-Men* (Fox Kids, 1992–1997); *Smallville* (WB and CW, 2001–2011); *Teen Titans* (WB and Cartoon Network, 2003–2006); *Teen Titans Go!* (Cartoon Network, 2013–present); *Young Justice* (Cartoon Network, 2010–2013) and more. Meanwhile, the most prominent superheroic girl, both in television and in television studies, remains *Buffy, The Vampire Slayer* (WB and UPN, 1997–2003). (See R. Wilcox, *Why Buffy Matters: The Art and of Buffy the Vampire Slayer* (London and New York: I. B. Tauris, 2005); and the open-access journal *Slayage* [Online: http://slayageonline.com/ [Accessed: February 25, 2015] for a small selection of the extensive critical exploration of this character.)
3. *The Power Pack* (Marvel Comics, 1984–1990).
4. *The Authority* (Wildstorm Comics, 1999–2010).
5. *The Uncanny X-Men* (Marvel Comics, 1963-Present). It should be noted that dozens of X-Men titles have existed over time. I cite this one as original and indicative, rather than comprehensive.
6. *The New Teen Titans* (DC Comics, 1980–1996).
7. *Kick-Ass* (Marvel Comics, 2008–2010).
8. G. Jones, *Men of Tomorrow: Geeks, Gangsters and the Birth of the Comic Book* (New York: Basic Books, 2004), pp. 270–277.
9. F. Wertham cited in G. Klock, *How to Read Superhero Comics and Why* (New York and London: Continuum, 2002), p. 32.
10. *All-Star Batman and Robin* (DC Comics, 2005–2008).
11. For a detailed critical account of the way this shifts toward "realism" functions in one particular cycle of superheroic narratives, see W. Brooker, *Hunting the Dark Knight: Twenty-First Century Batman* (New York and London: I. B. Tauris, 2012), pp. 89–133.

12. S. Hopkins, *Girl Heroes: The New Force in Popular Culture* (Pluto Press: Anandale, AUS, 2002), p. 3.
13. Y. Tasker, *Working Girls: Gender and Sexuality in Popular Cinema* (London and New York: Routledge, 1998), p. 69.
14. R. Kaveny, *Superheroes: Capes and Crusaders in Comics and Films* (London: I. B. Tauris, 2008); L. Robinson, *Wonder Women: Feminisms and Superheroes.* (London and New York: Routledge, 2004); D. Wolk, *Reading Comic: How Graphic Novels Work and What They Mean* (Cambridge, MA: Da Capo Press, 2007); B. Wright, *Comic Book Nation: The Transformation of Youth Culture in America* (Baltimore, MD: Johns Hopkins University Press).
15. C. Tookey, "Don't be Fooled by the Hype: This Crime Against Cinema is Twisted, Cynical and Revels in the Abuse of Childhood," *The Daily Mail*, April 2, 2010, http://www.dailymail.co.uk/tvshowbiz/reviews/article-1262948/Kick-Ass-Dont-fooled-hype–This-crime-cinema-twisted-cynical-revels-abuse-childhood.html, [Accessed March 21, 2014].
16. C. Driscoll, *Girls: Feminine Adolescence in Popular Culture and Cultural Theory* (New York: Columbia University Press, 2002), p. 7.
17. D. Kelly and S. Pomerantz, "Mean, Wild and Alienated: Girls and the State of Feminism in Popular Culture," *Girlhood Studies* 2:1 (2009), 2–3.
18. A. McRobbie, "Post-Feminism and Popular Culture," *Feminist Media Studies* 4:3 (2004), 255–256.

Filmography

13 Going on 30. Dir. Gary Winick, USA, 2004.
37°2 Le Matin/Betty Blue. Dir. Jean-Jacques Beineix, 1989.
A bout de soufflé. Dir. Jean-Luc Godard, France, 1960.
A Hard Day's Night. Dir. Richard Lester, 1964.
A mi madre le gustan las mujeres/My Mother Likes Women. Dir. Inés París and Daniela Féjerman, Spain, 2002.
A Room with a View. Dir. James Ivory, UK, 1985.
A Taste of Honey. Dir. Tony Richardson, UK, 1961.
Alien. Dir. Ridley Scott, USA, 1979.
All Over Me. Dir. Alex Sichel, USA, 1997.
Another Cinderella Story. Dir. Damon Santostefano, 2008.
Aparajito, Dir. Satyajit Ray, India, 1958.
Appropriate Adults. Dir. Julian Jarrold, UK, 2011
Apu Sansar, Dir. Satyajit Ray, India, 1959.
Atonement. Dir. Joe Wright, UK, 2007.]
Ayneh/The Mirror. Dir. Jafer Panahi, Iran, 1997.
Bacheha-ye Aseman/Children of Heaven. Dir. Majid Majidi, Iran, 1997.
Badkonake sefid/The White Balloon. Dir. Jafer Panahi, Iran, 1995.
Baise-moi. Dir. Virginie Despentes, France, 2000.
Batman Begins. Dir. Christopher Nolan, USA/UK, 2005.
Beat Girl, aka *Wild for Kicks.* Dir. Edmond T. Greville, UK, 1960.
Bella Martha/Mostly Martha. Dir. Sandra Nettelbeck, Germany/Austria/ Switzerland/Italy 2001.
Black Swan. Dir. Darren Aronofsky, USA, 2010.
Blood Diamond. Dir. Edward Zwick, USA, 2006.
Bonheur. Dir. Cédric Kahn, France, 1994.
Bridget Jones's Diary. Dir. Sharon Mcguire, UK, 2001.
Bring It On. Dir. Peyton Reed, 2000.
Broken. Dir. Rufus Norris, UK, 2012.
Buda az sharm foru rich/Buddha Collapsed Out of Shame. Dir. Hana Makmalbaf, Iran, 2007.
Bye Bye Blondie. Dir. Virginie Despentes, France, 2011.
Captain America. Dir. Joe Johnston, USA, 2011.
Catwoman. Dir. Pitof Comar, 2004.
Charlie's Angels. Dir. McG, USA, 2000.

Circumstance. Dir. Maryam Keshavarz, Iran, 2011.
Close Up. Dir. Abbas Kiarostami, Iran, 1990.
Come tu mi vuoi/As You Desire Me. Dir. Volfango De Biasi, 2007.
Comme t'y es belle!/Gorgeous! Dir. Lisa Azuelos, UK/Luxembourg/France/
Belgium, 2006.
Cracks. Dir. Jordan Scott, UK, Ireland, 2009.
Crazy/Beautiful. Dir. John Stockwell, USA, 2001.
Das Cabinet des Dr. Caligari. Dir. Robert Wiene, Germany, 1920.
Davandeh/The Runner. Dir. Amir Naderi, Iran, 1985.
Der Krieger und die Kaiserin/The Princess and the Warrior. Dir. Tom Tykwer,
Germany, 2001.
Dokhtari Ba Kafsh-Haye-Katani/The Girl in the Sneakers. Dir. Rasul Sadr Ameli,
Iran, 1999.
Don't Let Me Drown. Dir. Cruz Angeles, USA, 2009.
Down for Life. Dir. Alan Jacobs, USA, 2009.
Dr Zhivargo. Dir. David Lean, USA, 1965.
El Niño pez/The Fish Child. Dir. Lucía Puenzo, Argentina/France/Spain, 2009.
El ultimo verano de la Boyita/The Last Summer of La Boyita. Dir. Julia Solomonoff,
Argentina/Spain/France, 2009.
Elektra. Dir. Rob Bowman, USA, 2005.
Et toi, t'es sur qui?/Just about Love? Dir. Lola Doillon, France, 2008.
Ezra. Dir. Newston Aduaka, Austrial, France/Belgium/Nigeria, 2007.
Feuerherz/Heart of Fire. Dir. Luigi Falorni, Eritrea/Germany/UK, 2009.
Fires Were Started. Dir. Humphrey Jennings, UK, 1942.
Fish Tank. Dir. Andrea Arnold, UK, 2009.
Four Weddings and a Funeral. Dir. Mike Newell, UK, 1994.
Foxfire. Dir. Annette Haywood Cater, USA, 1996.
Foxfire. Dir. Laurent Cantet, France, 2012.
Frau Lehmann's Töchter. Dir. Carl Heinz Wolff, Germany, 1932.
Frères. Dir. Olivier Dahan, France, 1994.
Frozen. Dir. Chris Buck and Jennifer Lee, USA, 2013.
Geminis. Dir. Albertina Carri, Argentina/France, 2005.
Girl with Green Eyes. Dir. Desmond Davis, UK, 1964.
Girlfight. Dir. Karyn Kusama, USA, 2000.
Hadewich. Dir. Bruno Dumont, France, 2009.
Heathers. Dir. Michael Lehmann, USA, 1988.
Iron Man 3. Dir. Shane Black, 2013.
Johnny Mad Dog. Dir. Jean-Stéphane Sauvaire, France/Liberia, 2008.
Kassim the Dream. Dir. Kief Davidson, Uganda/USA, 2008.
Khane-ye doust kodjast/Where Is the Friends House. Dir. Abbas Kiarostami, 1987.
Kick-Ass 2. Dir. Jeff Wadlow, UK/USA, 2013.
Kick-Ass. Dir. Matthew Vaughn, UK/USA, 2007.
Kill Bill. Dir. Quentin Tarantino, USA, 2003.
King Kong Théorie. Dir. Virginie Despentes France, 2006.
Kyūtī Hanī/Cutie Honey. Dir. Hideaki Anno, Japan, 2004.

L'Ami de mon amie/My Girlfriend's Boyfriend. Dir. Eric Rohmer, France, 1987.
La Boum 2/The Party 2. Dir. Claude Pinoteau, 1982.
La Boum/The Party. Dir. Claude Pinoteau, 1980.
La Ciénaga/The Swamp. Dir. Lucrecia Martel, Argentina/France/Spain, 2001.
La mujer sin cabeza/The Headless Woman. Dir. Lucrecia Martel, Argentina/France, 2008.
La niña santa/The Holy Girl. Dir. Lucrecia Martel, Argentina/Italy/Netherlands/Spain, 2004.
La rabia/Anger. Dir. Albertina Carri, Argentina/Netherlands, 2008.
La Vérité si je mens!/Would I Lie to You? Dir. Thomas Gilou, France, 1997.
La vie au ranch/Chicks. Dir. Sophie Letourneur, France, 2009.
La Vie d'Adèle—Chapitres 1 & 2/Blue Is the Warmest Colour. Dir. Abdellatif Kechiche, France/Belgium/Spain, 2013.
Ladri di biciclette/Bicycle Thieves. Dir. Vittorio de Sica, Italy, 1948.
Lara Croft: Tomb Raider. Dir. Simon West, USA/UK/Japan/Germany, 2001.
Le Beau Serge. Dir. Claude Chabrol, France, 1959.
Les Coquillettes. Dir. Sophie Letourneur, France, 2012.
Les Roseaux sauvages. Dir. André Téchiné, France, 1994.
LOL (Laughing Out Loud). Dir. Lisa Azuelos, France, 2008.
Longford. Dir. Tom Hooper, UK, 2006.
Love, Concord. Dir. Gustavo Guardado, USA, 2012.
Love Streams. Dir. John Cassavetes, USA, 1984.
Make It Happen. Dir. Darren Grant, USA, 2008.
Mean Girls. Dir. Mark Waters, USA/Canada, 2004.
Mince alors! Dir. Charlotte de Turckheim, France, 2012.
Miss Congeniality. Dir. Donald Petrie, 2000.
Morvern Callar. Dir. Lynne Ramsay, UK, 2002.
Mulholland Drive. Dir. David Lynch, USA, 2001.
My Queen Caro. Dir. Dorothée Van Den Berghe, Belgium, 2009.
My Summer of Love. Dir. Pawel Pawlikowski, UK, 2004.
Naissance des Pieuvres/Waterlillies. Dir. Céline Sciamma, France, 2007.
Nān o Kūcheh/Bread and Alley. Dir. Abbas Kiarostami, Iran, 1969.
Nanook of the North: A Story of Life and Love in the Actual Artic. Dir. Robert. J. Flaherty, USA, 1922.
Never Back Down. Dir. Jeff Wadlow, USA, 2008.
Nūn o goldūn/A Moment of Innocence. Dir. Moshem Makmalbaf, Iran, 1996.
Pariah. Dir. Dee Rees, USA, 2011.
Pather Panchali. Dir. Satyajit Ray, India, 1955.
Persepolis. Dir. Marjane Satrapi, Iran/France, 2007.
Peter, Portrait of a Serial Killer. Dir. Skip Kite, UK, 2011.
Precious. Dir. Lee Daniels, USA, 2009.
Pretty Woman. Dir. Garry Marshall, USA, 1990.
Pride and Prejudice. Dir. Joe Wright, UK/France/USA, 2005.
Pulp Fiction. Dir. Quentin Tarantino, USA, 1994.
Quinceañera. Dir. Richard Glatzer and Wash Westmoreland, USA, 2006.

Real Women Have Curves. Dir. Patricia Cardoso, USA, 2002.
Rebelle/War Witch. Dir. Kim Nguyun, Canada, 2012.
Scusa ma ti chiamo amore/Sorry if I Love You. Dir. Federico Moccia, Italy, 2008.
See No Evil. Dir. Christopher Menaul, UK, 2006.
Sense and Sensibility. Dir. Ang Lee, UK/USA, 1995.
Shadow of a Doubt. Dir. Alfred Hitchcock, 1943.
She Monkeys/Apflickorna. Dir. Lisa Aschan, Sweden, 2011.
She's All That. Dir. Robert Iscove, USA, 1999.
Sib/The Apple. Dir. Samira Makhmalbaf, Iran, 1998.
Snow White and Seven Dwarves. Dir. William Cottrell, Wilfred Jackson, Larry Morey, Perce Pearce, and Ben Sharpsteen, USA, 1937.
Soldier Child. Dir. Neil Abramson, USA, 1998.
Something's Gotta Give. Dir. Nancy Meyers, USA, 2003.
Spring Breakers. Dir. Harmnoy Korine, USA, 2012.
St Trinian's. Dir. Oliver Parker, Barnaby Thompson, UK, 2007.
Stoker. Dir. Park Chan-wook, USA/South Korea, 2013.
Super. Dir. James Gunn, USA, 2010.
Suzanne. Dir. Katell Quillévére, France, 2012.
Terminator 2: Judgment Day. Dir. David Cameron, USA, 1991.
The Avengers. Dir. Joss Whedon, USA, 2012.
The Dark Knight Rises. Dir. Christopher Nolan, USA/UK, 2012.
The Dark Knight. Dir. Christopher Nolan, USA/UK, 2008.
The Devil Wears Prada. Dir. David Frankel, USA, 2006.
The Disappearance of Alice Creed. Dir. J Blakeson, UK, 2009.
The Exorcist. Dir. William Friedkin, USA, 1973.
The Girl on a Motorcycle. Dir. Jack Cardiff, UK/France, 1968.
The House Bunny. Dir. Fred Wolf, USA, 2008.
The Incredibles. Dir. Brad Bird, USA, 2004.
The Incredibly True Adventure of Two Girls in Love. Dir. Maria Maggenti, USA, 1995.
The Kids Are All Right. Dir. Lisa Cholodenko, USA, 2010.
The L-Shaped Room. Dir. Bryan Forbes, UK, 1962.
The Wizard of Oz. Dir. Victor Fleming, USA, 1939.
The Women. Dir. Diane English, USA, 2008.
Thirteen. Dir. Catherine Hardwicke, USA, 2003.
Titanic. Dir. James Cameron, USA, 1997.
Tomboy. Dir. Céline Sciamma, France, 2011.
Tout ce qui brille/All That Glitters. Dir. Hervé Mimran and Géraldine Nakache, France, 2010.
Tout est pardonné/All Is Forgiven. Dir. Mia Hansen-Løve, France, 2007.
Tout pour plaire/Thirty-Five Something. Dir. Cécile Telerman, France/Belgium, 2005.
Twenty-One. Dir. Don Boyd, UK, 1991.
Un Amour de jeunesse/Goodbye First Love. Dir. Mia Hansen-Løve, France, 2011.
Un giorno special/A Special Day. Dir. Francesca Comencini, Italy, 2012.

Une semaine sur deux (et la moitié des vacances scolaires/Alternate Weeks (And Half the Vacation). Dir. Ivan Calbérac, France, 2009.
Vi är bäst!/We Are the Best. Dir. Lukas Moodysson, Sweden, 2013.
Voces Inocentes/Innocent Voices. Dir. Lewis Mandoki, Mexico/Puerto Rico/USA, 2004.
War Child. Dir. Christian Karim Chrobog, USA, 2008.
We Need to Talk about Kevin. Dir. Lynne Ramsay, UK/USA, 2003.
Where's Mary? Dir. Tony Hickson, UK, 2005.
Wish You Were Here. Dir. David Leland, UK, 1987.
Women without Men. Dir. Shirin Neshat, Germany/Austria/France, 2009.
X-Men. Dir. Brian Singer, USA, 2000.
XXY. Dir. Lucía Puenzo, Argentina/Spain, France, 2007.
Yek ettefāq-e sāda/A Simple Event. Dir. Sohred Shaheed Saless, Iran, 1973.

TV SHOWS:
10 Years Younger. UK: Channel 4, 2004–present.
Batman: The Animated Series. USA: Fox, 1992–1995.
Birds of Prey. USA: Warner Brothers Television, 2002–2003.
Buffy, The Vampire Slayer. USA, Warner Brothers Television and United Paramount Network, 1997–2003.
Gossip Girl. USA: Warner Brothers Television, 2007–2012.
Sailor Moon/Bishōjo Senshi Sērāmūn. Japan: Toei Animation, 1992–1993.
Sex and the City. USA: HBO. 1998–2004.
Smallville. USA: Warner Brothers Television and the CW Television Network, 2001–2011.
Teen Titans Go! USA: Cartoon Network, 2013–Present.
Teen Titans. USA: Warner Brothers Television and Cartoon Network, 2003–2006.
The L Word. USA: Showtime, 2004–2009.
X-Men. USA: Fox Kids, 1992–1997.
Young Justice. USA: Cartoon Network, 2010–2013.

Contributors

Lucy Bolton is Lecturer in Film Studies at Queen Mary, University of London, and is the author of *Film and Female Consciousness: Irigaray, Cinema and Thinking Women* (Palgrave Macmillan, 2011). She is currently co-editing, with Julie Lobalzo-Wright, a collection of essays with the title *Lasting Stars: Images that Fade and Personas the Endure* (Palgrave Macmillan), and is also writing an article on the stardom of Grace Kelly and Ava Gardener in the film *Mogambo*. Other publications include a chapter on *The Hours* in *Hollywood Puzzle Films* (edited by Warren Buckland, Routledge 2014) and an entry on Nicholas Ray in *Fifty Hollywood Directors* (edited by Yvonne Tasker and Suzanne Leonard, Routledge, 2014). Her current research is for a monograph on cinema and the philosophy of Iris Murdoch, and she is also co-writing, with Catherine Wheatley, *An Introduction to Film Philosophy: Concepts, Forms and Theories* (Berghahn).

Clara Bradbury-Rance is in the final stages of an AHRCfunded PhD at the University of Manchester. Her research explores the problem of representation for lesbian studies by means of an intersection with queer and feminist theory, reading twenty-firstcentury films that embrace, reject, or confuse their readability as films about "the lesbian." Clara has been invited to present her work at UCL, Queen Mary, Manchester, Westminster, Stirling, Mount Holyoke, and the Cornerhouse. She also co-organizes the annual Sexuality Summer School at the University of Manchester. Clara is the author of "Querying Postfeminism in *The Kids Are All Right*" in Joel Gwynne and Nadine Muller, eds, *Postfeminism and Contemporary Hollywood Cinema* (Palgrave Macmillan, 2013) and a forthcoming chapter on *Nathalie* (Fontaine, 2003) and *Chloe* (Egoyan, 2010) in a collection on queer translation.

Samantha Colling is Research Degrees Assistant at the Manchester Institute for Research and Innovation in Art and Design and an Associate Lecturer in Film and Media at Manchester Metropolitan University. She has recently completed her PhD dissertation, fully funded by MIRIAD, titled "The Aesthetic Pleasures of Girl Teen Film." She is also currently involved in two AHRCfunded projects, one of which uses aspects of her research as part of an exhibition at the University of Leicester. Sam is particularly interested in the connections between popular entertainment, pleasure, affect, and emotion.

Lara Cox teaches in the department of Comparative Literature at the American University of Paris. She is a specialist of performance studies and gender studies. Her work retains a comparative focus on French and Anglophone (particularly the US) cultures. The performance media that she has published on include avant-garde theatre, cinema, and stand-up comedy and she has also explored the topic of queer performance in the archive in the French context.

Lisa Downing is Professor of French Discourses of Sexuality at the University of Birmingham, UK. She is the author of numerous books, articles, and chapters on sexuality and gender studies, film, and critical theory. Her book-length publications include *Desiring the Dead: Necrophilia and Nineteenth-Century French Literature* (Oxford EHRC, 2003), *Patrice Leconte* (Manchester University Press, 2004), *The Cambridge Introduction to Michel Foucault* (Cambridge University Press, 2008), *Film and Ethics: Foreclosed Encounters* (co-authored with Libby Saxton, Routledge, 2010), *Queer in Europe: Contemporary Case Studies* (co-edited with Robert Gillett, Ashgate, 2011), *The Subject of Murder: Gender, Exceptionality, and the Modern Killer* (University of Chicago Press, 2013), and *Fuckology: Critical Essays on John Money's Diagnostic Concepts* (co-authored with Iain Morland and Nikki Sullivan, University of Chicago Press, 2015).

Joel Gwynne is Assistant Professor of English at the National Institute of Education, Singapore, where he teaches courses on contemporary literature and feminism. He is the author/co-editor of several books, including *Sexuality and Contemporary Literature* (Cambria Press, 2012), *Erotic Memoirs and Postfeminism: The Politics of Pleasure* (Palgrave Macmillan, 2013), *Postfeminism and Contemporary Hollywood Cinema* (Palgrave Macmillan, 2013) and *Ageing, Popular Culture and Contemporary Feminism* (Palgrave Macmillan, 2014). His essays have appeared in *Women's Studies International Forum, Journal of Gender Studies, Journal of Contemporary Asia*, and *Feminist Theory: An International Interdisciplinary Journal*.

Fiona Handyside is Senior Lecturer in Film Studies and French at the University of Exeter, UK. She is the author of *Cinema at the Shore: The Beach in French Cinema* (Peter Lang, 2014) and the editor of *Eric Rohmer: Interviews* (University of Mississippi Press, 2013) and has published in several journals including *Screen* and *Continuum*. She is currently writing a book on the films of Sofia Coppola.

Mary Harrod is Assistant Professor in French Studies at the University of Warwick. She is the author of *From France with Love: Gender and Identity in French Romantic Comedy* (I. B. Tauris, 2015) and co-editor with Mariana Liz and Alissa Timoshkina of the collection *The Europeaness of European Cinema: Identity, Meaning, Globalization* (I. B. Tauris 2015,) and has published on European and Hollywood film and media in such journals as *Screen* and *Studies in French Cinema*.

Danielle Hipkins is Associate Professor of Italian Studies and Film at the University of Exeter. She has published on postwar Italian women's writing, cinema and gender, and is currently completing a book entitled *Italy's Other Women: Gender and Prostitution in Postwar Italian Cinema, 1942–1965*. She is also working on an AHRCfunded project on Italian cinema-going audiences of the 1940s and 1950s, and on contemporary cinema and girlhood in the context of postfeminism.

Deborah Martin is Senior Lecturer in Latin American Cultural Studies at University College London. Her research focuses on Latin American cultural production with a particular emphasis on cinema, and draws on a broad range of methodologies, including film theory, gender and sexuality studies, and childhood studies. Her articles have appeared in *Journal of Latin American Cultural Studies, Bulletin of Latin American Research* and *Hispanic Research Journal*, amongst others. She is the author of two books: *Painting, Literature and Film in Colombian Feminine Culture: Of Border Guards, Nomads and Women* (Tamesis, 2012), and *The Cinema of Lucrecia Martel* (MUP, forthcoming). Her current research focuses on representations of the child in Latin American cinema, and she is preparing a monograph on this topic to be published by Palgrave Macmillan.

Tim McNelis teaches in the Department of Communication and Media at the University of Liverpool. His PhD thesis, completed at the University of Liverpool, focused on the role that songs and musical performance play in regulating agency and constructing identity in US youth films. Tim's recent publications include a chapter on the meaning of anachronistic music in *Dirty Dancing*, published in the collection *The Time of Our Lives: Dirty Dancing and Popular Culture* (Wayne State University Press, 2013). He has also co-authored (with Elena Boschi) an article on audiovisual style in the films of Wes Anderson that appeared in the *New Review of Film and Television Studies* (2012) and a chapter on the meaning of visible playback technology in film, published in *Ubiquitous Musics* (Ashgate, 2013).

Margherita Sprio is Senior Lecturer in Film History and Theory at University of Westminster. She is the author of *Migrant Memories: Cinema and the Italian Post War Diaspora in Britain* (Peter Lang, 2013), which is a cultural history of Italian migration to Britain and focuses on the relationship between cinema, cultural memory, and migrant audience consumption. She works on film practice and theory as well as the relationship of film theory to photography, contemporary art, and philosophy. Her particular research interests relate to the politics of cinema and art, globalization and diaspora, cultural/sexual difference and transnationalism. She has also written about Iranian cinema, realism, performance, and film history and has contributed chapters in various books, which include "The Terrain of Subculture in *Silences of the Palace* (Mofida Tlatli, 1994)," in Layal Ftouni and Tarik Sabry, eds. *Arab Cultural Studies: Mapping the Field* (I. B. Tauris, 2015). She has also contributed to different journals including *Journal of British Visual Culture* and *Third Text* and is currently working on a book about Women and Experimental Cinema in Britain.

Kate Taylor-Jones is Senior Lecturer in East Asian Studies at Sheffield University. She is the author of *Rising Sun, Divided Land: Japanese and South Korean Filmmakers* (Wallflower; Columbia, 2013), and founding editor-in-chief of the *East Asian Journal of Popular Culture*. Forthcoming publications include an AHRC funded study on Colonial Japanese Cinema (Bloomsbury Press) and a study on bride kidnapping in contemporary global visual culture.

Martin Zeller-Jacques is Lecturer in Film and Media at Queen Margaret University. His research focuses on serial narratives in contemporary media, especially television drama and superhero franchises, and he also pursues research on gender and sexuality in film and television. He has previously published chapters in several edited collections, and has contributed to several volumes of *The Directory of World Cinema*.

Index